Poets in Progress

THEODORE ROETHKE
ROBERT LOWELL
STANLEY KUNITZ
RICHARD WILBUR
RICHARD EBERHART
WILLIAM DE WITT SNODGRASS
HOWARD NEMEROV
J. V. CUNNINGHAM
RANDALL JARRELL
W. S. MERWIN
DENISE LEVERTOV
LOUIS SIMPSON
ANNE SEXTON

POETS
IN
PROGRESS

A Reprint, Augmented
Critical Prefaces to Thirteen Modern American Poets

EDITED BY EDWARD HUNGERFORD

Northwestern University Press 1967

NOTE UPON THIS PRINTING

THE *Foreword* below, as it was written for *Poets in Progress* in 1962, explains the origin of these *Prefaces*. To the original ten I have now added three more which were printed in *The Tri-Quarterly* soon after the book appeared. The three are by Yohma Gray on Louis Simpson, Beverly Fields on Anne Sexton, and Ralph Mills on Denise Levertov—the latter as revised for inclusion in his *Contemporary American Poetry* and reprinted here with the permission of Random House.

In the reissue of a volume such as this, several problems spring to mind. The title, appropriate for poets who in 1962 were "in the full flight of their careers," is now, with the deaths of Roethke and Jarrell, sadly inappropriate; but to change it would look like a mere sales pitch—old book, new market. Updating? When the book first appeared, the authors had revised their earlier work to take account of new poems. But a book of critical opinions isn't an escalator constantly going up—especially with thirteen writers riding it. Another question: should the bibliographies list new books (quite a lot, all counted)? I decided no. The critical appraisals were made without the knowledge of these later works, and time should have a stop where the critic stopped.

What has let *Poets in Progress* sell out and go into paperback? Maybe people liked it because it wasn't very professional—just some writers, astray from their specialties, writing about poets they enjoyed—poets of a generation coming up, with critical judgments still open, nothing static. My own pleasure came—and is now renewed—from talking poetry with my thirteen writers. In my *Notes on the Contributors* I have updated their careers and my own pleasant recollections of them as persons.

E.H.

1967

FOREWORD

Perhaps there is no such thing as modern poetry—only modern poets. This book is about ten living American poets. Though a few of them began publishing before the Second World War, their reputations are in the main post-war, some of them post-Korean War.

The ten articles, or earlier versions of them, first appeared in Northwestern University's *The Tri-Quarterly,* beginning in the Fall of 1958 with Ralph Mills' "Toward a Condition of Joy: Patterns in the Poetry of Theodore Roethke." Each issue of the magazine since then has contained an article written for the series upon an invitation from the editor to members of Northwestern University's English department—some of the writers now scattered from Dublin to California. Each article is concerned with critical appraisal and with some analysis of separate poems, but all are primarily prefaces—invitations to read a set of poets who are in the full flight of their careers.

Choices were personal, with only this limitation, that a poet should have published in book form so that his poetry is available beyond the journals. Manner and form too were a matter of choice, except that each writer was asked to include some full-length poems and a liberal quotation from others in order that the created poem and the act of judgment might confront each other in the reader's presence.

All the poets so chosen have recently published, some so short a time ago that even those articles written within the last few months needed to be brought up to date a little. In order to keep up with Mr. Roethke, Mr. Mills decided to rewrite his article altogether; and Mr. Staples, second in the magazine series, revised his considerably to keep up not only with Mr. Lowell but with himself, as he has just completed a book on the poet, to be published this spring. In only one instance has the editor chosen to reprint an article without some revisions for timeliness. Mr. Torchiana sent me his estimate of new poetry by Mr. Snodgrass, but I haven't included it, since his original article, written in a personal fashion around *Heart's Needle*, should be read as it was first conceived.

The poets proved to be in the full flight of their careers indeed—almost embarrassingly full for their critics. New poems and new books were coming out fast. For his first article Ralph Mills was able to read advanced copy of the English edition of Roethke's *Words for the Wind;* Lowell kindly sent Hugh Staples the poems about to appear in his *Life Studies,* and Robert Harvey was able to work with the proof for *New and Selected Poems* by Howard Nemerov, the volume then in printing at the University of Chicago Press. All of the poets chosen were vigorously writing. Some were good enough to send along new poems to accompany the articles.

By good luck and the good will of publishers we kept abreast of the poets' output, but were not able to keep up with their reputations. Mr. Walter Rideout missed by a few hours the chance to include in his essay the news that Mr. Jarrell's *Woman at the Washington Zoo* had just won the National Book Award—our press had already begun printing his article. Mr. Hagstrum's article came off the press on the day of the announcement of the Pulitzer Prize for Mr. Kunitz's *Selected Poems.* (However, with better luck, the magazine, the poet, and the announcement of the honor all appeared on campus the same afternoon.) The news of the Pulitzer Prize for *Heart's Needle* came when the issue containing Torchiana's essay on the book was at the mailing office. Since our articles on Roethke and Lowell appeared almost simultaneously with *Words for the Wind* and *Life Studies*, we were of course too late to mention the many honors (including National Book Awards for both poets) which followed soon after the publication of those books. In our series we knew for certain that the word *contemporary* meant contemporary. All poets and all reputations were on the go.

Other poets might well have been included. It is disappointing that no one chose a poet from the California group, beat or not beaten. And there are many others whose work is making a stir in the circles of those who read contemporary poetry. Perhaps a second series, if this proves useful to those who like some direction and suggestions in their reading, may make up for unintended slights. But for the present publication in book form a time limit seemed desirable. To be of value in a wider world than the magazine reached, these essays should be read while the opinions are freshly spoken and the books with which they deal still new. This printing by a university press is another mark of the increasingly close relationship of press, professor, and poet on the American campus.

In my explanation of the book it remains only to point out that while our critics are in their field professional, here their choices were by no means professional. Each choice represents an individual enthusiasm for a living poet whom the writer likes to read. Hagstrum, for instance, is a scholar in the literature of the eighteenth century in England, and Stanley Kunitz, on whom he writes, is a long way from the eighteenth century anywhere. Nor can Richard Wilbur, the subject of Frederic Faverty's essay, be counted among Faverty's Victorians.

"It is necessary," said Rimbaud, "to be absolutely modern." But many people don't want to be absolutely modern, and every day tells us why. Moreover, it is difficult to be modern. The act of a new confrontation is hard. It is as hard in the reading of poetry as in other matters, and this difficulty is the subject of considerable protest. Perhaps we protest too much.

Today no one expects to be able to read in the advancing sciences with the ease possible when Huxley was explaining the nineteenth century revolutions in geology and biology. Poetry, like contemporary physics, proceeds from an increasingly complex awareness, and its revolutions have been commensurate. Perhaps it is fair to say that for persons unwilling to accept the rebellions in all the arts which broke out with especial violence from about 1904 to 1914, the reading of poetry since Arnold, Swinburne, and Hardy will never be wholly possible. But it seems to me that, with a few exceptions, poets of the past decade have finally assessed and assimilated those rebellions, and external unorthodoxies are no longer a difficulty. Internally, however, the directed explanation and the clearly stated or clearly implied meanings of traditional poetry have gone indeed. Today the poet expects his reader to probe through his taut metaphors and, often without the aid of plainly identifiable circumstances or even of leading transition, to find his way into an intense, inner, and sometimes private experience. The assumption, and I think it is necessary and valid, is that human nature is such that the subtlest inner experience can be shared if not by all at least by some, and if not at once, then as further experience becomes available. A just corollary is that since in a whirling world the range of experienced sensation and knowledge able to be shared from person to person is limited, to any given reader a given poem may prove impenetrable. Let a reader make that admission and he will be comfortable and able to rejoice at what he does find available to him. The poets in this volume are men of our times, intelligent, perceptive, gifted, articulate, and with a high degree of availability.

EDWARD HUNGERFORD

1962

CONTENTS

Poets in Progress

I
THEODORE
ROETHKE:
THE
LYRIC
OF
THE
SELF

RALPH J. MILLS, JR.

Le vent se lève! . . . il faut tenter de vivre!
L'air immense ouvre et referme mon livre . . .
　　　　　　　　　　—Paul Valéry

I

ONE of the dangers of any age that has produced important writers and literary revolutions such as our own is that the artists of generations immediately subsequent to the seminal one may not receive the attention they deserve. The focus of readers turns upon the task of assimilating the pioneers, the originators of new styles; and there follows a neglect of younger poets working in the light of the radical changes initiated by their predecessors. Several rough but distinguishable phases can be remarked in twentieth century poetry: one includes the post-symbolist revolutionaries who firmly established a modern tone and style—Eliot, Yeats, Pound, Rilke, Valéry, Stevens; another divides three ways, the first two developing the inheritance of their forerunners

(Auden, Spender, Day Lewis in England, Tate, John Peale Bishop, Stanley Kunitz in America), the other in romantic reaction to this legacy (Dylan Thomas, George Barker, Kathleen Raine, David Gascoyne); a third consists of American poets who first became known during the second World War, among whom are Randall Jarrell, Karl Shapiro, Robert Lowell, and Theodore Roethke. Of these poets, Roethke has, it seems to me, demonstrated the most restless and exploratory impulse, a desire continually to plumb new areas of experience and to alter his style in accord with his discoveries. As a result of this impulse and his fine lyric gifts, the body of his writing has a strong cumulative effect upon the reader, for each successive stage of his work—and I mean thematically speaking, too—grows naturally out of the former. Reading his latest poems, one feels the weight of earlier ones as an actual presence. By means of this closely woven pattern, there is built up a scheme of meanings and values, what we might call a universe of discourse, in which the poems themselves fit and are comprehended.

Roethke's first book, *Open House* (1941), impresses the reader at the very start with this poet's natural ability to sing, his sharp, compact lines, his fundamental rhythmic sense. One is sure, having seen some of these short lyrics and descriptive pieces, that Roethke could never have stopped *here;* flexibility and incipient progress lurk everywhere under the surface of the words. In the title poem, one of the best in the volume, he announces the theme that will continue to occupy him and the artistic personality that is inseparable from it:

My secrets cry aloud.
I have no need for tongue.
My heart keeps open house,
My doors are widely swung.

An epic of the eyes
My love, with no disguise.

My truths are all foreknown,
This anguish self-revealed.
I'm naked to the bone,
With nakedness my shield.
Myself is what I wear:
I keep the spirit spare.

The anger will endure,
The deed will speak the truth
In language strict and pure.
I stop my lying mouth:
Rage warps my clearest cry
To witless agony.[1]

The art proposed in these stanzas is peculiarly autobiographical, "naked to the bone," and, we might say, assumes the appearance of a journal—kept with great
pain—which traces the path of a sensitive mind from
bondage into the freedom of the open air. It seems as if
much of the poetry evolves from a kind of curative effort
on the poet's part—the exorcism of a demon, T. S. Eliot
would call it—determining the direction his work will
take. The pattern which emerges visibly from the writing as a whole is seen to fall into stages ranging from the
psychological to the visionary and near-mystical. Such a
classification must necessarily slight some excellent light
verse and children's poems that appear peripheral to the
author's main concerns. Roethke sets out upon a journey
in his poems, a research into the origins of the psyche
sometimes resembling the classical ordeals of legendary
heroes since it involves a descent into the underworld of
the mind, a confrontation of all the perils this voyage

creates to the integrity of self. Having passed through these subterranean distances where the past history of the individual stands still and weighs secretly upon him, Roethke leads the way back into the world; the regenerated spirit discovers the physical universe anew. The development of Roethke's poetry is a record of the spirit's mutations, its division from nature and expansion into love and illumination, its final, anagogical disposition.

The series of brief poems opening *The Lost Son* (1948) serves as an introduction to later and longer pieces in the same book. Roethke has always stressed the eye as the most important organ (see his "Prayer"); and it is the eye of microscopic power trained on the minute, thriving vegetable life and mineral realm of the earth that determines the range and character of sensibility here. These poems remind us in part of Rimbaud's *Les Illuminations* or Whitman's *Leaves of Grass* not so much in subject matter and not at all in technique but because they are an affront to our habitual forms of perception. We are forced to look at things differently or reject the poetry altogether. The labor urged on us demands that we strip away those winding cloths of category and convention with which we deaden our sense of life, and that we regain our simplicity of vision: the belief in human possibility. Lying flat on the soil, our eyes level with the ground, we begin again in the poems with the elements of the natural world. Our origins are linked by correspondences with those elements. If this procedure of close attention to budding plants and tiny creatures clashes with our pretensions to adult dignity, Roethke shows us in "Cuttings (Later)" that such observation has a striking relevance to our own estate:

This urge, wrestle, resurrection of dry sticks,
Cut stems struggling to put down feet,

What saint strained so much,
Rose on such lopped limbs to new life?

If we disclaim recognition of this struggle, we either fail
to tell ourselves the truth or have not risen to life.
Roethke constantly forces on us the images of grace and
defection.

As he has often pointed out in commenting on his own
writings, Roethke's youth was spent around his father's
greenhouses in Michigan; and he absorbed their atmosphere and the minutiae of plant and vegetable life with
an intensity, an affinity that has transformed them into
both literal facts and dominant metaphors of his poetry.
Early influenced by his reading of Wordsworth, John
Clare, and Whitman, and later by Leonie Adams,
quickly enough he found poetic counterparts to spur his
personal fascination with the details and processes of
nature. There is a human lesson to be learned that starts
with a humility towards the lower orders of life and
the knowledge of connections we have with them. True
growth requires us to return along the way we came and
touch once more the roots from which we sprang:

When sprouts break out,
Slippery as fish,
I quail, lean to beginnings, sheath-wet.

Such imagery identifies man with a process in the
natural world and relates him to the stubborn fecundity
of the entire creation. This assertion of existence is evident in a poem like "Root Cellar" where

Nothing would give up life:
Even the dirt kept breathing a small breath.

The shorter poems of this period are all devoted to what
Roethke calls "the minimal." Their recurrent themes and
metaphors furnish a basis for more ambitious efforts and
point to new departures. In a fine poem called "trans-
planting," we watch young plants set down in fresh
soil and, as if through the eye of a camera equipped with
a timing device, see them unfurl and bloom:

> Watching hands transplanting,
> Turning and tamping,
> Lifting the young plants with two fingers,
> Sifting in a palm-full of fresh loam,—
> One swift movement,—
> Then plumping in the bunched roots,
> A single twist of the thumbs, a tamping and
>   turning,
> All in one,
> Quick on the wooden bench,
> A shaking down while the stem stays straight,
> Once, twice, and a faint third thump,—
> Into the flat-box it goes,
> Ready for the long days under the sloped glass:
>
> The sun warming the fine loam,
> The young horns winding and unwinding,
> Creaking their thin spines,
> The underleaves, the smallest buds
> Breaking into nakedness,
> The blossoms extending
> Out into the sweet air,
> The whole flower extending outward,
> Stretching and reaching.

Roethke has realized how the same striving upwards is an
essential movement of the spirit in man. This per-

ception led him, in a series of longer poems, to explore the relationships between the unfolding inner life of the person and the objects and forces of physical nature. What is merely a proposed analogy between human and natural processes in earlier poems approaches identity in the ones that follow.

II

These longer poems, which extend and deepen Roethke's previous interests, appear as a full sequence in *The Waking* (1953), a volume which won for its author the Pulitzer Prize. In a feat of imaginative re-creation and poetic skill, he dramatizes by means of a technique close to the novelist's interior monologue the consciousness of a child as it slowly ascends from the mysterious regions of its origin toward a complete apprehension of the world and communion with it. As the body grows, the spirit grows with it; and the inter-action of the two, with the added consideration of the lives and things outside which impose upon the self, create the drama of the poems. An intimate connection with the animal, vegetable, and mineral levels of the universe is disclosed; and along with it, a tension in the human person between a persistent desire for his whole existence and a contrary pull downwards to death or the inanimate. In order to realize within the poems the immediacy of this evolution of self and spirit, Roethke turned away from the stricter forms of his preceding work to the looser form of what I have already indicated as a dramatic internal monologue—dramatic because it registers the impression of sensations from without on a shifting physiological and spiritual life within until there is a kind of dialectical arrangement between them. Thus these poems contain abrupt changes:

Tell me, great lords of sting,
Is it time to think?

When I say things fond,
I hear singing.

("O Lull me, Lull me")

the conflict of opposites:

A worm has a mouth.
Who keeps me last?
Fish me out.
Please.

God give me an ear. I hear flowers.
A ghost can't whistle.
I know! I know!
Hello happy hands.

("Where Knock Is Open Wide")

and unexpected juxtapositions everywhere:

Such music in a skin!
A bird sings in the bush of your bones.
Tufty, the water's loose.
Bring me a finger. This dirt's lonesome for grass.

("Give Way, Ye Gates")

In spite of superficial difficulties, which disappear once the reader surrenders himself to the purpose and rhythm of the poet's undertaking, we notice the same simple and precise diction, the familiar musical gifts that mark Roethke's art. If the poems seem to lack the order we found in *Open House*, this lack must be attributed to the fluid reality they render. And so the adjustments demanded of us are more extreme than before. Entering the child's mind, we have to adopt a literalness in our apprehension and discard the adult's acquired skepticism. The world, from the new point of view Roethke provides, is transformed into a densely populated, because animistic, place where normal distinctions of object and subject, consciousness and unconsciousness, will and instinct are abolished, and synesthesia is an accepted mode of perception. Perhaps the license for such a radical departure in poetry can best be explained by a recent remark of the poet. "We must permit poetry to extend consciousness," Roethke says, "as far, as deeply, as particularly as it can, to recapture, in Stanley Kunitz's phrase, what it has lost to some extent to prose. We must realize, I think, that the writer in freer forms must have an even greater fidelity to his subject matter than the poet who has the support of form." [2] Roethke, as a reading of his collected verse will prove, has labored in both these provinces; most of his newer poems display his fascination with experiment in "freer forms," as do the poems of the childhood sequence.

The poems, then, are composed on a rationale wholly their own, a logic nearer that of the dream or the ellipsis of thought and sensation than the calculating intelligence. Individually, they constitute stages of a journey into the hidden corners of the mind, the memories beneath everyday conscious thought; and so, too, they participate in a different temporal dimension by disturbing the apparently dormant experiences of the past. Roethke's poetic enterprise here involves him in something like the interpretation of the many layers of writing on a palimpsest; each one draws him farther back in time and into more obscure circumstances. But the journey is made with direction and, we feel, even with necessity. It is an attempt to gain a perspective on the general movement of personal existence from its remote beginnings by finding the "lost son" and recovering the moments of that long-abandoned life.

It would be simple on the basis of this description to discount these poems as clinical matters or the raw stuff of psychoanalysis, whereas they are nothing of the sort. However private the resources on which Roethke has called, the problems of understanding details of separate poems seldom appear to come from faults of privacy. Maybe the problems which arise are due to our own carelessness or impatience in reading. At any rate, a statement Roethke wrote for inclusion in *Twentieth Century Authors* should help to clarify the poet's intention:

> I have tried to transmute and purify my 'life,' the sense of being defiled by it, in both small and formal and somewhat blunt short poems, and, latterly, in longer poems which try in their rhythms to catch the very movement of the mind itself, to trace the spiritual history of a protagonist (not 'I,' personally), of all haunted and harried men; to make in this series . . . a true and not arbitrary order which will permit many ranges to feeling, including humor.[3]

The universal character of Roethke's protagonist compels our participation in these inner travels. We are turned into partial actors of the drama his poems relate.

The uncovering of childhood exposes old sores; and anxiety over the questions of death, God, isolation, sexuality, and parental relations bulk large in these poems. An inclination to get up and out of the morass of such disturbances is the most pronounced characteristic of the protagonist, but he can attain this release only by facing directly all the hazards and powers—usually psychic ones —that endanger the gradually developing spirit. "The Lost Son" is possibly the most representative poem of the sequence for our purposes, because it contains within its carefully made order the major themes of the entire group, and so forms a paradigm of the inward journey. The plan of the poem falls into several sections which trace the narrator's progress: departure; the quest—with its accompanying ordeals; the return to a new harmony; the protagonist's expectation of another phase.

Any suspicion that "The Lost Son" follows the same cyclical motion as certain other works of modern literature and ends no farther on than it began ought to be dismissed, for the poem records the trial and the decided advance of the spirit. Beginning, ominously enough, with suggestions of death, gloom and ugliness, the poem drops us into the midst of the child's pursuit of freedom and singular identity, a pursuit frustrated by the continued shocks which experience administers the frail equilibrium of his psychic life:

> At Woodlawn I heard the dead cry:
> I was lulled by the slamming of iron,
> A slow drip over stones,
> Toads brooding in wells.

The proximity of destruction and the riddle of his own nature lure the protagonist into action, and he engages himself fully in the search for liberation:

> Which is the way I take;
> Out of what door do I go,
> Where and to whom?

But confusion dogs his tracks, for the animistic universe where each thing has an independent and ambiguous nature is nothing if not deceptive; like the magical forests of fairy tales, it presents more false leads than true paths. The creatures and plants and other elements populating this world, even the friendliest ones, haunt him, and yet he must inquire of them the way out. He seeks among the smallest creatures some reliable guides, though not always with the happiest results:

All the leaves stuck out their tongues;
I shook the softening chalk of my bones,
Saying, Snail, snail, glister me forward,
Bird, soft-sigh me home.

Under the prevailing conditions, movement offers the only relief available to the agonized spirit, which is also heir to the complaints of the flesh. The protagonist's search brings him at last to "the pit," in the section of the poem named after it, and there he reaches the lowest and most dangerous point in the journey. In fact, the pit, which needs partially to be viewed as a female symbol, signifies the place of origins but has now become a sign of defeat, even of death. As the protagonist approaches there to ask the fundamental question about life— "Who stunned the dirt into noise?"—he is answered with images of the womb and of birth, "the slime of a wet nest." A harsh music of warning jangles his nerves, accompanied in section three, "The Gibber," by further alienation from his surroundings, sexual dilemmas, and shrill discord:

Dogs of the groin
Barked and howled,
The sun was against me,
The moon would not have me.

The weeds whined,
The snakes cried,
The cows and briars
Said to me: Die.

At the edge of annihilation, the protagonist passes through the "storm's heart" and glides beyond it into a state of calm, another level of existence. The spirit, having survived the threats to its growth, leaps forth in a gesture of exultation at the sheer pleasure of being:

These sweeps of light undo me.
Look, look, the ditch is running white!
I've more veins than a tree!
Kiss me, ashes, I'm falling through a dark swirl.

Body and spirit revel in their newly won harmony. The freed spirit, no longer fighting for its independence, dissolves all conflicts with the material world about it and, instead, elevates the things of the world by bringing them into communion with itself. The greenhouse, with its rich store of life, serves as the scene of this revelation and symbolizes both the unity and the potentiality of existence. The regenerative process is caught in the images of flowers:

The rose, the chrysanthemum turned toward the light.
Even the hushed forms, the bent yellowy weeds
Moved in a slow up-sway.

In the final section of the poem, the protagonist meditates on his experience. This is "an in-between time" when he can do nothing but await further activity of the spirit. The imagery of the passage recalls *Ash Wednesday* and *Four Quartets,* and this is unquestionably purposeful, as it is in "The Meditations of an Old Woman," which closes *Words for the Wind.* But Eliot's poems treat spiritual development as the result of prayer, contemplation, and self-denial. In Roethke's scheme, such development is the fruition of a *natural* struggle and is religious only in a much broader sense. The narrator hesitates to classify his experience; he will admit of no more than an indefinable visitation. I think it is clear that in stating his own attitude Roethke is replying to Eliot's:

Was it light?
Was it light within?
Was it light within light?
Stillness becoming alive,
Yet still?

The allusion to Eliot's "still point of the turning world" seems obvious, but a certain amount of parody in these lines prevents them from being taken as a literal echo of the elder poet. Whatever generates the spiritual odyssey in Roethke's poem comes apparently from within, not from an external divine source:

A lively understandable spirit
Once entertained you.
It will come again.
Be still.
Wait.

That spirit does return, again and again, in this poet's writings. Though Roethke continues to be preoccupied with the progress of the spirit, the conclusion of his sequence of monologues, with their radical technique, enables him to move off in a different direction. He does, of course, deal with the isolated self again in later poems, but in general the themes of childhood are replaced by mature considerations of love, death, and the larger meanings of human existence in the world.

III

With *The Waking* (1953), Roethke brought together a selection of his earlier verse and a number of new poems, some of them indicating a sharp departure from self-contemplation. These were, of course, the love poems;

and more of them have appeared since, so that a section of *Words for the Wind* is devoted to an entire group. If we think of these poems solely in terms of the spirit, however, we shall misread them, for many are erotic and sensual. All the same, they do signify another stage of that theme: the change from consideration of self to fascination with the other. The woman of these poems is various. Sometimes she assumes the form of a wraith or entrancing spectre; sometimes she is purely physical. Her place in the poems can only be called that of the female or the opposite or the other, since her role involves metamorphosis. Observation of her beauties frequently means for the poet a rapport with creation:

> The breath of a long root,
> The shy perimeter
> Of the unfolding rose,
> The green, the altered leaf,
> The oyster's weeping foot,
> And the incipient star—
> Are part of what she is.
> She wakes the ends of life.
>
> ("Words for the Wind")

In some way, this beloved possesses the elusive secrets of existence and partakes of all that is. The style of these poems differs greatly from the psychological ones, but Roethke has certainly incorporated the informality and the discipline required by his previous experiments in these new pieces.

Fulfillment in love is the subject of a quartet of lyrics, "Four for Sir John Davies," which extends the search for integration and harmony we saw in "The Lost Son" from an internal, psychological process to union with the beloved. Drawing its basic metaphor of dancing from Davies' sixteenth century poem, *Orchestra*, which explains the hierarchical order of the universe through that figure, and from Yeats, who saw in the dance an image of sexual and spiritual reconciliation, the poem leaves the poet's isolated dancing at the start to discover something of a transcendent completion in which both lover and beloved share. In the opening portion, the poet celebrates the vital energies of creation and of his own dance, but his movements are occasionally humorous and lack agility and purpose:

> I tried to fling my shadow at the moon,
> The while my blood leaped with a wordless song.
> Though dancing needs a master, I had none
> To teach my toes to listen to my tongue.

In spite of the joy of his single dance, which offers him the feeling of kinship with *things*, the poet seeks a deeper human relationship. The attraction for his newly found partner begins between "animal and human heat," but we soon realize that the meeting of the lovers physically has created a spiritual state corresponding to it.

> Incomprehensible gaiety and dread
> Attended all we did. Behind, before,
> Lay all the lonely pastures of the dead;
> The spirit and the flesh cried out for more.
> We two, together, on a darkening day
> Took arms against our own obscurity.

As traditionally befits such lovers, they receive, in the poem's third part, one identity. They remind us of that pair in Donne's "The Canonization" whose pure devotion to one another divorces them from the public world and invests them with a sacred or mystical aura, for here also, Roethke tells us, "the flesh can make the spirit visible." So this dance, though it originates in human love, is anything but ordinary and mundane. The vertical movement of the dancers and the successive alterations they undergo in their ascent lend the poems a religious quality, but only in a personal or loose way. It cannot be denied that the experience of love at its most intense which the poems portray is explicitly defined by the author as an event of the spirit, and, furthermore, an event of such magnitude that the lovers' connection with the cosmos is completely revised. And in "The Vigil," the concluding poem, Dante's paradisiacal vision is introduced to set off Roethke's own version of an encounter with the eternal; but this seems, as it did in "The Lost Son," a condition of inward blessedness, the gift of Eros rather than of God. What the poet calls elsewhere "a condition of joy," this moment renders the universe transparent to perception and mysteriously transfigures the couple:

The world is for the living. Who are they?
We dared the dark to reach the white and warm.
She was the wind when wind was in my way;
Alive at noon, I perished in her form.
Who rise from flesh to spirit know the fall:
The word outleaps the world, and light is all.

Roethke's poetry is dedicated much of the time to a search for moments like this. But such ecstatic assertions of being do not hide an inability to face the realities of human life. The later verse collected in *Words for the Wind* [4] (1958) and the poems which have appeared in magazines after that book demonstrate the poet's effort to enlarge the range of his work, as well as to consolidate his gains in theme and style.

It is obviously impossible within this introductory essay to give a suitable or clear impression of the richness and variety of all of the more recent poetry of Roethke. He has been accused in the past few years of falling into, first, imitations of Yeats, then of Eliot; yet both these charges appear simple-minded and are founded on poor reading or a failure to understand the poet's aims. For a period Roethke uses Yeats as a point of departure for his own attitudes, and "The Dying Man" sequence is sub-titled as a memorial to Yeats. Even in that poem, though, we can hardly think the following passage—except for the third and possibly the second lines—sounds very reminiscent of the Irish master:

> The edges of the summit still appal
> When we brood on the dead or the beloved;
> Nor can imagination do it all
> In this last place of light: he dares to live
> Who stops being a bird, yet beats his wings
> Against the immense immeasurable emptiness of things.

There are, of course, some poems which bear the marks of Yeats' influence; "Four for Sir John Davies" is one of them. For a further discussion of this matter, the reader should consult Roethke's own remarks in his essay "How to Write Like Somebody Else," in the *Yale Review*.

The question of Eliot is a rather different one and centers around the group of five poems called "Meditations of an Old Woman," with which Roethke concludes *Words for the Wind*. Composed very freely with a prose-style line, the poems are sometimes said to be derivative from *Four Quartets*. Maybe so, though the influence of Whitman has seemed to me greater here, both in style and attitude, and this opinion the poet has recently confirmed in a letter to me. Yet the confusion is understandable when we recognize that the poems are in part

—and in part only—an answer to *Four Quartets*. The old woman, though she is not a fictitious speaker and was a relative of the poet in life (as Roethke told me in a recent conversation), serves as an opposite to the mature Eliot in his poems. And the reflective conclusions at which she arrives have little in common with those of Eliot; in fact, some passages, like the following from "What Can I Tell My Bones?" can only be read as a direct answer to him—with slight overtones of parody:

It is difficult to say all things are well,
When the worst is about to arrive
It is fatal to woo yourself,
However graceful the posture.

Loved heart, what can I say?
When I was a lark, I sang;
When I was a worm, I devoured.

The self says, I am;
The heart says, I am less;
The spirit says, you are nothing.

Old age and the approach of death are themes of both Roethke's and Eliot's poems, but their final attitudes diverge widely. In contrast to the asceticism of *Four Quartets*, Roethke's old lady finally embraces in her memory and imagination the entire spectrum of life, its pleasures and delights, its sufferings and disappointments included. It is, at last, a series of poems which do more than merely affirm the unevenness of human existence; indeed, they celebrate the beauty of its variety and the horizons its possibilities open to view.

Though the narrator of the poem cannot be exactly identified with the poet, she is, in large measure, a voice for Roethke's beliefs. As I understand his use of her for dramatic purposes, she owes her *poetical* existence to what he makes her say; and, in her own life, she apparently coincided in outlook with the author. The poems shift with her mind's changing currents, touching on incidents and thoughts of a long life, and introducing many of Roethke's constant images and metaphors: the sun, the wind, the tiny creatures of earth, flowers and seeds and grass, water, and so on. But the range of the poem is not narrow; here is a brilliant and savage passage on the modern forms of destruction:

> I think of the self-involved:
> The ritualists of the mirror, the lonely drinkers,
> The minions of benzedrine and paraldehyde,
> And those who submerge themselves deliberately in
>   trivia,
> Women who become their possessions,
> Shapes stiffening into metal,
> Match-makers, arrangers of picnics—
> What do their lives mean,
> And the lives of their children?—
> The young, brow-beaten early into a baleful silence,
> Frozen by a father's lip, a mother's failure to answer.
> Have they seen, ever, the sharp bones of the poor?
> Or known, once, the soul's authentic hunger,
> Those cat-like immaculate creatures
> For whom the world works?

Perhaps the closing lines, full of the affirmative beauty of the world and the magical transformation or re-birth which the spirit works in man, indicate the lyrical power Roethke can command even in an informal order:

> The sun! The sun! And all we can become!
> And the time ripe for running to the moon!
> In the long fields, I leave my father's eye;

And shake the secrets from my deepest bones;
My spirit rises with the rising wind;
I'm thick with leaves and tender as a dove,
I take the liberties a short life permits—
I seek my own meekness;
I recover my tenderness by long looking.
By midnight I lover everything alive.
Who took the darkness from the air?
I'm wet with another life.
Yea, I have gone and stayed.

The great beauty of this passage is quite characteristic of Roethke's recent verse; however, his newer poems are of many sorts. Some describe what Roethke calls the motions of the soul; others, such as the splendid "Meditation at Oyster River" (which appeared in *The New Yorker*) carry on the line of development opened up by "Meditations of an Old Woman." Without any doubt, Roethke is one of the most considerable American poets of the past half-century: his increase in range, power, and variety promise the kind of writing we must call major.

NOTES

[1] All quotations of poetry, unless otherwise specified, are taken from Theodore Roethke: *Words for the Wind* (New York: Doubleday and Co., 1958), with the permission of the publisher.

[2] "Some Remarks on Rhythm," *Poetry*, 97, 1, October 1960, p. 45.

[3] Stanley Kunitz: *Twentieth Century Authors: First Supplement* (New York: H. W. Wilson Co., 1955), p. 837.

[4] This collected edition of Roethke's poems received the Bollingen Prize and the National Book Award.

II
BEYOND
CHARLES
RIVER
TO
THE
ACHERON:
AN INTRODUCTION
TO THE POETRY
OF ROBERT LOWELL

HUGH B. STAPLES

THE poet's problem in any age is to resolve the conflict between his sense of form and the audacity of his imagination. A sense of form implies a knowledge of tradition and an acknowledgment of decorum. Rebelling against these restrictive influences is the poetic impulse, which strains against the limits of language. Some of the younger American poets have tended toward one of these extremes or the other, so that we are offered, for example, the uncontrolled ululations of Allen Ginsberg or the restrained, refined and often rather pallid verse of Richard Wilbur. The poetry of Robert Lowell, however, presents us with a pattern of controlled violence and regulated disorder: his poems are a mixture of fury and grace. By addressing his intellect to the most serious themes, and by submitting his imagination to the guiding forces of the main poetic tradition, Lowell has risked more than most of the poets of his generation, and where he has been successful, he has achieved more. As the judicious Randall Jarrell has said (in a review of *Lord Weary's Castle*): ". . . one or two of these poems, I think, will be read as long as men remember English."

Much of Lowell's best work is difficult. Many of his poems are interpretations of American history or speculations of a theological nature, but his treatment of these familiar themes often requires a knowledge both of his personal religious and intellectual career and of his topical allusions. Again, his diction appears conventional enough at first glance—drawn as it often is from the Bible or from his illustrious predecessors, but, like Eliot, Lowell has adapted traditional allusions to his own uses, so that their connotations take on unexpected meanings in context. His style is sometimes harsh, grating and monosyllabic, but he makes poetry out of it as an artisan fits particles of jagged glass into a beautiful mosaic.

Like his famous relatives, James Russell and Amy, Robert Lowell bears a name as old as the Puritan theocracy itself. The name is often associated with the rather staid intellectual tradition of nineteenth-century Boston Brahmanism. Yet the individual members of the family have often opposed convention. One has only to remember, for example, the educational revolution effected by President A. Lawrence Lowell of Harvard, or his sister Amy's advocacy and practice of free verse, to realize that the family has been as concerned with modifying tradition as with maintaining it. In a similar way, the poetry of Robert Lowell reflects a talent originating out of and in contention with the atmosphere of "cold roast Boston" and of New England Calvinism in general.

Lowell's life, like his poetry, has been unconventional. Born in Boston in 1917, Robert Trail Spence Lowell, Jr., after a childhood on Beacon Hill (charmingly portrayed in his autobiographical prose essay *91 Revere Street*), entered the exclusive St. Mark's preparatory school, where the poet Richard Eberhart was one of his instructors. Harvard was perhaps inevitable, but he soon transferred to Kenyon College, where John Crowe Ransom was forging a new critical tradition and shaping the careers of important young men, Randall Jarrell and Peter Taylor among them. After his graduation from Kenyon in 1940, Lowell's career took further unexpected turns. The son of a retired naval officer, Lowell was indicted in 1943 for failure to obey the Selective Service Act; and, the grandson of a noted Episcopal minister—the first headmaster of St. Mark's—he was converted to the Roman Catholic Church in his twenty-third year. His religious attitude is displayed in his early poetry; his refusal to join the Army arose out of the belief that indiscriminate bombing of the civilian population of Europe had so altered the character of the war as to make it morally indefensible. Lowell describes his predicament in a late poem, "Memories of West Street and Lepke," this way:

> Ought I to regret my seed time?
> I was a fire-breathing Catholic C.O.,
> and made my manic statement,
> telling off the state and the President, and then
> sat waiting in the bull-pen
> beside a Negro boy with curlicues
> of marijuana in his hair.[1]

Upon conviction, he was sentenced to a year and a day in Federal prison. (The phrase "a year and a day" may sound poetic, but it is to indicate the penalty for a felony—more than a year—thus depriving the prisoner of his future privileges—among them voting rights.) Of this term, Lowell served five months. In the following year, 1944, there appeared his first book of poems, *Land of Unlikeness*—its title taken from the *Confessions* of St. Augustine, and its Latin epigraph: *Inde anima dissimilis Deo inde dissimilis est et sibi* ("Insofar as the soul is unlike God, it is unlike itself") from the sermons of St. Bernard on the *Song of Songs*. The unique edition of this work, issued by the Cummington Press, numbers 250 copies and is one of the truly rare books of our day. This volume was expanded in 1946 into the larger collection, *Lord Weary's Castle*. As a result of the critical acclaim that greeted the latter, Lowell received official recognition as a leader of the younger generation of poets in the form of an appointment as Consultant in Poetry at the Library of Congress, a Guggenheim Award, and the Pulitzer Prize for Poetry. Since then he has been on the faculty of various colleges, including the University of Iowa, Kenyon College, and Boston University, where he became Associate Professor in 1960. His later work includes *The Mills of the Kavanaughs* (1951), which displays an increasing emphasis on narrative poetry, *Life Studies* (1959), a series of autobiographical poems for which Lowell won the National Book Award in 1960, and a verse translation of Racine's *Phèdre* (1961). A collection of adaptations from Continental poets, called *Imitations,* is scheduled for publication in the autumn of 1961. One index of Lowell's contemporary reputation is the fact that all three of his major volumes of verse are currently available in paper-back editions.

In view of Lowell's heritage, it is not surprising to find that much of his poetry is dominated by a sense of the past. Again and again in his earlier poetry he plays variations on a central theme—the failure and death of the Puritan tradition. His antagonism to Calvinism is explicit in "After the Surprising Conversions," which deals with the religious hysteria touched off by the fire-and-brimstone sermons of Jonathan Edwards. In this poem, Lowell weaves together phrases taken from the preacher's own letter to excoriate what he takes to be narrow-minded bigotry:

> At Jehovah's nod
> Satan seemed more let loose amongst us; God
> Abandoned us to Satan, and he pressed

Us hard, until we thought we could not rest
Till we had done with life. Content was gone.
The breath of God had carried out a planned
And sensible withdrawal from this land;
The multitude, once unconcerned with doubt,
Once neither callous, curious, nor devout,
Jumped at broad noon, as though some peddler groaned
At it in its familiar twang: "My friend,
Cut your own throat. Cut your own throat. Now!
Now!" [2]

Similarly, "Children of Light" is a protest against the
Puritan mentality that could justify the slaughter of the
Indians in the name of religion—a theme more fully de-
veloped in "At the Indian Killer's Grave." But for
Lowell, man's inhumanity to man and his immersion in
materialism are not only destructive to the individual
souls; they account for the general decay in all aspects of
the culture as well. Thus the sonnets "Concord" and
"Salem" are respectively analyses of the failure of New
England's intellectual and mercantile tradition, and even
the fine elegy for his grandfather, "In Memory of Arthur
Winslow," is also a lament for the unfulfilled promise of
the Founding Fathers' dream.

Austin Warren, in a review of *Lord Weary's Castle*,
refers to Lowell as "a Boston poet" and it is true that one
of the problems in his poetry for the non-Bostonian
reader is that of local allusion. He blandly assumes that
references to swanboats, Phillips House, and the Public
Gardens will be familiar to his readers. Lowell's concern,
however, is by no means limited to the New England
scene. A minor though consistent strain in his early poetry
is the exploration of themes drawn from European and
classical history, as in such poems as "Dea Roma," "The
Exile's Return," "Napoleon Crosses the Berezina," and in
his adaptations from the work of other poets, "Charles the

Fifth and the Peasant" (Valéry), "War" (Rimbaud),
"The Shako" (Rilke) and "The Ghost" (Sextus
Propertius). In later years, Lowell lived much abroad,
with the result that his interpretations of European history and literature have broadened and deepened. "Beyond the Alps" (from *Life Studies*) records the impact
of the European tradition, both ancient and modern, on
an American sensibility that is at once impressionable,
sophisticated and learned. The breadth of Lowell's interest
in European literature is reflected in the range of poets
whose work he has adapted for the forthcoming *Imitations:* Leopardi, Heine, Baudelaire, Rimbaud, Rilke,
Montale and Pasternak. Additionally, his lifelong absorp-
tion in the classics has found poetic fruition in the magnificent rendering of *Phèdre,* which captures the spirit of
Racine's drama in a racy contemporary idiom.

In spite of Lowell's somewhat Jamesian fascination with
the meaning of the Old World for the New, his roots
remain in New England. Like the Episcopalian grandfather for whom he was named, he often gives the impression of preaching from a text (contained in an epigraph). His emotions and ideas are presented against the
background of contemporary society and tested in the
perspective of history. In this he is in direct contrast to
such a poet as Roethke, whose game of animal, vegetable
and mineral is seldom played in so large an arena. Some
of Lowell's poems, such as "In Memory of Arthur Winslow" and "The Quaker Graveyard in Nantucket" (dedicated to his cousin, Warren Winslow, dead at sea) obviously have been inspired by personal tragedy, but the
implications of these poems extend beyond their contexts.
Note, for example, the ease with which he moves from
the mundane to the transcendental in these lines from
"In Memory of Arthur Winslow":

Grandfather Winslow, look, the swanboats coast
That island in the Public Gardens, where

The bread-stuffed ducks are brooding, where with tub
And strainer the mid-Sunday Irish scare
The sun-struck shallows for the dusky chub
This Easter, and the ghost
Of risen Jesus walks the waves to run
Arthur upon a trumpeting black swan
Beyond Charles River to the Acheron
Where the wide waters and their voyagers are one.[2]

Similarly, "The Quaker Graveyard in Nantucket" is an elegy in the great tradition, in that the lament for the death of his cousin moves to the larger consideration of the nature of God and salvation. Lowell often adopts the role of a Christian mystic; he regards himself as a seer— an agency for revelation. Nearly all of the poems in his early volumes have this vatic quality. "I am a red arrow on this graph of Revelations," he cries in "Where the Rainbow Ends," and a sense of impending judgment is never very remote from any of these poems. Like the Yeats of "The Second Coming," Lowell sees the modern world marching toward some dreadful Armageddon. The contemporary scene is all slither, flux and chaos; its characteristic mood is that of nightmare and disorientation; as he puts it in "Colloquy in Black Rock":

All discussions
End in the mud-flat detritus of death.[2]

With the Psalmist, Lowell is constantly asking, "What is man, that Thou art mindful of him?" and there is something of Job's apprehension of the Divine power in elemental forces, as well as a faith that needs no justification in lines like these from his apostrophe to the sea in "The Quaker Graveyard":

Mart once of supercilious, wing'd clippers,
Atlantic, where your bell-trap guts its spoil
You could cut the brackish winds with a knife
Here in Nantucket, and cast up the time
When the Lord God formed man from the sea's slime
And breathed into his face the breath of life.
And blue-lung'd combers lumbered to the kill.
The Lord survives the rainbow of His will.[2]

If there is here the threat that God has forgotten man, the
corollary is that man, having forgotten God, has lost
the capacity for repentance, and history consequently becomes a sordid, meaningless charade, as in Lowell's redac-
tion of Breughel's famous picture "The Blind Leading
the Blind":

A land of mattocks; here the brothers strode,
Hulking as horses in their worsted hose
And cloaks and shin-guards—each had hooked his hoe
Upon his fellow's shoulder; by each nose
The aimless waterlines of eyeballs show
Their greenness. They are blind—blind to the road
And to its Maker. Here my father saw
The leadman trip against a pigpen, crash
Legs spread, his codpiece split, his fiddle smash . . ."[2]

And the disorder of society at large has its analogue in
personal relationships, so that love turns to lust, as in the
"Adam and Eve" section of "Between the Porch and the
Altar":

                              Your market-basket rolls
With all its baking apples in the lake.
You watch the whorish slither of a snake

That chokes a duckling. When we try to kiss,
Our eyes are slits and cringing, and we hiss;
Scales glitter on our bodies as we fall.

The quest for love between man and woman ends in the
incest of "The Death of the Sheriff" and of "Her Dead
Brother," the insanity of "Thanksgiving's Over," the
suicide of "The Mills of the Kavanaughs," or the sheer
animality of the *Life Studies* poem "To Speak of Woe
That Is in Marriage." In all of these poems, the characters move in an atmosphere of hallucination and disorder—a reflection on the personal level of the frenzy
that has overtaken a sinful world.

At different stages of his career, Lowell has sought for
a principle of order in all this chaos, and in his earlier
period, especially, has found it in religious faith. His attitude toward religion is neither simple nor consistent, nor
is it often expressed in conventional terms. In some of his
earliest poems he traditionally invokes the intercession of
the Virgin, yet his manner is idiosyncratic, as in "A
Prayer for my Grandfather to Our Lady":

O Mother, I implore
Your scorched, blue thunderbreasts of love to pour
Buckets of blessings on my burning head
Until I rise like Lazarus from the dead.[8]

Similar language informs such equally unorthodox devo-
tions as "On the Eve of the Feast of the Immaculate Conception" (where the Virgin is addressed as "Celestial
Hoyden,") or "The Wood of Life"—both from *Land of
Unlikeness*. Randall Jarrell has put the matter this way:

Lowell reminds one of those heretical enthusiasts,
often disciplined, and occasionally sanctified or ex-

communicated, who are more at home in the Church Triumphant than in the church of this world, which is one more state.

Whatever Lowell's personal and formal commitments to Roman Catholicism may be, or may have been, there is in his poetry an underlying note that can only be called, in the fundamental sense of the word, Protestant. His religious sympathies, in fact, seem to be in accord with the heroine of his poem "Mother Marie Therese"—an aristocratic and cultured nun who sees no discrepancy between her pursuit of refined worldly pleasures and the rule of her order, with the result that she is characterized in her funeral sermon as "an emigrée in this world and the next."

In *Life Studies,* furthermore, Lowell has turned away from religious themes to find in his personal career material for fresh creative activity. In many ways, these new poems stand in striking contrast to his earlier achievement. The poems of his youth are complicated and sometimes cryptic, but those of his latest phase are disarmingly intelligible on a first reading, though their full meaning is revealed only through more careful scrutiny. In re-assessing his relationships to the people in his life, Lowell has used the microscope rather than the stereopticon, and to this new material he brings an attitude of detachment that is sometimes whimsical, but more often frightening in its psychological clarity and truth. The earlier voice of prophecy, often strident and insistent, has yielded to a calmer tone of middle-aged reminiscence: "These are the tranquillized *Fifties,* and I am forty," he says in "Memories of West Street and Lepke." Yet these poems, for all their lucid intellectual objectivity, are really intimate; some of them seem to be confessionals. For the first time in his career, Lowell deals with his own emotion for its own sake; what he reveals are his feelings about his youthful non-conformity, his father and mother, grandparents, and his wife, to whom at the age of forty-one he addresses his first love poem.

The personal candor and pungency of Lowell's latest manner can be seen in the poem "Home After Three Months Away":

Gone now the baby's nurse,
a lioness who ruled the roost
and made the Mother cry.
She used to tie
gobbets of porkrind in bowknots of gauze—
three months they hung like soggy toast
on our eight foot magnolia tree,
and helped the English sparrows
weather a Boston winter.

Three months; three months!
Is Richard now himself again?
Dimpled with exaltation,
my daughter holds her levee in the tub.
Our noses rub,
each of us pats a stringy lock of hair—
they tell me nothing's gone.
Though I am forty-one,
not forty now, the time I put away
was child's play. After thirteen weeks
my child still dabs her cheeks
to start me shaving. When
we dress her in her sky-blue corduroy
she changes to a boy,
and floats my shaving brush
and wash-cloth in the flush . . .
Dearest, I cannot loiter here
in lather like a polar bear.

Recuperating, I neither spin nor toil.
Three stories down below,
a choreman tends our coffin's length of soil,
and seven horizontal tulips blow.
Just twelve months ago,
these flowers were pedigreed
imported Dutchmen; now no one need
distinguish them from weed.
Bushed by the late spring snow,
they cannot meet
another year's snowballing enervation.

I keep no rank nor station.
Cured, I am frizzled, stale and small.[1]

This poem, like many of its companion pieces in *Life Studies,* seems low-keyed in tone; its impact depends on understatement. The three month absence has been more than geographical; from the context of other poems in this sequence it is clear that Lowell's return is not merely to his home but to reality itself after an extended period of treatment in "McLeans"—the mental hospital described in the preceding poem, "Waking in the Blue." One would expect a note of jubilation, a sense of release, but in contrast to the analogous case of W. E. Henley's "Discharged" we have a mood of contemplative meditation, not rhapsody.

On a first reading, the very casual attention to rhyme and meter and the flat, homely diction make the poem seem almost formless, even disorganized; its subject seems to amount to little more than a kind of associative inventory of domestic detail. But a closer examination reveals here that, as in the earlier work, Lowell's art is of the variety that conceals art. Each word and phrase has been chosen with great skill, and the apparently disjunctive flow of sense impressions has been fused into a consistent, unified pattern. The poem as a whole, far from being a mere celebration of trivia, is actually a profound and moving attempt on Lowell's part to re-assess his relationship to his daughter, his family and to himself, to rediscover a principle of order in his life, to counterbalance the remorseless flux of reality with some unvarying element of stasis and fixity.

Thus the images of control and governing (the "lioness who ruled the roost"; the poet's explicit identification with Richard III—the phrase is from Cibber—his daughter's levee; her suit of corduroy) operate in the poem to suggest order. Similarly, the heavy instance on numbers and images of measurement reflect a compulsion to order his universe (of which his home is the microcosm) in terms of mathematical certainty. After the dislocation of mental illness, Lowell is trying to make sure that "things add up."

To this pattern of fixity in the poem is juxtaposed an antagonistic series of images of metamorphosis. The pork-rind has become soggy toast (this unattractive image is presented early in the poem because Lowell wants to use it as a metaphor for himself in the closing lines); the poet is "forty-one, not forty now" (his birthday is March 1); his daughter, though she retains her old endearing feminine habits, is changed to a boy both in costume and behavior; the tulips have gone through their own cycle of rebirth and death in "our coffin's length of soil." (Vis-à-vis the tulips, note Lowell's old penchant for achieving concentration through a pun:

> Bushed by the late spring snow,
> they cannot meet
> another year's snowballing enervation.)

The poem ends, characteristically, in a paradox: Lowell feels that he has regained mental health and control only at the expense of vital energy; he seems to have exchanged one kind of life-in-death for another. His attainment of an uneasy truce with reality is appropriate to both his exhausted state of partial recovery and his poignant apprehension of the meaning of middle age. The poem is right in its context; Lowell's revelation (thought by some reviewers to be too personal) is moving because of its complete sincerity. This delicate blending of joy at the implied continuity of life, symbolized by his daughter, and sadness in the realization that all things suffer the effects of process, time and change is achieved with a skill that is eloquent testimony that he has retained all his earlier power, but that in middle age he has changed the direction of his career to find in his own private life fresh material for inspiration.

NOTES

[1] Reprinted from *Life Studies* (copyright 1956, 1959, by Robert Lowell) with the permission of the publishers, Farrar, Straus and Cudahy, Inc.

[2] From *Lord Weary's Castle*, copyright 1944, 1946, by Robert Lowell. Reprinted by permission of Harcourt, Brace and World, Inc., and Faber & Faber, Ltd.

[3] From *Land of Unlikeness*, The Cummington Press, 1944. Copyright 1944 by Robert Lowell.

III
THE
POETRY
OF
STANLEY
KUNITZ:
AN
INTRODUCTORY
ESSAY

JEAN H. HAGSTRUM

STANLEY KUNITZ provides his readers with the excitement, rarely encountered in modern poetry, of exploring both the guilty and the joyful recesses of the personality. Of guilt alone, we have perhaps had more than our share, and the pilgrimage from sin to salvation has become—who would have believed it a generation ago?—almost fashionable. But relatively few have moved, as Mr. Kunitz has in his thirty-year poetic career, from darkly morbid psychic interiors to a clean, well-lighted place, where personality is integrated through love and art—love that draws nourishment from the unabashedly physical and art that, though complex, rests on the honest simplifications of life.

I

Though Kunitz's literary life and manner are difficult, one of his central ideas is extremely simple. He has said, "Let life happen to you . . . Life is right," and he believes that modern neurosis in part stems from the morbid separation of art from life that characterizes our culture. The naked prose statements will impress only those who admire the dignified Johnsonian ability to state without fear of triteness the essential commonplaces of life and art. But expressed in his poetry the same idea possesses verbal vigor and imagistic shock, especially in that series of brilliant life-death antitheses whose polarities constitute the major contention of his major poetry.

In the early poetry the negative or life-denying side of the contrast receives the greater emphasis and is embodied in the important image of the skeleton and in other images that cluster about it. Kunitz imagines bones as clean, hygienic, disinfected, shapely, sharp—the

> bonecase (melted down)
> Shimmers with scaly wit— [1]

but irrevocably and horribly dead. The death-image is composed not of decay, blood, exposed viscera, smells of disintegration, but of harsh, dry, and defined things like needles, spines, spikes, sand, stones, leafless branches, scalpels, peeled nuts, and shadows on the wall. In "The Surgeons" death is symbolized by skillful, professional savages who open the brain of a child, dissipate its dreams, and cut away all pity and love. These men of knife and bone are systematic, amputating men who hate tradition and passion and whose despair of the future matches their scorn of the past.

Kunitz's symbols of life, which seem to predominate in the later poems, are better if one prefers the constructive and wholesome to the bitterly angry. The old-clothes man, unlike the surgeons, does not create but mobilizes wounds. He collects the decaying coats behind the door, the scraps and rags of past experience—dead ambitions, buried love, lost innocence. But this tatterdemalion army, as ragged as Jack Falstaff's, is an invincibly human one:

> Let
> The enemies of life beware
> When these old clothes go forth to war.

In a recent poem, "The Thief," in which the poet curses a *ladrone* who picked his pocket clean in a crowded Roman train, Kunitz gives his favorite antithesis an auto-biographical context. The unpleasant loss evokes recol-lections of both historical Rome and the poet's own per-sonal Rome, which he remembers from the lantern slides shown at school. But that Rome, he now knows, was a "pedagogic lie," and the careful reader of Kunitz sees that that Rome ("the frozen pure") has become a symbol of stony, skeletal death. But the real Rome, with its elbowing mobs, its thieves, its jogging *carrozze,* and its stones baroquely shaped by Bernini, is all motion, im-pure like emotion, flawed by mutability,

> and yet thereby
> More lovely and more graced, perhaps
> More true.

Kunitz likes the blooming, bacterial rot the surgeon cuts away to expose his dead and flinty surfaces. For the poet, the blood, the guts, the "bubbling brain, exploding life's gray tumor," and the "green-celled world" where our "blind moulds" kiss have their compensatory side: they blaze with life as well as death. Alexander Pope recoiled in horror from the crawling maggoty world which in the *Dunciad* he created to symbolize Grub Street. But Kunitz finds decay a pre-condition of existence, the very com-post in which life sprouts:

> In fierce decay I'll find a stripe
> Of honey sweetening the tart

Old brain. I shall not know again such ripe
Beauty of the burst, dark heart.

Kunitz believes, in Gospel phrase, that "Except a corn of
wheat fall to the ground and die, it abideth alone; but
if it die, it bringeth forth much fruit":

I lie awake, hearing the drip
Upon my sill; thinking, the sun
Has not been promised; we who strip
Summer to seed shall be undone.

Now, while the antler of the eaves
Liquefies, drop by drop, I brood
On a Christian thing: unless the leaves
Perish, the tree is not renewed.

II

Kunitz has said in prose that "every poem must be loaded
with a full charge of experience" and in verse,

I, being rent
By the fierce divisions of our time, cried death
And death again, and my own dying meant.

We cannot, without more information than we now
possess, trace the poetry back to its biographical source.
But as critics we must ask that unsophisticated, essential,
and difficult question: does the poetry have on it the
bloom of first-hand experience?

Kunitz was born in 1905 of Russian-Jewish parents, and
in his verse there is the shadowy outline of a changing
response to his Jewish heritage. The following early

lines seem to sound a note of revolt against the family and its traditions:

> Now I must tread the starry wrack
> And penetrate the burning sea.
> Iscariot, I may come back,
> But do not wait for me.

In "For the Word is Flesh" the poet apparently confesses to hearing "the fierce/Wild cry of Jesus on the holy tree" at the very moment he says to his dead father that he has

> of you no syllable to keep,
> Only the deep rock crumbling in the deep.

And the impression from the earlier poetry is confirmed by a comment on his boyhood days in one of his latest poems,

> For nothing pleased me then in my legacy.

World War II seems, from the evidence of the poetry and from that alone, to have restored the poet's ties with his personal past, for the following lines must surely be autobiographical (The man of the first lines is, I believe, Hitler, the ancestors of the third and following lines are his immigrant parents, and the second paragraph refers to the Nazis, persecuting the Jews and perhaps also invading Russia):

> When I stand in the center of that man's madness,
> Deep in his trauma, as in the crater of a wound,
> My ancestors step from my American bones.

There's mother in a woven shawl, and that,
No doubt, is father picking up his pack
For the return voyage through those dreadful years
Into the winter of the raging eye.

One generation past, two days by plane away,
My house is dispossessed, my friends dispersed,
My teeth and pride knocked in, my people game
For the hunters of man-skins in the warrens of
   Europe,
The impossible creatures of an hysteriac's dream
Advancing with hatchets sunk into their skulls
To rip the god out of the machine.

Two of Kunitz's best poems, "For the Word is Flesh"
(from the 1930 volume) and "Father and Son" (from
the 1944 volume), represent strongly diverse responses to
antithetical father-images, or, if the biographical identifi-
cations I propose are wrong, antithetical responses to the
same father-image, or perhaps something more complicated than either of these alternatives. (The two poems
are obviously now intended to be read together since
they are printed on opposite pages in the 1958 volume.)
The earlier poem belongs to the period of Kunitz's impatience with his heritage—or lack of one—and his horror at the surgically produced skeletons of modern life.
Among these enemies of life he has placed his father—
or at least a generic father whom the speaker of the poem
addresses—now a lipless skeleton:

Let sons learn from their lipless fathers how
Man enters hell without a golden bough.

It may be relevant to note that Kunitz's father died a suicide at thirty-eight, a few weeks before his son was born,

and to quote the poet's comment, "Of my father I know almost nothing except that he was a free-thinker and a Mason who left behind a collection of good books."

In the later father-poem tenderness has replaced anger. This poem, I suggest hesitantly, is addressed not to Kunitz's father but his stepfather, Mark Dine, "of all men I have known . . . the gentlest," who lived with the family only six years before he died of a heart attack. The stepson was then fourteen. In the poem from which I quote here only the last paragraph, the spirit of Mark Dine has been transmuted to unalloyed poetic gold:

> At the water's edge, where the smothering ferns
>   lifted
> Their arms, "Father!" I cried, "Return! You know
> The way. I'll wipe the mudstains from your clothes;
> No trace, I promise, will remain. Instruct
> Your son, whirling between two wars,
> In the Gemara of your gentleness,
> For I would be a child of those who mourn
> And brother to the foundlings of the field
> And friend of innocence and all bright eyes.
> O teach me how to work and keep me kind."
> Among the turtles and the lilies he turned to me
> The white ignorant hollow of his face.

The two father-poems also represent responses to the poet's national and religious heritage. In the first he confesses that he "cannot blur/The mirrored brain with fantasies of Er," but in the second a suffering and chastened man seeks wisdom in the Gemara of his father's gentleness.

Kunitz's love poetry has always been perceptive and persuasive. Neither Puritanical or prurient, it never stridently tempts us to eat forbidden fruit. It has sometimes been tremblingly tender, as in "Night-piece," when men sigh good night,

> put out their bodies like a light,
> And set their brains adrift upon their blood,

and urge, "Let us be shy again like feathered things"; and sometimes jealously amorous as in "The Science of the Night," when the lover, his manhood lying on a rumpled field, his beloved sprawled carelessly in sleep, imagines that she returns to people and places he has never known.

Kunitz's poetry introduces two Ladies, an Early Lady and a Later Lady, who must correspond to his experience in the subtle way that art always corresponds to the reality out of which it springs. The Early Lady is imprecisely outlined. She appears fleetingly in the surrealist landscape of the first poems; and the experiences in which she figures are frustrating ones, not unlike the situation in Gertrude Stein's most beautiful story, *Melanctha*, in which one lover's love is too early and the other's is tragically too late:

> For love is coming or is passing by,
> And none may look upon her features plain.

> How shall these tarry, how shall these meet,
> When he must remember and she forget?
> Her baby-heart is running down a street
> Already ended, his to a place not yet.

The Later Lady has provided both lover and artist with his deepest fulfillments. Although a person of an earlier secret life lived apart from his own and although a person of a wild, adventuring spirit for whom the boldest

astronomical imagery may even be restrained, this Lady
has also evoked the most delicate, urbane, and courtly
poetry Kunitz has as yet written. The Lady, herself an
artist, transforms the raw music of life to measured
harmony; metaphysical of mind, she provokes and ap-
preciates the subtlest intellectual joke. But even the Early
Lady—a Dark Lady who spoke the serpent's word—
is never really lost to life and experience. She may, like
the ooze of souls, be too virulent to die. She may be one
of the blind wounds the old-clothes man comes to
mobilize. In any event, she has taught the poet a hard,
hard lesson:

> We learn, as the thread plays out, that we belong
> Less to what flatters us than to what scars.

III

Kunitz has published three volumes of poetry, in 1930,
1944, and 1958. *Intellectual Things,* the first of these,
contained fifty poems, most of them short lyrics in the
modern metaphysical manner made fashionable by T. S.
Eliot.

The bold images and scenes remind one of Donne, but
the urbane language, the exquisitely flowing music, and
the syntactical precision recall Marvell. Donne's sense of
evil in the marrow, his moral and psychological frankness,
his imaginative originality in combining geography,
mathematics, science, and statecraft with love-making and
worship—all these have their impressive counterparts in
Kunitz. But Donne serves a modern purpose; and his
tight, though outrageously literal scholastic logic, his firm
sense of intellectual outline, his essential fidelity to nature
even when his combinations disfigure its surface, Kunitz
distorts into an imagistic surrealism that provides intense experience without providing paraphrasable mean-

ing. Man dissolves in a cooking vat of chemicals that stands alone on a crumbling rock. A poetic speaker compares himself to a crystal bead in a crystal ball, "So pure that only Nothing could be less." Twilight invades a room in which glowing lions congregate and in which the poet, also tawny, awaits the approach of night, as the day and his heart spill their blood to slake his lips, when suddenly the moon, tawny like man and lion, materializes at the door. A human body swells in corruption until in death it becomes a whale that, like a derelict vessel, is pillaged by the curious. Lovers eat their ecstatic hearts and kiss in "complicate analysis of passionate destruction." The poet creeps deep into his own self, where he lies on the burning plumage of an angel and so lives his entire life all at once.

In thus delineating Kunitz's surrealist landscape, I have been guilty of separating image and context. In its proper place the imagery does more than shock. It attacks the modern simplifications of human nature that reduce it to one dimension and omit the vital parts. Kunitz's outrage is that of the anti-body against a destroying foreign presence. Blood, organ and sinew swell in protest, and a feverish brain tries to expel the attackers of our vital centers.

"Single Vision," which I have chosen to represent the 1930 volume, is so tightly coherent that it must be quoted in full. The action seems to be this: one of Kunitz's surgeons, a lost man, rises in a resurrection scene that recalls Donne and, in one image—though if there was conscious intent it must have been to draw a contrast— Piero della Francesca's great painting in which Christ rises with a banner in his hand. The rising man is a Kunitzian skeleton, taught to reject love and the blood and to refine away the flesh. But as he rises, persisting life rises with him and all that goes with life—the unused evil in the bones, the stain of reality on the brain, and the pride of blood unimaginably unfurled at his side. In sympathy with these life-symbols, the skeleton, now in remorse, sheds the tears of the soul and then slips into the silence of the bony and dusty grave which modern, life-disinfecting, hollow men have prepared for him:

Before I am completely shriven
I shall reject my inch of heaven.

Cancel my eyes, and, standing, sink
Into my deepest self; there drink

Memory down. The banner of
My blood, unfurled, will not be love,

Only the pity and the pride
Of it, pinned to my open side.

When I have utterly refined
The composition of my mind,

Shaped language of my marrow till
Its forms are instant to my will,

Suffered the leaf of my heart to fall
Under the wind, and, stripping all

The tender blanket from my bone,
Rise like a skeleton in the sun,

I shall have risen to disown
The good mortality I won.

Directly risen with the stain
Of life upon my crested brain,

Which I shall shake against my ghost
To frighten him, when I am lost.

Gladly, as any poison, yield
My halved conscience, brightly peeled;

Infect him, since we live but once,
With the unused evil in my bones.

I'll shed the tear of souls, the true
Sweat, Blake's intellectual dew,

Before I am resigned to slip
A dusty finger on my lip.

In 1944 Kunitz's second volume of verse, *Passport to the War*, appeared, containing fifty poems in all, twenty-six of which had not before appeared in book-form and twenty-four of which were re-published from the earlier volume. Lines like

The silence unrolling before me as I came,
The night nailed like an orange to my brow,

and others, recalling early De Chirico,

Through portal and through peristyle
Her phantom glides, whose secret mouth,
The absence of whose flagrant smile,
Hangs on my chimney like a wreath of cloud,

show that the earlier metaphysical-surrealist manner continues. But it is now combined with themes of contemporary political and social reality; and a new style of expression, that may suggest Robert Frost, introduces greater colloquial flexibility and greater human warmth. Anger remains, but it is a satirical anger aimed at recognizable targets: Hitler, the Nazis, the Bitch Goddess Success, military men of any nation, and a new, dangerously pervasive savagery. "Reflections by a Mailbox," "Night Letter," and "Father and Son"—unfortunately all too long to quote in full—add new power to the old without obliterating the Kunitzian signature, which remains unmistakable throughout his entire career.

The best moments are still those that explore the individual's soul. The new social themes remain languid until they disturb the psyche. But though not notable in themselves as programs of action or ways of life, the new social reality has brought drama and scene into sharper focus even in the metaphysical moments. Consider the increased intensity of that stunning poem about evil in the dream and in the soul, "The Fitting of the Mask," the inspiration for which Kunitz seems to have derived from a passage he greatly admired in Rilke's *Journal of My Other Self*. I quote the poem entire as an example of the new power of the 1944 collection:

"Again I come to buy the image fated."
"Your valued image, sir, and that's a pity,
Is gone, I mean the youth, the undefeated,
Whose falcon-heart, winged with the golden shout
Of morning, sweeps windward from his native city,
Crying his father's grief, his mother's doubt."

"You knew I cared, and that I'd come for him;
The traffic hindered me; you should have known."
"Ah there, that's bad! But my poor memory's dim
As a bell that rings the tide in; I lose track

Of things to keep and things to sell, and one
Can never be quite certain who'll come back."

"Enough! There was another face, a bright
Pathetic one I'll take, from whose wild stain
Of sympathy a man could borrow light."
"Our catalogue describes him 'Fool of Love,
Fragile and dear, tinctured with mortal pain,
Buys grain of his grain and eats the chaff there-
of.' "

"Your cataloguer has the cynic touch,
But I'll forgive him. Is our business over?"
"Be patient, sir. You would not thank me much
Or recommend my baffling merchandise
If I should offer this unblessed believer,
This torn-cheek, with the chasm in his eyes."

"Old man, I'm in a hurry to proceed,
And everyone, you know, must wear a mask.
Give me a countenance to meet my need
Or malice will expose me at the dance."
"Oh sir, we'll try, but it's no easy task
To make adjustments to your circumstance;

And now, while my assistant turns the key
And in the windows now the lights go out,
For it is closing time irrevocably
Until new features sit upon the forms,
I'll sing a little ditty to the ghost
That occupies this world of empty frames.

[*Sings:*]
Good-fellow's lost among our Psychic Cases,
The Angry Man has turned a ghastly blue,

Munich exhausted all our Judas-faces.
And what are we to do, and what to do?
The Optimist was mangled in a sock,
The rats conferred and ate The Wandering Jew,
There's nothing left that's decent in our stock,
And what are we to do, and what to do?

But look!—here's something rare, macabre, a true
Invention of the time's insomniac wits.
Perhaps we ought to sell it to the zoo.
Go to the darkening glass that traps your shames
And tell me what you see."
                    "O Prince of Counterfeits,
This is the Self I hunted and knifed in dreams."

Kunitz's *Selected Poems 1928–1958* contained eighty-five poems, of which one-third were new and the remaining were republished from the two earlier volumes. The latest poems make the old metaphysical boldness even bolder and intensify the already unparaphrasable imagistic intensity. At the same time, the long colloquial line of 1944 has now become a marvel of flexible strength. Suffusing these familiar effects is a golden romanticism that had earlier been only a hesitant *soupçon* of better things to come—a strain that from the beginning invoked poets of the romantic generation, notably Blake.

The title *Intellectual Things* (1930) was adapted from Blake's famous sentence, "For the tear is an intellectual thing," which Kunitz used as the epigraph of that volume. In a memorable phrase Kunitz defined the "tear of souls" (in contrast to modern, dry-as-dust, skeletal powder) as the "true sweat, Blake's intellectual dew." Some four poems in that volume, none of which Kunitz has chosen to reprint, are vaguely Blakean and romantic: "Death in Moonlight," "Sad Song," "Thou Unbelieving Heart" (which contains lovely lines but may not be as fully integrated as at first appears), and "Elemental Metamorphosis" (which contains a stronger recollection of Wordsworth's "Three Years She Grew" and "A Slumber did my Spirit Seal" than of anything in Blake). But except for certain lines these poems did not achieve the magic of the *Songs of Innocence and Experience* because they are too lush or because they remain flat and smooth and imprecise, like the romantics at their least impressive. In "Open the Gates" of the 1944 collection, however, Kunitz, perhaps unconsciously, has achieved an effect in the first two stanzas that is authentically Blakean—but recalling not so much the purely lyrical Blake as the verbal-visual Blake of emblems like the frontispiece to *Jerusalem* or the haunting "Death's Door":

Within the city of the burning cloud,
Dragging my life behind me in a sack,
Naked I prowl, scourged by the black
Temptation of the blood grown proud.

Here at the monumental door,
Carved with the curious legend of my youth,
I brandish the great bone of my death,
Beat once therewith and beat no more.

In the 1958 volume the Blakean strain grows into something fresh and lovely: in the poem to the delicate white mouse, "The Waltzer in the House"; in the emblematic allegory, "The Way Down"; in the exquisite "As Flowers Are," a lovely poem that draws on the wars and loves of the flowers—Erasmus Darwin refined into quintessential Blake; but above all in that delicate aubade, "When the Light Falls," a poem of urbane compliment which combines Ben Jonson's courtly, classical elegance and Blake's power of deep and elemental suggestion:

When the light falls, it falls on her
In whose rose-gilded chamber
A music strained through mind
Turns everything to measure.

The light that seeks her out
Finds answering light within,
And the two join hands and dance
On either side of her skin.

The lily and the swan
Attend her whiter pride,
While the courtly laurel kneels
To kiss his mantling bride.

Under each cherry-bough
She spreads her silken cloths
At the rumor of a wind,
To gather up her deaths,

For the petals of her heart
Are shaken in a night,
Whose ceremonial art
Is dying into light.

Kunitz's poetic virtuosity is such that it fully vindicates his own aesthetic belief that meaning in verse is "a product of the total form." But like his peers and even his betters, he is not an absolutely impeccable craftsman, and there are some fifteen separate occasions on which one reader grieved in reading the latest collection, from which the poet has excluded what he considers his earlier failures—grief usually over a word, line, or image, only rarely over an entire poem or one of its crucial sections.

Kunitz has said that "there is only one artist, the true, recurrent, undying wanderer, the eternally guilty, invincibly friendly man." It is tempting to apply that sentence to its author. The joyous love lyrics, the austere but amiable reviews of younger men's work, his comments on his teaching experiences, in which he has delighted in engaging the inquisitive spirits of even the faltering beginners—all this makes us want to say of him that he must be "an invincibly friendly man."

As poet Mr. Kunitz appears also as the "eternally guilty" man:

> But why do I wake at the sound,
> In the middle of the night,
> Of the tread of the Masked Man
> Heavy on the stairs . . . ?
> Agh! I am sometimes weary
> Of this everlasting search
> For the drama in a nutshell,
> The opera of the tragic sense,
> Which I would gladly be rid of.

But Mr. Kunitz need not be embarrassed. "Complicate" guilt is one of his most excitingly exploited themes, absolutely without the theatricality he seems to impute to it in the lines just quoted.

What can Kunitz mean when he calls the artist the "true, recurrent, undying wanderer," and can this part of the sentence also be applied to him? I think it can, and I judge it to mean that a poem—to interpret Kunitz by Kunitz—"repeats for us man's spiritual ascent, identifying whoever shares in its beauty with those obscure thousands under the hill of time [this image Kunitz has used more than once in his poetry] who once climbed . . . and climb again the forbidding slope." That is, a true work of art is a kind of secular All Souls' Day sacrament, that brings us into communion with struggling men of all days and ways, with dead poets who have celebrated those struggles, and with the heroes of myth and legend who have memorably embodied them for the whole race. "The Approach to Thebes" reveals the true poetic "wanderer" in the full meaning of Kunitz. Oedipus, who speaks the lines of the poem, has encountered and overcome the Sphinx. He now approaches Thebes, about to become its king—not joyfully but in solemn sadness since a prophetic vision reveals to him the horrors that will with the years be heaped upon his head. But he comes prepared: the winning of the Sphinx has irrevocably tied him to life itself. In overcoming her, he has mastered it:

> In the zero of the night, in the lipping hour,
> Skin-time, knocking-time, when the heart is pearled
> And the moon squanders its uranian gold,
> She taunted me, who was all music's tongue,
> Philosophy's and wilderness's breed,
> Of shifting shape, half jungle-cat, half-dancer,
> Night's woman-petaled, lion-scented rose,
> To whom I gave, out of a hero's need,
> The dolor of my thrust, my riddling answer,
> Whose force no lesser mortal knows. Dangerous?
> Yes, as nervous oracles foretold
> Who could not guess the secret taste of her:
> Impossible wine! I came into the world
> To fill a fate; am punished by my youth
> No more. What if dog-faced logic howls
> Was it art or magic multiplied my joy?
> Nature has reasons beyond true or false.

We played like metaphysic animals
Whose freedom made our knowledge bold
Before the tragic curtain of the day:
I can bear the dishonor now of growing old.

Blinded and old, exiled, diseased, and scorned—
The verdict's bitten on the brazen gates,
For the gods grant each of us his lot, his term.
Hail to the King of Thebes!—my self, ordained
To satisfy the impulse of the worm,
Bemummied in those famous incestuous sheets,
The bloodiest flags of nations of the curse,
To be hung from the balcony outside the room
Where I encounter my most flagrant source.
Children, grandchildren, my long posterity,
To whom I bequeath the spiders of my dust,
Believe me, whatever sordid tales you hear,
Told by physicians or mendacious scribes,
Of beardless folly, consanguineous lust,
Fomenting pestilence, rebellion, war,
I come prepared, unwanting what I see,
But tied to life. On the royal road to Thebes
I had my luck, I met a lovely monster,
And the story's this: I made the monster me.

The sensitive and trained reader of these lines cannot
escape believing that the Sphinx of the legend the poet
has made to correspond profoundly to the Later Lady of
the love-lyrics and that therefore Oedipus must be, in
ways too deep to follow, a richly autobiographical character. The poem virtually equates the mastery of the
lovely monster with the mastery of life itself, and that
equation measures both the difficulties and the rewards
of the conquest.

Kunitz has said, "No poetry is required of any of us.

Our first labor is to master our worlds." No poetry is indeed required, but it is most welcome when, like that of Stanley Kunitz, it authentically reports the breaking and the making of a poet and his world.

NOTES

¹ All poems quoted in whole or in part are copyrighted by Stanley Kunitz and printed with his permission and the permission of Little, Brown, and Company publishers of Mr. Kunitz' *Selected Poems, 1928–1958.*

IV
"WELL-OPEN EYES": OR, THE POETRY OF RICHARD WILBUR

FREDERIC E. FAVERTY

"Everything in the world is strange and marvellous to well-open eyes. This faculty of wonder is the delight . . . which leads the intellectual man through life in the perpetual ecstasy of the visionary. His special attribute is the wonder of the eyes. Hence it was that the ancients gave Minerva her owl, the bird with ever-dazzled eyes." (José Ortega y Gasset, *Revolt of the Masses*.) [1]

FOR a comparatively young poet, Richard Wilbur (b. 1921) has received considerable recognition from official quarters: the Harriet Monroe Prize in poetry, 1948; the Oscar Blumenthal Prize, 1950; the Edna St. Vincent Millay Memorial Award, 1957; the National Book Award, 1957; and the Pulitzer Prize, 1957. In recognition of his promise as well as his achievement he has been granted fellowships by the Guggenheim Foundation (1952) and by the American Academy of Arts and Letters (1945). Currently he is a professor of English at Wesleyan University.

One of his central interests has been animals, an interest that culminated in *A Bestiary*, compiled by Wilbur and illustrated by Alexander Calder (Pantheon Books, Inc., 1955). In this work there are thirty-three separate treatments: the frog, the dog, the fly, the spider, the hawk, the whale, etc. Fabulous animals like the centaur, the mermaid, and the unicorn are also included. For each creature there are four or five brief descriptions in prose or verse drawn from the voluminous literature on animals, from ancient books like Aesop's *Fables* and Pliny's *Natural History* to the works of contemporaries like Richard Eberhart and Marianne Moore. A few of the poems are Wilbur's own; some, like the one on the pelican, are his translations from other languages.

For more than a thousand years the *Bestiary* was one of the chief reference books on animals. In the earliest form of the work, *The Physiologus* of the second century, the legendary attributes ascribed to animals were given symbolical interpretations. By ingenious parallels the lion and the whale, for example, were shown to represent Christ. In many a medieval tapestry the unicorn dominates the scene. According to legend, it was an exceedingly dangerous beast; yet at sight of a virgin it would approach gently and place its head in her lap. So, Christ, mightiest of celestial beings, took on human form in the womb of the Virgin Mary. Animal allegories of this sort were favored by the Greek and Latin Church Fathers: Origen, Ambrose, Jerome, and Augustine. Through their influence the *Physiologus* came to be translated as the *Bestiary* into most of the west European vernaculars. Wilbur draws particularly upon the Middle English *Bestiary*. For translation from the twelfth century Anglo-Norman Philippe de Thaun's *Bestiaire* he selects "The Pelican," in which sophistication and naïveté are skilfully blended. The father pelican angered by the attacks his infant offspring make upon him, slays them. Moved by compassion he returns after three days, draws blood from his side and sprinkles it upon the lifeless forms. The little birds revive. In similar fashion, mankind condemned to death has been restored to life through the shedding of Christ's blood.

In definition and range, however, Wilbur's *Bestiary* goes far beyond its medieval original. It includes classical and modern accounts that have no trace of allegory. Thorstein Veblen's diatribe on "the filthiest of the domestic animals," the dog, is an example. Of Wilbur's translations, one of the best is "A Prayer to Go to Paradise with the Donkeys," by the late nineteenth century French poet, Francis Jammes. In its humble subject, its simple diction, and its unquestioning faith, it recaptures something of the charm of the middle ages. Wilbur's faithful translation deserves to be quoted in full:

When I must come to you, O my God, I pray
It be some dust-roaded holiday,
And even as in my travels here below,
I beg to choose by what road I shall go
To Paradise, where the clear stars shine by day.
I'll take my walking-stick and go my way,
And to my friends the donkeys I shall say,
'I am Francis Jammes, and I'm going to Paradise,
For there is no hell in the land of the loving God.'
And I'll say to them: 'Come, sweet friends of the
   blue skies,
Poor creatures who with a flap of the ears or a nod
Of the head shake off the buffets, the bees, the
   flies . . .'
Let me come with these donkeys, Lord, into your
   land,
These beasts who bow their heads so gently, and
   stand
With their small feet joined together in a fashion

Utterly gentle, asking your compassion.
I shall arrive, followed by their thousands of ears,
Followed by those with baskets at their flanks,
By those who lug the carts of mountebanks
Or loads of feather-dusters and kitchen-wares,
By those with humps of battered water-cans,
By bottle-shaped she-asses who halt and stumble,
By those tricked out in little pantaloons
To cover their wet, blue galls where flies assemble
In whirling swarms, making a drunken hum.
Dear God, let it be with these donkeys that I come,
And let it be that angels lead us in peace
To leafy streams where cherries tremble in air,
Sleek as the laughing flesh of girls; and there
In that haven of souls let it be that, leaning above
Your divine waters, I shall resemble these donkeys,
Whose humble and sweet poverty will appear
Clear in the clearness of your eternal love.[2]

In his own animal poems, only a few of which are included in the *Bestiary*, Wilbur strikes an original note. He takes for his themes such things as the locust's song in "windless summer evenings," the southern flight of blackbirds in autumn, the death of a toad. Unlike Aesop, he provides no narrative, no moral; unlike Pliny, he is not concerned mainly with the animal's attributes, real or fabulous. In each instance, his animal is a medium through which he moves to larger, deeper issues. The poem about the locust, or cicada, rests upon a paradox. The cicada's song has always puzzled and delighted men; "chanters of miracles" have even taken it for a sign. Yet, as the scientist Fabre proved, the cicada cannot hear. In trying to catch in words the impression that the flight of blackbirds makes upon him, he discovers the shifting nature of reality, learns

By what cross-purposes the world is dreamt.

In imagination he follows the dying toad as it sinks back toward its origins in primal oceans, toward "cooling shores," and "lost Amphibia's emperies." But the particular and profounder quality of these animal poems is illustrated best, perhaps, in "A Grasshopper," which appeared in *The New Yorker*, August 22, 1959. The familiar and invidious contrast with the ant has no place in this poem. There is no sermon on industry *vs.* idleness. Instead, the poem is an attempt, and a successful one, to catch the stillness of a summer day, the peace that for "a brief moment" descends on a field of grass, when a grasshopper pauses on a chicory leaf. The leaf rocks briefly under the weight and then is still. The quiet spreads to the surrounding flowers. The wind shrinks away. All cries fade out. Peace seems to extend "to the world's verge." But suddenly, and with no apparent purpose, the grasshopper leaps away, "giving the leaf a kick." By a kind of chain reaction, the grasses begin to sway again, the cricket's cry is heard, the entire field awakes. So, the macrocosm is shown in the microcosm. In little, the incident illustrates the larger ebb and flow of things, the universal alternation of opposites which is the dance of life, the cosmic harmony.

The *Bestiary* can be used to indicate another aspect of Wilbur's work, the equal attraction that comic and serious themes have for him. Under "The Fly" he has an entry drawn from Laurence Sterne and another drawn from William Blake. Uncle Toby in Sterne's *Tristam Shandy* is of so gentle a disposition that he has "scarce a heart to retaliate upon a fly." Having caught a particularly large and persistent one that has buzzed around his nose through dinner, he ceremoniously conveys it to the window, and after a long, grandiloquent, semi-Biblical speech of forgiveness and benediction, sets it free. The passage is remarkable for its lightness of touch and its comic overtones. A striking contrast is provided by Blake's serious thoughts on the same subject:

Little Fly,
Thy summer's play
My thoughtless hand
Has brush'd away.

Am I not
A fly like thee?
Or art not thou
A man like me?

For I dance,
And drink, & sing,
Till some blind hand
Shall brush my wing.

That Wilbur includes selections from authors so different in type as Sterne and Blake indicates a range of interests that is to be found also in his own work—his translations and his original poems.

It is significant that among French authors the two with whom Wilbur is most concerned are Molière and Voltaire. For sophisticated repartee, the satiric give-and-take of drawing-room conversation, few plays in the world's repertory can match Molière's *Misanthrope*. And Wilbur's translation of the play (Harcourt, Brace, and Company, Inc., 1955) is as lively as any thus far in English. Furthermore, it is done in verse, preserving, as Wilbur says, "the frequently intricate arrangements of balancing half-lines, lines, couplets, quatrains, and sestets." All this, too, without sacrifice of accuracy and faithfulness to the original. How difficult such a feat is the Italians recognize in their adage, "*traduttore, traditore*." Too frequently the translator is a traitor. In Wilbur's English dress, however, Molière's epigrams retain their polish and their poison. The double-edged nature of the satire—the simultaneous ridicule of society on the one hand, and its chief critic, Alceste, on the other—is admirably maintained. For conversational ease and naturalness combined with deadly verbal thrusts, as in a duel, no scene surpasses the one in which two drawing-room belles, Arsinoé and Célimène, tear each other's reputations to shreds. It is the scene that Wilbur selects for inclusion in his collection, *Poems 1943–1956* (Faber and Faber, 1957). The play as a whole shows his genuine talent as a translator.

After his success with Molière, he was a natural choice when Leonard Bernstein and Lillian Hellman wanted someone to write the lyrics for *Candide,* their comic operetta[3] on Voltaire's famous philosophical romance. Of all the spirited and amusing lyrics, the best is "Pangloss's Song," Wilbur's contribution, on which the opera closes. Through the ravages of syphilis, Pangloss the philosopher of optimism, has lost an eye, and his nose is half eaten away. Yet he remains faithful to his philosophy, still sings a song of praise to the Goddess of Love in this best of all possible worlds:

Dear boy, you will not hear me speak
    With sorrow or with rancour
Of what has paled my rosy cheek
    And blasted it with canker;
'Twas Love, great Love, that did the deed
    Through Nature's gentle laws,
And how should ill effects proceed
From so divine a cause.

Sweet honey comes from bees that sting,
    As you are well aware;

To one adept in reasoning,
   Whatever pains disease may bring
Are but the tangy seasoning
   To Love's delicious fare.

Columbus and his men, they say,
   Conveyed the virus hither
Whereby my features rot away
   And vital powers wither;
Yet had they not traversed the seas
   And come infected back,
Why, think of all the luxuries
   That modern life would lack!

All bitter things conduce to sweet,
   As this example shows;
Without the little spirochete
   We'd have no chocolate to eat,
Nor would tobacco's fragrance greet
   The European nose.

Each nation guards its native land
   With cannon and with sentry,
Inspectors look for contraband
   At every port of entry,
Yet nothing can prevent the spread
   Of Love's divine disease;
It rounds the world from bed to bed
   As pretty as you please.

Men worship Venus everywhere
   As plainly may be seen;
The decorations which I bear
   Are nobler than the Croix de Guerre,

And gained in service of our fair
And universal Queen.[4]

There is a sprinkling of poems of the light and humorous
sort in each of Wilbur's books thus far published. Two
clever couplets, for example, are devoted to Dr.
Samuel Johnson's kicking a stone in refutation of
Berkeley's idealistic philosophy ("Epistemology"). Don
Quixote riding abroad in search of glory and adventure
comes to a crossing and allows his horse to choose the
way. The horse, wiser than the master, heads back for the
barn ("Parable"). A graceful dancer pirouettes on a
museum wall ("Museum Piece"). It is a painting by
Edgar Degas who once bought an excellent El Greco

To hang his pants on while he slept.

Degas, to whom Wilbur devotes two poems ("Museum
Piece" and "L'Étoile"), is not the only painter, however, to
interest him. "My Father Paints the Summer" is another
poem on the kindred art. Eugène Delacroix receives a
tribute in "The Giaour and the Pacha." A painting by
Bazille is the subject of "Ceremony." And Pieter de
Hooch's art inspires "Objects" and "A Dutch Courtyard."
In the work of these painters it is evident that Wilbur
finds principles operative that are of value, also, to him as
a poet. There is, for example, the peculiar power the
painter Pieter de Hooch has of making "objects speak."
This power Wilbur also possesses. From many possible illustrations, "Driftwood" can be selected as representative.
Cast up by the sea, at rest finally on the sand, a few
gnarled relics have a tremendous significance. They tell
of years of growing in the forest; of service as mast, or
oar, or plank; of eventual ship-wreck; of floating in deep
waters by which they were "never dissolved"; of being
"shaped" and "fitted" by ocean tides until now they have

                    the beauty of
Excellence earned.

To the present generation faced by so many difficult
problems, these relics should have a special meaning,
for through all their ordeals—the wrecks and the wash of
the seas—they have preserved their "ingenerate grain."

In his *Weltanschauung* Wilbur does not belong to the
school currently in fashion. Today the reigning favorites
are the authors who possess the tragic vision. There is a
revival of interest in Hawthorne and Melville with their
sombre musings. Dostoevsky's schizophrenics and psycho-
paths, characters who have lost their spiritual bearings,
are taken to be the forerunners of twentieth century man.
The dominant philosophy in Europe is existentialism,
which has its origin partly in Nietzsche's dictum, "God
is dead." Existentialism's leading exponent is the French
philosopher Sartre, whose first novel, *Nausea* (1938), expresses in its very title his attitude toward existence. And
the titles of the French novelist, Camus, who in 1957
won the Nobel Prize for literature, are similarly revealing: *The Outsider* (1942), *The Plague* (1947), *The Fall*
(1956). Among German writers of the twentieth century, few have received more attention than Kafka,
whose story "The Metamorphosis" is representative. In it
the chief character, Gregor Samsa, is filled with such con-
tempt for himself, and so strongly desires to evade his responsibilities, that he longs to become, and in fact does
turn into a cockroach.

For these dark readings of the human enigma there is,
of course, considerable basis in twentieth century experience. Camus never allows us to forget "that over a period
of twenty-five years, between 1922 and 1947, 70 million Europeans—men, women, and children—have been
uprooted, deported, and killed." It is no reflection on these
powerful writers, however, to say that their philosophy
is not the only one possible. At other times, or in other

places, or by a different light existence may be viewed more favorably. For Wilbur, at any rate, black is not the only color, nor anguish the only theme. A writer's view of life depends largely on his temperament. And in temperament Wilbur differs from Sarte, Camus, and Kafka. Not that he is deaf or blind so far as social, political and economic questions are concerned. He, too, has witnessed the world conflict of the 'forties. In "Mined Country" he describes the aftermath. War, he says, "hits at childhood more than churches." In "First Snow in Alsace," the gutted buildings and the ammunition dumps are gradually covered and changed by the snowfall. And a mile or two outside the town, the snow also

> fills the eyes
> Of soldiers dead a little while.

He refers in passing to such things as the Negro problem, and "the single-tax state" ("Water Walker"). Five of his quatrains berate the Philistines in the suburbs ("To an American Poet Just Dead"). But he is not at his best on these subjects. They lie on the periphery of his thought.

Essentially, Wilbur's note is one of affirmation. He is attracted, for example, by an Italian fountain ("A Baroque Wall-Fountain in the Villa Sciarra"), by the carved fauns at their innocent games. They never grow weary of the sun. They are happy in the loose waterfall and spray,

> Reproving our disgust and our ennui
> With humble insatiety.

It is possible, Wilbur implies ("A Problem from Milton"), that men reflect too much on the nature of things, do not enough enjoy the natural phenomena of which they are a part, the life force evidencing itself in the coiled vine, the lush tree, the comber dashing itself on the rocks. Adam in Eden was the first offender. Not content simply with being, he lost Paradise in his attempt to understand it. For splendid vitality there is no better example than the sea

Whose horses never know their lunar reins.

As Ortega y Gasset says in the passage quoted at the beginning of this article, "Everything in the world is strange and marvellous to well-open eyes." Unquestionably, Wilbur would meet with the Spanish philosopher's approval. For he discovers the strange and the marvellous in the commonest objects. Like the painter, Pieter de Hooch, whom he admires ("Objects" and "A Dutch Courtyard"), he is entranced by the way in which a courtyard seems to burn in the sun, finds pleasure in "true textures," "true integuments," magic in "the weave of a sleeve." Even the lowly potato inspires a lyric ("Potato") ten stanzas long.

Yet he is aware, as Wordsworth earlier was aware, that when he invests the commonplace with magic, he half perceives and half creates the objects of his vision. In "My Father Paints the Summer," the setting is a beach hotel on a chilly, rainy July day. While the other guests shiver by the "lobby fire," the father in his room puts on canvas his conception of the perfect season. It is "a summer never seen," having its origin in the heart, for

Caught summer is always an imagined time.

On occasion, as in "La Rose des Vents," the poet may be too prone to journey to the lands of his imagining, to

cultivate the "roses of the mind." His lady calls him back
to reality so that he may

> tend the true
> The mortal flower.

Deep within the heart of reality, however, dwells the
miraculous, requiring for its perception no perversion or
distortion of things, only "well-open eyes." This is the
theme of "Praise in Summer":

> Obscurely yet most surely called to praise,
> As sometimes summer calls us all, I said
> The hills are heavens full of branching ways
> Where star-nosed moles fly overhead the dead;
> I said the trees are mines in air, I said
> See how the sparrow burrows in the sky!
> And then I wondered why this mad *instead*
> Perverts our praise to uncreation, why
> Such savour's in this wrenching thing awry.
> Does sense so stale that it must needs derange
> The world to know it? To a praiseful eye
> Should it not be enough of fresh and strange
> That trees grow green, and moles can course in clay,
> And sparrows sweep the ceiling of our day? [5]

Many of Wilbur's works are songs of praise. His love
poems, delicate and restrained, trace the forms the
beautiful takes in its many changes ("A Simile for Her
Smile" and "The Beautiful Changes"). Reading in the
Notebooks of G. M. Hopkins he comes upon a quotation
from another poet: "The young lambs bound/As to the
tabor's sound." And at once he thinks of Nijinsky's "marvellous mid-air pause" in his dancing; the amazing sure-

footedness of the dining-car waiter "in the shaken train"; Hamlet's thought and Flaubert's speech—all instances of grace that he remembers with pleasure ("Grace"). And along with "Grace" his tributes to "Clearness," "Lightness," and "Ceremony" should be mentioned. In effect, they are what he calls one of his poems, a "Conjuration."

From all these examples cited, it is evident that Wilbur is a versatile poet. Nothing has been said of his verse forms and metres, but they are as varied as his themes, and as skilfully handled. He is deeply and widely read in at least two literatures, English and French. In his techniques as in his subjects he sometimes draws upon earlier authors: Nash, Traherne, Milton, La Fontaine, Baudelaire, Valéry. But always he supplies his own distinctive touch, beats his own music out. In the difficult and insufficiently appreciated art of translation he is a master. Most of all, in his own, original work he imparts to the familiar an air of newness and strangeness. He is what Ortega y Gasset desires—an intellectual man who has not lost the sense of wonder. He is one of those poets of whom in a recent anthology Robert Frost says that they "need live to write no better, need only wait to be better known for what they have written."

NOTES

[1] Quoted under "The Owl" in *A Bestiary*, compiled by Richard Wilbur, illustrated by Alexander Calder (Pantheon Books, 1955).

[2] From *Things of This World*, copyright, 1956, by Richard Wilbur. Reprinted by permission of Harcourt, Brace and Company, Inc.

[3] *Candide: A Comic Operetta Based on Voltaire's Satire*. Book by Lillian Hellman. Lyrics by Richard Wilbur [and others]. Random House, 1957.

[4] Reprinted by permission of the author and of Random House, Inc.

[5] From *The Beautiful Changes and Other Poems*, copyright, 1947, by Richard Wilbur. Reprinted by permission of Harcourt, Brace and Company, Inc.

V
THE
POETRY
OF
RICHARD
EBERHART

PETER L. THORSLEV, JR.

It is absurd to wince at being called a romantic poet.
Unless one is that, one is not a poet at all.

Wallace Stevens, in Opus Posthumous

RICHARD EBERHART's life has been almost as varied as his
poetry, rising sometimes to poetic adventure, then sinking
again to the seemingly prosaic. He was born (1904) and
raised in the small town of Austin, Minnesota, and it
was from there that he went to Dartmouth, where he
received his B.A. in 1926. He capped his undergraduate
education with a trip around the world on a tramp
steamer, working as a deck-boy, chipping rust from sun-
glaring decks or stoking coal in engine-rooms with tem-
peratures well over 100 degrees, and visiting strange
oriental cities. He completed his education at St. John's
College, Cambridge (B.A. 1929, M.A. 1933), and at Harvard; but during this time he also took a year off to become tutor to the son of Prajadhipok, the King of Siam.
He then returned to the more conventional teaching of
English at St. Mark's School, Southboro, Massachusetts,

until the outbreak of the Second World War. During the war, he served in the U. S. Navy, in aircraft gunnery for part of the time; after the war, he joined the Butcher Polish Company, of Boston. While rising in six years from assistant manager to vice president, he found time to write, among other things, some *Helpful Hints for Homemakers* (on the virtues of Butcher wax). In 1952, however, he returned to teaching again, and after serving at a number of colleges as lecturer, he has settled down to be Professor of English and Poet in Residence at Dartmouth, his alma mater. He has served as Consultant in Poetry to the Library of Congress, and is a member of the National Institute of Arts and Letters.

Recognition has come to Eberhart rather as a slow growth or accretion than as sudden fame. His first volume of verse, *A Bravery of Earth,* appeared in England in 1930, and since that date six more volumes have appeared, in England and America, the latest being his *Collected Poems: 1930–1960.* His honors include the Harriet Monroe Memorial Award, the Shelley Memorial Prize (1951), and a grant from the National Institute of Arts and Letters.

From the first his reviews have been "mixed"; their general tenor could be summarized in the nursery rhyme: "When he is good, he is very, very good;/And when he is bad, he is horrid." Such a reaction on the part of critics is not in itself remarkable, I suppose; a poet who writes such lines as these: "My being being being's essence, a mathema" ("The Magical"), or "Will will will him his own, a fabled ease" ("Sestina"), certainly risks offending the sensitive ears of his critics. Such verbal pyrotechnics perhaps distract more than they convey. (Admittedly much of Eberhart's verse reads like a poetry of inclusion, rather than of selection or exclusion. In his criticism and casual pronouncements he has not expressed much respect for the care-filled revision, for the serious second

thoughts which would perhaps excise such lines as
these.) But what is more remarkable in these reviews is
the tone which Eberhart's critics assume. In the face of
his successes they remain curiously inarticulate, almost
in awe; with his "failures," on the other hand, they are
never condescending, or merely disappointed: they become petulant, exasperated, almost infuriated. It is as if
somehow they were personally involved, and personally
betrayed. To put it another way: with much contemporary poetry one is pleased or annoyed, surprised by an unexpected felicity or a clever image, or mildly irritated
because so much cerebration seems to yield so little; and
just below the level of consciousness hovers the question:
But does it all really matter? With Eberhart's poetry this
question never occurs; the reader is immediately aware
that what is being said, with whatever success, does indeed matter, both to himself and to the poet. One may
sometimes question the felicity of the expression, but one
is never tempted to question the validity of the experience.

The qualities just indicated—the reliance on first
thoughts or on "inspiration," the emotional intensity, the
earnestness, and the assertive moral and personal sincerity
—are, I think, enough in themselves to suggest what I
believe to be Eberhart's first most distinctive characteristic: he is in a way a twentieth-century Romantic.
Now "Romantic" is a nebulous and dubious epithet, not
less so because in the last forty years it has been more
often used as a pejorative than as a neutral descriptive
term. Still, the Romantic Movement was an historical
phenomenon with some measure of coherence; and it is a
matter of record that every literary movement since 1830
has either allied itself with one or the other of the great
Romantics, or, more commonly in this century, defined
itself in its opposition to all Romanticism.

But Eberhart is a Romantic, I believe, in an even more

definite sense than Stevens implies in the assertion I have used as an epigraph. First, Eberhart is a nature poet, and what is more, he is a nature poet who would not object to being called one. Furthermore, he has allied himself with no twentieth-century (and therefore almost *ispo facto* anti-Romantic) school of poetry, and the poets who most obviously influenced him, especially in his earlier years, are three of the greatest Romantics: Blake, Wordsworth, and Whitman. Finally, and most important, the themes of his poetry, the problems which have concerned him most vitally from his first volume to his last, are problems posed first in their modern form by the great Romantic poets, and when Eberhart offers solutions to these problems they are often modified and modernized Romantic solutions.

Like all nature poets Eberhart frequently takes some object of everyday nature—a beast, a bird, an insect, or a flower: any sharply-defined natural phenomenon—as the central image around which to organize a poem meant to illustrate some facet of human or social experience. Nature poetry of this sort is at least as old as medieval bestiaries, or as those "emblem-books" of the earlier days of printing, whose major attraction was allegorical and moral illustrations, with short verses below to amplify the pictured text. And nature poetry of this sort is still popular in American letters: Marianne Moore draws lessons from seagulls or fishes; Richard Wilbur has compiled a modern *Bestiary*; and of course Robert Frost images forth truths of man and nature from birches, or butterflies, or cows in apple-time.

Some of Eberhart's poems of this sort resemble Frost's even in their ironic or whimsical conclusions: two wasps found wintering on a New Hampshire tree, brought into the kitchen, and breathed upon by the poet (like God on Adam's dust), come quivering to life. One wasp dares to attempt to fly, but dazed, it falls and is crushed accidentally by the poet's boot. The other, safer and sager, remains to become a pet; and Eberhart concludes: [1]

The moral of this is plain.
But I will shirk it.
You will not like it. And
God does not live to explain.

("New Hampshire, February")

In another poem of the same period the poet finds wisdom in contemplating the "large soft cows" in a warm barn. The cow has "learned the lesson of the pacifist," that of passive sufferance. Eberhart concludes ironically:

If acceptance after the storms of decades
Is the ounce of wisdom in electrified flesh,
Philosophy can end in the eye of a cow.

("Burr Oaks: The Barn")

Others of these "emblem" poems seem to come closer, in theme and in spirit, to the poems of Blake. The dry husk of the sloughed skin of a cicada leads the poet to consider life, change, and perfect death-like form, and to question "What eternal hovers in/Him?" ("The Largess"); and the sight of a "tight lizard on a wall" leads him to ask ultimate questions—"What the protection, who the protector?"—like Blake's in "The Tiger." Even cancer cells under a microscope, in their "spiky shapes," become an image of the poetic imagination, of the "fixed form in the massive fluxion."

One of these poems, although not printed until 1953, was actually written much earlier, and is almost unique in that it seems reminiscent of the woods and of the history of Eberhart's native Minnesota. He must often have seen this soft, white fungus with its single flower in the groves and pastures around Austin. The lyric spells out no explicit moral, and its meaning is left to spiral out from Indians and ghosts to the evanescence of all human life and dreams. The poem is entitled "Indian Pipe":

Searching once I found a flower
  By a sluggish stream.
Waxy white, a stealthy tower
  To an Indian's dream.
  This its life supreme.

Blood red winds the sallow creek
  Draining as it flows.
Left the flower all white and sleek,
  Fainting in repose.
  Gentler than a rose.

Red man's pipe is now a ghost
  Whispering to beware.
Hinting of the savage host
  Once that traveled there.
  Perfume frail as air.

But Eberhart is by no means alone among contemporary poets in his use of animal or floral "emblems"; he is more particularly the nature poet in his celebration of the sheer sensuous and sensual pleasures in the physical world around him. In this he comes close, in spirit, at least, to Wordsworth, or to the Whitman of "Song of Myself." Eberhart's first volume of poetry, *A Bravery of Earth* (1930), opens and closes with the lines:

This fevers me, this sun on green,
On grass glowing, this young spring.

The whole volume is really one long poem in four parts, and it forms something unique in twentieth-century

American verse, I believe: it is a spiritual autobiography of a poet, and its obvious model is Wordsworth's *Prelude*. Not in style or diction, certainly; Eberhart's short lyric lines, with their irregular rhymes and rhythms, are very much his own. But the stages in the poet's spiritual growth are remarkably like those Wordsworth describes in the *Prelude*. The "first awareness" is of life as will, as sensual force, the "fever" of the sun and of the world of energy and sub-intellectual life: much the same as the feeling for nature which Wordsworth describes in his youthful climbing over the Cumberland hills, or along the banks of the Wye. The "second awareness," however, is an intellectual disillusionment caused by analytic reason, which makes the world seem a dull and deadly mechanism, drained of will or purpose (Wordsworth describes a similar experience in his student life at Cambridge). Gradually, however, the poet grows into the light of a new manhood, "a bravery of earth," and this "third awareness" brings a new understanding not only of nature, but of man in nature—a vision of purpose and of human "destiny" which owes much, I think, to Whitman.

The elemental joy in physical nature is admittedly more characteristic of Eberhart's early poetry; still, enough of it remains to add a special poignancy to such later poems as "Recollection of Childhood" or "If I could only live at the Pitch that is near Madness." In the latter poem he laments the fact that in taking on manhood he has come "into the realm of complexity,"

Where nothing is possible but necessity
And the truth wailing there like a red babe.

But sometimes even in his mature poetry he can achieve a pure nature lyric such as "Now is the/Air made of Chiming Balls," in which the delight in all of the senses is unclouded by analytic reason or moral second thoughts, as he sees that "The stormcloud, wizened, has rolled its rind away"; that "seeds, assuaged, peep from the nested spray," and "the sun"

> Begins to dress with warmth again every thing.
> The lettuce in pale burn, the burdock tightening;
> And naked necks of craning fledglings.

An even later poem, "Summer Landscape," with its delicate observation and its richly sensuous imagery and sleepy rhythms, reminds one somehow of Keats' ode "To Autumn"—perhaps because of the swallows, although here, with their quick movements, their "playing/ About the barn like brightest minds," they contrast sharply with the placid life around them: the algae on a stagnant pool, which become a "green mantle, a spreading tone," or even the snake, which "will hold his poise, then glide away." And, as the "waves of clover-ether triumph," the poet promises that "The moonlight will be as good as the hot day."

Nevertheless, such joy in uncomplicated nature is relatively rare in Eberhart's latest poetry; he moves on to consider themes and problems more complex and tragic. The "second awareness" comes for him as it came for the first Romantics; and nature and man, which seem simple and unified in childhood, break into the complexities of adult life. In Blake's terms, we move from innocence to experience, and the new "awareness" becomes painful and intense. The Romantics did not, after all, come by their mature "single visions" easily (in Blake's terms again): at first the old certainties of the Enlightenment broke into polar opposites, and what they found was rather a painful duality in man—between blood and mind, between passion and analysis, between imagination and reason; and a corresponding duality in the world of things—between nature as life and organism, and nature as mechanical necessity. When the Romantics arrived at a new unity, a new vision of the world as one (and the Romantics were, generally speaking, the last who dared a monist metaphysics), it was usually through a higher and dialectic synthesis in the realm of spirit, a new mystic vision which transcended both blood and the mind, both organism and mechanism. Wordsworth found his new unified vision in a Nature in which all things were transformed into spirit, but a spirit which seems often rather bloodless and passionless. Blake's synthesis is perhaps more modern in that he refused to relinquish the world of the flesh in the realm of the spirit: his God created both the tiger and the lamb. In this respect, Eberhart is closer to Blake, I think, than to Wordsworth.

For these Romantic themes (Romantic in their origins, at least) form the subject-matter of many of Eberhart's best poems. In some of these he laments the disillusionment, the loss of wonder, which comes when life is probed by analytic reason:

> It is man did it, man,
> Who imagined imagination,
> And he did what man can,
> He uncreated creation.

> There is no tree in my arm,
> I have no hounds in my feet,
> The earth can soothe me and harm,
> And the lake of my eyes is a cheat.   ("Maze")

In a much later "animal" poem, "Seals, Terns, Time," the poet illustrates man's dual nature by picturing himself balanced in a boat on the surface of the sea, drawn between the seals, those "blurred kind forms/ That rise and peer from elemental waters," and the terns, wheeling gracefully in the free blue of the sky.

In his earlier poetry Eberhart does sometimes discover a unity in organic nature, at the heart of things, but when he does, it is not the moral and personal Nature of Wordsworth. One of his longer poems, describing a walking trip through Wordsworth's lake country, appeals in turn to all of the senses, and the hurried, short, and irregular lines seem even to catch something of the breathlessness of mountain-climbing. The poem culminates in a mountain-top experience on Helvellyn, perhaps parallel to Wordsworth's on Snowdon, but Eberhart does not see Wordworth's "emblem of a mind . . . that broods over the dark abyss"; he feels instead that

> A surge of demonic energy unites
> Blood and the bitter world-vitality
> As the flaying and flayed being ignites
> In elemental passion intensity
> Satanic, angelic, one harmony
> Of immense glory like fire clinging
> A blaze of terrible immediacy
> The wild blood of freedom singing . . .
>
> ("Four Lakes' Days," IV)

In later poems, this transcendent unity is often more quiet, if no less terrible—a white hardness, like what he sees in the eye of a "Sea-Hawk," a "piercing, inhuman perfection/ . . . A blaze of grandeur, permanence of the impersonal."

But in a very few of his latest poems Eberhart comes close to that vision of a unity in organic nature which is so peculiarly Blakean—in that vein which Middleton Murry, speaking of Keats and Blake (and, perhaps more appositely, of D. H. Lawrence) called an inverted "this-worldly" mysticism, because, paradoxically, it sees a "transcendent" unity not by denying the flesh, the senses, and things of the earth, but by reaching through the senses to the blood. Such a poem is "Thrush Song at Dawn," the concluding poem in *Great Praises* (1957), a poem which seems to me entirely successful. The fourth stanza echoes the Immortality Ode, and the idea of a "lost purity" is perhaps also Wordsworthian, but the substance of the poem has more of D. H. Lawrence, and the image with which the poem closes carries the same tenor as that poet-as-Aeolian-harp image so popular with all of the Romantics:

Bird song is flute song and a glory
Of the morning when the sun unascending
Holds his other glory of mentality

And the dawn has not the mental mockery
But the birds from sweet subconscious wells
Pierce through all barriers to sense,

They send and giving sing divinity,
So sweetly charged with subterranean meaning
They are like angels in the morning

Come from ancient time, a fast enchantment,
To bless our mortal songless weakness
And trail a vocal glory all the day.

I would not be a bird, but I would hear
Deep in some lost purity, beneath the mind,
There in the sweet, dark coil of time,

As in a mother, the thrush as saviour,
And sovereign mediator; or any other
Lung-red singing: richness propounds confusion,

The pleasure that will never cease to be
Where we are played upon without a fault
By magic tones we love but do not have to know.

Another way to face the central issue of the duality in
man and nature is to approach it obliquely, by probing
the ultimate mystery of death; and this theme was also
a favorite of the Romantics. A realization of the evanescence of sensuous beauty in the face of death is the central agony of Keats' greatest odes; his solution was esthetic, in an eternal beauty which transcends time and
death, but which also, unfortunately, transcends life. The
life-long development of Shelley's thought can be traced
in his changing attitudes toward death, and when he
found his peace, it was in the concept of an impersonal
immortality, in returning cycles of nature as in the "Ode
to the West Wind," or in the more fully developed neo-
Platonism of "Adonais." But it was for a belated minor
Romantic, Thomas Lovell Beddoes, that death as an in-
soluble mystery became almost an obsession; and when
he could no longer make a cosmic Jacobean joke of it (as
in *Death's Jest-Book*), he twice attempted suicide, and
at last succeeded.

I don't mean to imply that Eberhart has been influenced
by Beddoes, nor that he shares the earlier poet's pessi-
mism; but still Eberhart is the first poet since Beddoes,
I think, for whom death has become such a persistent
theme. His concern is not merely with death as a concept,
or as a mystic attraction (although in such a poem as
"The Soul Longs to Return Whence It Came" death is
an attraction), but with death and decay as a brutal
physical fact. With a characteristic "metaphysical shudder" Marvell once wrote "The grave's a fine and private
place,/ But none I think do there embrace." In Eberhart's poetry, however, dead lovers do indeed embrace, as
in the first part of "Suite in Prison":

. . . they sink deeper in abysmal love
And in the slowest satisfying lust
Are tightened, till they get great regiments
Of babes with petal spears to pierce the air.

Sometimes this preoccupation with death seems only a defiant attempt to see "some beauty even at the guts of things" ("When Golden Flies upon My Carcase Come"); sometimes Eberhart seems to take a Shelleyan consolation in the fact that death and decay are after all only a return to nature: nothing alive is ever wholly lost. This seems to be the conclusion of "For a Lamb," a description of a dead lamb on a hillside, "propped with daises," which has returned to the wind and the flowers; or of the beautiful and quiet "Rumination," in which the poet concludes that Death will "blow his breath/ To fire my clay, when I am still."

But the poet cannot always find such solace in the thought of death as a return to living earth. From a strictly human point of view, the tragedy remains, and this is the theme of Eberhart's most famous and most often anthologized poem, "The Groundhog." It is another animal-emblem poem, but in this case the picture is of a dead body in a summer field, and a dead body paradoxically alive with decay. Changing attitudes toward death, in a series of visits to the tiny body in the fields, give the poem its structure. On the first visit, the poet is filled with an intense love and an intense loathing at the sight of fierce nature at work in the decaying flesh, the "immense energy of the sun." The second visit is made in the "strict eye" of Autumn, and an intellectual wisdom has controlled the fierce energy but has also left the earth and the body a "sodden hulk," bereft of meaning (as in the poet's earlier "second awareness"). On the third visit the poet sees only a bit of hair and bleached bones, "beautiful as architecture," as he achieves at last the indifference of spirit. But still the pathos remains, and when three years later there is no sign of the groundhog, the poet stands and thinks of the evanescence of all human life, "of China and of Greece,"

> Of Alexander in his tent,
> Of Montaigne in his tower,
> Of Saint Theresa in her wild lament.

Still, even in this vision of death, a kind of fierce mystic joy is possible, an impassioned acceptance of the impersonal, of death and decay. This attitude is more than mere resignation: it is the affirmation which comes to the heart of tragedy. One of Eberhart's lyrics which illustrates this mystic experience also shows his poetry at its most intense, and I think perhaps at its best. The diction is simple and the imagery is disciplined, but this seems only to heighten by contrast the intensity of the feeling:

> Imagining how it would be to be dead,
> Until my tender filaments
> From mere threads air have become
> And this is all my consciousness
> (While like a world of rock and stone
> My body cumbersome and big
> Breathes out a vivid atmosphere
> Which is the touchless breach of the air)
> I lost my head, and could not hold
> Either my hands together or my heart
> But was so sentient a being
> I seemed to break time apart
> And thus became all things air can touch
> Or could touch could it touch all things,
> And this was an embrace most dear,

Final, complete, a flying without wings.
From being bound to one poor skull,
And that surrounded by one earth,
And the earth in one universe forced,
And that chained to some larger gear,
I was the air, I was the air,
And then I pressed on eye and cheek
The sightless hinges of eternity
That make the whole world creak.

In the nature of things, however, such intensely subjective mystical experiences are necessarily brief and infrequent, and they don't provide moral truths to live by.
Eberhart's final message is closer to a quiet humanism, an
acceptance of the mystery of things, and a faith in the
ultimate spiritual perseverance of man's love for man. In
one of his latest poems ("What Gives," first printed in
Collected Poems), as a child of the twentieth century
who has lived through two world wars and what has
come between and after, Eberhart writes of the "absolute"
which he has "tortured out in fifty years." He is tentative,
to be sure—"I do not know, but think will show the
same"—but this is what he concludes:

Strength grows and throws around us holy love.
It is this I count on to the end of time.
Love is the end of knowledge, and sublime.

More frequently his optimism is tempered to a wry
stoicism, as in the last stanza of "Anima":

It is the perdurable toughness of the soul
God and nature make us want to keep;

The struggle of the part against the whole.
Each time we take a breath it must be deep.

There could be a danger in too much emphasis on Eberhart's neo-Romanticism, I suppose. In the first place, such an emphasis may seem to imply that his verse is derivative in style and idiom, when this is not at all the case. Then, too, although those of his poems which I think are most likely to survive are concerned with personal themes—themes which are Romantic, in the best and broadest sense of the term—he has also upon occasion written on topical subjects, especially in some war poems and in his recent experiments in verse drama.

However much his poems share common themes with other Romantic poets, Eberhart's style and idiom are nevertheless always his own. His lines are short, his rhymes oblique or infrequent, and his rhythms intentionally irregular, but within these limits he shows a quite extraordinary range. Some of his lyrics are fluent, with simple unaffected diction, and in almost regular metric stanzas. The beauty of these poems, I think, as is the case with many of Blake's short stanzas or with Wordsworth's "Lucy" poems, lies in the reader's appreciation of restraint, of the tension between the apparently artless simplicity of the verse and the intensity of the controlled emotion. A few isolated lines which stick in my mind will perhaps illustrate the point: "And music a broken Ilium"; or, "Calm is but the end of a poem"; or, when the poet speaks of himself and of his art as

Locked in this lone discipline
Against the world's decay.

At the other extreme of his range, Eberhart writes many poems which, like the lyrics of Gerard Manley Hopkins, are crowded with stressed monosyllables and often almost choked with alliterative consonants, in which the effect seems to be to compress into each line as much poetry as possible. An extreme example is the youthful and experimental "Four Lakes' Days," which, in spite of some striking images, is perhaps a little too Hopkins-like, with its compressed and distorted grammar and syntax and its strings of adjectives and nouns made adjectives.

References to current events of our time—political, economic, or social—were comparatively rare in his poetry all through the thirties, but the Second World War and his involvement in it did break into his poetry in the forties. He also began to collect war poems by other poets, and in 1948 he edited, together with his friend Selden Rodman, an anthology of these entitled *War and the Poet*. One of the poems anthologized was Tennyson's translation of the Old English "Battle of Brunanburh," and it may have been this poem which inspired the style of Eberhart's longest war poem, "Brotherhood of Men." The poem is an attempt to write a brief epic account of the death march of Bataan, and it is written in the style of Old English verse, in which the principle of coherence is not rhyme or quantitative meter, but recurring patterns of stressed alliterative syllables. Of his other less ambitious war poems few reach the level of his personal and "Romantic" lyrics, I think, but some of them, including the often anthologized "Fury of Aerial Bombardment" and the later "A Young Greek, Killed in the Wars," achieve a considerable force of compassion, restrained by the irony of understatement and of prosaic diction and detail.

Eberhart's more recent incursions into the field of verse drama also demonstrate both his interest in poetic experimentation and his concern with topical themes. In 1950 he was one of the founders and subsequently the first president of The Poet's Theatre, in Cambridge, Massachusetts, and the fruits of this new interest were two verse dramas, one, "The Apparition," printed in *Poetry* (Chicago), in 1950, and the second, "The Visionary Farms," printed in *New World Writing* in 1953. Both of these are experimental "discussion" dramas, in which the play within the play is watched and commented upon by "Spectators" on the stage. The first is really a short "mood" play, the only action being a brief encounter between a salesman in a hotel and a bewildered young girl who wanders into his room on a caprice, talks with him for a while over a few drinks, and then disappears again into the hallway. The second play, "The Visionary Farms," is more ambitious, and has been successfully produced four times, most recently at the University of Cincinnati. On one level, this drama is an incisive and sometimes humorous satire on hucksterism in the person of "Hurricane" Ransome, the recklessly ambitious manager of a midwestern firm, who, it turns out, has embezzled somewhat more than a million dollars from the company, and thus left Fahnstock, the half-owner of the company and the protagonist of the drama, on the verge of financial ruin. Read on another level, the play becomes a broad indictment of our American "ad-man" civilization, which perverts the ideals and the very personalities of all of the characters in the play. The drama is intentionally episodic and undramatic; as one of the choric "spectators" puts it, the purpose of the play is rather to "keep vile actions off, and bring on thoughts/ To estimate these matters to a standstill."

These verse dramas, however, remain interesting experiments, and any summary estimate of Eberhart's achievement so far must stand on the basis of the considerable quantity of lyric poetry which he has published since 1930.[2] His faults, in my opinion, lie at his extremes. In a very few poems, his verse seems to me not to rise above the prosaic. In one long poem entitled "The Kite," for instance (*Hudson Review*, Summer, 1956), he spends many introductory stanzas versifying instructions for the assembly of his kite "emblem"; and however these lines are read, they seem to me to remain something less than poetry (this poem was pointedly omitted from *Collected Poems*). More frequently, Eberhart's stanzas are crammed with figures and images which go off in the reader's mind like Roman candles; but, like all such fireworks, they sometimes leave no very lasting impression on the darkness. Fortunately, most of Eberhart's lyrics stand between these extremes. Some of the quieter ones are centered on a single image, or are unified by a tightly-controlled line of logical or psychological argument; in others, the very intensity of the expressed thought or emotion seems to fuse the varied images into a single vivid impression.

Among contemporary American poets who often seem either academic and a little tired, or else full of fire and wildly anti-intellectual, it is a pleasure to read a poet like Eberhart, who has, I think, something of the virtues of both camps: a keen intelligence, but also a warm humanity and a genuine inspiration.

NOTES

[1] Quotations are by permission of the poet and of Oxford University Press (New York) and Chatto and Windus Ltd. (London). All of the poems cited are included in Eberhart's *Collected Poems, 1930–1960.*

[2] This judgment will have to be revised when the University of North Carolina Press publishes a collection of Eberhart's new and old verse dramas in July of 1962.

VI
HEART'S NEEDLE: SNODGRASS STRIDES THROUGH THE UNIVERSE

DONALD T. TORCHIANA

THE name Snodgrass may sound novel for a sparkling new poet, but William DeWitt Snodgrass not only glories in his name, he also hymns it, apostrophizes it in his first volume of poetry, *Heart's Needle* [1] (New York, 1959), which has already won the Pulitzer Prize in poetry for 1960, not to mention the $1000 Ingram-Merrill Award, the Longview Foundation Award, and the Poetry Society Award, Special Citation. Trained in the poetry workshop of the State University of Iowa, Snodgrass, now in his mid-thirties, was Quaker-born, reared in Beaver Falls, Pennsylvania, and has since followed one of the likely paths for the contemporary American poet. He took himself through Geneva College, endured the Navy and America's last romantic invasion of the world in World War II, and turned up soon after in Iowa City, resplendent in cast-off Navy costume, great head of hair and flowing beard, and properly abstracted poet's eye. Now, considerably clipped, he is an established poet, a family man, and a teacher at Wayne State University in Detroit. Unprepossessing as this background may seem—Robert Lowell in the blurb calls the workshop "the most sterile of sterile places"—*Heart's Needle* is something of a triumph. At its calm, insistent best it has both credo and style:

> "The world's not done to me;
> it is what I do;
> whom I speak shall be;
> I music out my name
> and what I tell is who
> in all the world I am."

I

In 1948, when I first set eyes on Snodgrass, Iowa City was still basking in its self-inflicted glory as the Athens of the Midwest. It was a retired-farmer's town and county seat, with a leisurely bus line, a good hospital, and a university of outlandish maverick decency. The school also aspired to be as creative as the state's more celebrated hogs. And it was. In short, after the war, it was just the place for as seedy a group of graduate students in arts and letters as ever fell off the Rock Island Line. Working for advanced degrees in literature and the fine arts, they gave the school a name certainly less deplorable, if not more exciting, than that swished about by the famed Scotch Highlanders, corn-fed lassies of 18 or so, who droned about in what seemed to be the year-long football season. Snodgrass was one of this pride of painters, writers, actors, musicians, sculptors, and critics that gave the university what class it had. The more orthodox, timid graduate student, like myself, was generally too swamped during the day with the traditional demands of advanced work to see much of them. But outside of class our lives were often joyously the same.

We lived in a pleasant half-world of hockshops, all night restaurants, Quonset huts or breezy rooming houses variously called the Empty Arms, the Flop House, or Gus's. To augment the G.I. Bill or the money from an occasional stint of teaching, we used to wash dishes, dig ditches, feed the mice and dogs in University Hospital, or mop the floors, rent boats on the sluggish Iowa River, tote parcels at Christmas time, sell blood to the Catholic Hospital, clerk in a drummers' hotel, sling hash, thresh wheat, or cheer our wives as they went off to work in the morning. To punctuate this grey round of study and subsistence, we could always slide into Joe's Airliner, where the fraternity mob bemused itself in beer, or Kenney's, haunt of the slender-wristed crowd, or the Antlers, a laborers' bar which boasted a blind piano player. We usually went to the last, if only for the fights. Then there was the frequent two-day poker game heavily attended by the poets. We also had a basketball team—one year Walter Van Tilburg Clark played on it. Nor should I omit the sprawling literary set-tos in the invariable small rooms, filled with shouts and whispers, with the reproduction of Rouault's "The Old King" on some wall, the inevitable name-dropping, and large quantities of Old Tub, an obscure Beam whiskey, downed. Yet there was also the half-finished novel, the rough draft of a story, the unread source-book, the type-script of poems, the crated pictures, or the last chapter of a thesis sitting in the next room.

The personalities were just as gaga. Aside from the usual run of intense New Yorkers, edgy disciples of the Southern Fugitives, and spruced-up rubes (me) from small Midwestern colleges, there were some real stars, especially among the writers. One was a Golden Gloves heavyweight who had also been a star reporter; another had been a sax man in the Krupa band. Don Peterson, a poet, had toured with a French basketball team. His friend, Herb Wilner, a short-story writer, had been captain of the Brooklyn College football team.

Two others systematically swindled a crackpot economist out of $20,000 that he sank into a newspaper they edited, which piled up under a porch. Many were from Harvard, Yale, and Princeton. One had driven a Marshall Field truck. Another, a graduate of West Point, ate on 75 cents a day and drove an $8.00 car, for awhile; his triumph came when his first volume of poems was reviewed as the work of a most disciplined artist. Two more were millionaires' sons, or acted as if they were. Many had elaborate marital lives. Just as many had been shot at in the war. Some got too deep in the sauce. Snodgrass suffered through a divorce.

I usually spotted him as he climbed the Flop House stairs to play chess with a friend of ours named Ace Levang, or when he was heading through campus for the writers workshop. This complex of versifiers and writers that he mixed with could, on occasion, be an especially arrogant, slow-smiling lot of empire builders. They had long before canonized the metaphysicals and French symbolists, and were most solemn about the sanctity of Flaubert, Stendhal, and James. The Authorized Version was Empson's *Seven Types of Ambiguity*, the Logos was to be found in the *Kenyon Review*, usually in the pronouncements of Tate ("Allen") or R. P. Warren ("Red"). *All the King's Men* enjoyed an enormous vogue; and then it was that F. R. Leavis was known for wit. For the more enterprising, such visiting writers as Robert Lowell offered the more exotic fare of Catullus, Villon, St. John of the Cross, Rilke, Kafka, and Lorca. There was also a bit of log-rolling. When the *Western Review*, Iowa's little mag, wasn't pontificating about teachers-as-writers or writers-as-teachers (I can't remember which), like Addison and his little Senate it sat attentive to its own applause and pushed the local boys rather heavily. Then too, there came that breathless moment when Iowa fell heir to the O. Henry Awards, the annual selection of prize stories. It was announced in the next volume that eight of the best twenty-three short stories for 1954 had been done by Iowa writers.

There were bound to be casualties in such a system. One graduate now edits the fiction of a slick magazine in New York City and affects gym shoes in the winter. Another in Chicago has taken to correcting the unsophisticated notions of young "beat" writers. One married a swimmer and wrote a novel about girls' dormitories. Several have made $100,000 inroads into Hollywood. Another at Bard drapes himself in open shirts and suntans and fondles his Phi Beta Kappa key conspicuously in public. One is a JP in Greenwich. A number have sold out to San Francisco and are holed up in the State College there. A director got himself into *Life* by memorializing the Iowa war dead and thereby added a new terror to modern warfare. But Snodgrass and a few others survived. They have written what appear to be a number of excellent poems. In doing so they have justified, I think, all the superficial irritations I've listed. For when Snodgrass evokes the dark straggling parks, the tinny Quonset huts, the stinking marshes, spring roads or drifting midnight snow, the July 4th tornado of 1953, the humming hospital corridors, and the God-awful neglected specimens in the school museum, he not only conjures up the buried life we loved—what other word can I use?—but he also blesses it with a rare elegance and authority. Thus to trace the order and development of his poetry is also to accept much of the folly and pretension of those days as finally accidental, ultimately irrelevant to that golden buckle on the Corn Belt . . . that Athens.

II

These landmarks dot the nineteen individual poems that complement the "Heart's Needle" cycle in Snodgrass's volume. The poems are arranged in chronology of subject but may be more handily viewed according to their easily demarked themes: memories of Navy service and home town; an early disintegrating marriage; new love and second marriage; and then, finally, the poet's successful assertion of integrity amid the stately, indifferent groves of academe. Very daringly, very triumphantly, filled with memories of his child riding on his shoulders, he can at last chant aloud in self-intoxication the final refrain from the poem "These Trees Stand . . .":

> If all this world runs battlefield or worse,
> Come, let us wipe our glasses on our shirts:
> Snodgrass is walking through the universe.

The early record of war return, home town, and broken marriage is painful. Throughout such poems as "Returned to Frisco, 1946," "MHTIS . . . OU TIS," "Home Town," "Orpheus," and "The Marsh" runs the theme of alienation in the No Man's land of postwar America or in an increasingly chilly marriage. If not his most successful poems, they nonetheless demonstrate Snodgrass' assimilation of what he has called the "symbolist-metaphysical" tradition taught at Iowa and his subsequent pushing on to a more relaxed, laconic idiom of his own. Take, for instance, "Returned to Frisco, 1946." It celebrates the homecoming accorded returned U. S. seamen some time after the war's conclusion. Their grand view is that of the unholy garbage peddled by hucksters of the old lies, a people for whom sailors are amorous, steak-eating "pigs along the rail." This charming vista of rewon freedom and choice, illusory as ever, is focused in the final ironic image:

> Off the port side, through haze, we could discern
> Alcatraz, lavender with flowers. Barred,

The Golden Gate, fading away astern,
Stood like the closed gate of your own backyard.

"MHTIS . . . OU TIS" takes the central pun of the
Odyssey, IX, for its pivot and then casts up what will
become a familiar paraclete, the psychiatrist, in the poet's
verse. This man, R. M. Powell, whom Snodgrass never
saw in a new experimental psychotherapy, is eulogized
in the sestet of the sonnet as the "dead blind guide" who
led him to drop his disguise as No Man and name his
name. Perhaps the subject is a fairly standard one—the
torment of a regimented life dedicated to killing; defiant
repudiation; the disguises of adequacy cast aside for the
painful acceptance of self. Still, the poem is notable.
For all its tangled obscurity and somewhat highfalutin
allusion, it specifies Snodgrass' unaltered trust in the
defiant mind and his gathering resolve to name his own
name. "Home Town" turns much the same divided light
on the poet's origins. Written late in 1956, the poem allows Snodgrass, against his will, to turn his back on the
ancient challenges of small-town America: the glittering
dare of sex pursuit and the swaggering approval of boys
of all ages. These lures are dressed out in verses picturing
the endless night prowl of sheathed adolescents, whom
we no longer hang but keep in school, through the
perpetual carnival of their days. Returned after fifteen
years, the poet has not stilled his fear nor his desire for
these illusions. Hence he asks himself:

Pale soul, consumed by fear
of the living world you haunt,
have you learned what habits lead you
to hunt what you don't want;
learned who does not need you;
learned you are no one here?

The same question is posed in "Orpheus" and "The Marsh." This time it touches even closer to home. It touches his first marriage. The one poem employs the Orpheus myth, a ready identification for husband and poet. It also clearly identifies the underworld of his marital difficulties with the image of our largely uninhabitable twentieth-century cities. The ashes of civic spirit, war rubble, gangland, poverty, municipal bribery, all these unacknowledged pledges of the cash nexus that we substitute for humanity, become the homesite for her who cannot love. The hope is that man and wife who do not love, who do not trust or know each other, may yet return to light otherwise. So the modern Orpheus begs the dark powers for the return of his bride in the radical fleshliness from which she has fallen, as did Eve, turned into stone:

> "I sing, as the blind beggars sing,
>   To ask of you this little time
>   —All lives foreclose in their due day—
>   That flowered bride cut down in Spring,
>   Struck by the snake, your underling."

But she wavers. He, despite his resolve, doubts. He turns; she is gone. Fear again has forced the question, which questioned the will. "The Marsh" tries to answer it. And this implied answer is unapologetically pulsing, forthright like the heart or like the poet's later cardinal spokesman or like the bright splash of red that adorns the covers of his volume. Lingering near what was in real life a swamp on the road to Cedar Rapids, which is to say the worst swamp possible, writing the poem while proctoring a test for a colleague (exams can be worthwhile), Snodgrass quietly surveys the bog of his marriage:

Swampstrife and spatterdock
lull in the heavy waters;
some thirty little frogs
spring with each step you walk;
a fish's belly glitters
tangled near rotting logs.

Over by the gray rocks
muskrats dip and circle.
Out of his rim of ooze
a silt-black pond snail walks
inverted on the surface
toward what food he may choose.

You look up; while you walk
the sun bobs and is snarled
in the enclosing weir
of trees, in their dead stalks.

This world of dead limbs, ensnared sunlight, and faded yellow lilies in the mud is indeed a world of "swampstrife," where a suspiciously bardlike snail must proceed unnaturally to sustain himself. In this mess, the question forces itself upon the poet in the last two lines:

Stick in the mud, old heart,
what are you doing here?

and is answered in the asking.

If this bitter theme of the tormented will was not usually so neatly taken by the throat as in "The Marsh," the subsequent love poems to his second wife, Janice, leave no doubt of Snodgrass' growing joy. Orpheus becomes Papageno of *The Magic Flute*; pride overtakes

rejection; while in a poem like "Song," the self-righteous
proprieties of an enforced union yield to a much more
splendid bed-rattling matrimony. The amorous landscape of toadstools and clipped lawns is replaced by
that of root, tree, and soil. Powerfully domestic and erotic,
these love poems are probably best represented by the
stanzas of "Winter Bouquet" that celebrate a reunion
with Janice. I am probably overimpressed with this
sublime and cockeyed mixture of fragile stems, parched
seeds, squalling brats, aerial sensuality, and wintry sunshine, but I really don't care. Here are the first and last
of its three stanzas:

> Her hands established, last time she left my room,
> this dark arrangement for a winter bouquet:
> collected bittersweet, brittle stemmed Scotch bloom,
> perennial straw-flowers, grasses gone to seed,
> lastly, the dry vaginal pods of milkweed.
> These relics stay here for her when she's away.
>
> Now, she's home. Today I lifted them, like charms
> in the March sunshine to part the pods and blow
> white bursts of quilly weedseed for the wide arms
> and eyes of the children squealing where they drift
> across the neighbors' cropped lawns like an airlift
> of satyrs or a conservative, warm snow.

The authority of these "relics"—surrounding a Snodgrass gone to seed, then transformed by love into delights
for children on more constrained beds of grass—is part
of a human recovery also established in "The Operation."
In the first stanzas of that poem, Snodgrass doubtless stays
too close to the standard version of the hospital. He also
tends to overwrite, perhaps in an effort to counter the
obvious. Thus the props of masked attendants, staring

crowd of bedraggled patients, and self-identification with forlorn Pierrot and schoolgirl at her first sacrament over-play the theme of guilt purified through sacrifice. Snodgrass himself admits to having been deep in psychosomatic literature at the time. His second wife was also supporting him. And the screaming child in the background of the second stanza is at once too pat, and, perhaps, even too obviously personal. Yet to say this is only to admit the success of the concluding stanza:

> Into flowers, into women, I have awakened.
> Too weak to think of strength, I have thought all
>   day,
> Or dozed among standing friends. I lie in night, now,
> A small mound under linen like the drifted snow.
> Only by nurses visited, in radiance, saying, Rest.
> Opposite, ranked office windows glare; headlamps,
>   below,
> Trace out our highways; their cargoes under dark
>   tarpaulins,
> Trucks climb, thundering, and sirens may
> Wail for the fugitive. It is very still. In my brandy
>   bowl
> Of sweet peas at the window, the crystal world
> Is inverted, slow and gay.

His recovery into "radiance," recalling Snodgrass' other paeans to human sunshine, also recovers the world. And that world, concentrated in the flowered brandy bowl, a gift from Jan, is also transformed and purified. Geo-metric glare and charted ways, other dark burdens under wraps, even those also pursued by guilt, are caught in this makeshift vase of flowers. There all have their rush and bitterness broken, "inverted, slow and gay," into still-ness.

After such wholeness, Snodgrass' resulting poetic stand is something to behold. For all I know, it marks a new series of attitudes in American poetry. For example, it can establish the new poet, the university poet, only to recall us to an ancient ideal of education that has all but disappeared. It also condemns our bustling, moneyed civilization only to expose it as less vigorous and alive than the poet. And it mocks the received belief in America's world superiority only to show us to be a world minority of frightened upstarts who deny our souls and content ourselves with looking down. I think specifically of the poems "A Cardinal," "April Inventory," and "The Campus on the Hill."

Leaving Iowa and its creative life, where poetry might be regarded as a living craft rather than as a dead subject, where you might even learn among friends, Snodgrass found Cornell dull. There is no other word, at least not for a poet, to describe a world where little if any creative work is done. "The Campus on the Hill" derives from his life in Ithaca. Recalling Karl Shapiro's earlier "University," Snodgrass' poem is nevertheless sharply different. Shapiro scored the University of Virginia for its treachery to Jefferson's ideal. With an eye on Ezra Cornell, who was a Quaker, Snodgrass scores "the children of the *nouveaux riches*" for the neglected tendance of their souls. In condemning them, he really condemns the dominant America of the Fifties, that one great static, monolithic, irresponsible suburb perched variously and imperturbably near New York, Chicago, Cleveland, St. Louis, Los Angeles—everywhere:

Tomorrow has broken out today:
  Riot in Algeria, in Cyprus, in Alabama;
Aged in wrong, the empires are declining,
  And China gathers, soundlessly, like evidence.
What shall I say to the young on such a morning?—

Mind is the one salvation?—also grammar?—
No; my little ones lean not toward revolt. They
Are the Whites, the vaguely furiously driven, who
  resist
Their souls with such passivity
As would make Quakers swear. All day, dear Lord,
  all day
They wear their godhead lightly.

"April Inventory" is even more outrageous. Behind it lies a year of meditating the monstrous examination in literary history for the Ph.D. in English at Iowa. There were also trips to the university dental clinic; Mahler's *"Lob des Hohen Verstands,"* taught to one Rachel Chester, a most promising young painter; lessons in moth lore and affection for Jan's daughter by an earlier marriage; and then a dying old man, Fritz Jarck, whom Snodgrass tended in the hospital. From this unpromising assortment emerged a poem that brazens forth a song of sweetness and humility in education that sets it once again aglimmering in the world that sounds and shines. Here is the whole thing:

The green catalpa tree has turned
All white; the cherry blooms once more.
In one whole year I haven't learned
A blessed thing they pay you for.
The blossoms snow down in my hair;
The trees and I will soon be bare.

The trees have more than I to spare.
The sleek, expensive girls I teach,
Younger and pinker every year,
Bloom gradually out of reach.

The pear tree lets its petals drop
Like dandruff on a tabletop.

The girls have grown so young by now
I have to nudge myself to stare.
This year they smile and mind me how
My teeth are falling with my hair.
In thirty years I may not get
Younger, shrewder, or out of debt.

The tenth time, just a year ago,
I made myself a little list
Of all the things I'd ought to know,
Then told my parents, analyst,
And everyone who's trusted me
I'd be substantial, presently.

I haven't read one book about
A book or memorized one plot.
Or found a mind I did not doubt.
I learned one date. And then forgot.
And one by one the solid scholars
Get the degrees, the jobs, the dollars.

And smile above their starchy collars.
I taught my classes Whitehead's notions;
One lovely girl, a song of Mahler's.
Lacking a source-book or promotions,
I showed one child the colors of
A luna moth and how to love.

I taught myself to name my name,
To bark back, loosen love and crying;
To ease my woman so she came,

To ease an old man who was dying.
I have not learned how often I
Can win, can love, but choose to die.

I have not learned there is a lie
Love shall be blonder, slimmer, younger;
That my equivocating eye
Loves only by my body's hunger;
That I have forces, true to feel,
Or that the lovely world is real.

While scholars speak authority
And wear their ulcers on their sleeves,
My eyes in spectacles shall see
These trees procure and spend their leaves.
There is a value underneath
The gold and silver in my teeth.

Though trees turn bare and girls turn wives,
We shall afford our costly seasons;
There is a gentleness survives
That will outspeak and has its reasons.
There is a loveliness exists,
Preserves us, not for specialists.

But it is a cardinal, in the poem of the same name, that makes the poet's credo explicit. Fleeing the unnatural rhythms of marching air cadets, superturnpikes, soaring golf balls, and airplane engines—all the cadences of so-called free enterprise, that ring any campus—the poet finds himself alone at last, free to tinker with his own rhythms. He spies a cardinal and first identifies the bird with "the ancient pulse of violence" that lies beneath the slogans and rhythms he has just escaped. But then he sees deeper. In doing so he shoots beyond the occasionally easy indictments of his earlier poems. The cardinal, after all, has a tough, tenacious grip on life, sings his claim with shrill eloquence. And so must all singing creatures, saith the poet:

Selfish, unorthodox,
they live upon our leavings.
Boys or cats or hawks
can scare them out of song.
Still, long as they are living,
they are not still for long.

Each year the city leaves
less of trees or meadows;
they nest in our very eaves
and say what they have to say.
Assertion is their credo;
style tells their policy.

III

Before turning to the "Heart's Needle" cycle, I probably ought to say something about Snodgrass' technique. The themes and development I have just loosely sketched, with their casual insistence that the university be considered part of the larger world, are gripped by a technical mastery rare even among academic poets. To be sure, Snodgrass has gone to school with Auden, Robert Lowell, and Marianne Moore. His wit is that of most modern poets. He can load his poems with the best of them. His verses abound with the metaphoric crockery of mid-century life, realistic diction, symbolic landscapes, double-dealing language, outrageous puns, partial rhymes, stretches of dead-pan prose, syllabic metres, sudden line breaks, accent groupings, and a most polished surface. But he has not stopped there, as have so many of his workshop compatriots. He has assimilated his influences; these devices are not ends in themselves. He doesn't play solemn games with words, and hence with life. Nor is his facility that of the schoolboy at his exercises. You don't find Snodgrass hymning a dull Georgia boyhood or a weekend in Des Moines in the borrowed cadences of Yeats's "The Tower" or in the variegated language of Stevens' "The Comedian as the Letter C." He knows better. It is true that he owes most of what he knows about poetry to his Iowa training; he also recognizes the danger of turning that learning into dogma. In his current effort to write poetry in the larger tradition of Wordsworth, Hardy, and Chaucer, he has gone beyond his Iowa mentors, especially after working with Randall Jarrell at Colorado. Consequently, you can find in his work the unabashed presence of Midwest farmland, the deceptively simple rhythms and statements of nursery rhymes, along with many an unblushing use of such words as "loveliness" and "gentleness." This combination of hard indirection and simplicity gives a tone of dreamy precision to his work, especially in his momentary human scenes, like snowdrops in water, that are so full of implications. The last stanza in "At the Park Dance," for instance, offers a metallic image of the solar system, borrowed from his little girl's game of jacks, and brushes it against the momentary touch of a child's finger:

> Beyond, jagged stars
> are glinting like jacks hurled
> farther than eyes can gather;
> on the dancefloor, girls
> turn, vague as milkweed floats
> bobbing from childish fingers.

And so it is, a dance of stars and girls, infinite and finite, cold and tender, vague and permanent.

My second example is the fifth poem of the "Heart's
Needle" series:

> Winter again and it is snowing;
> Although you are still three,
> You are already growing
> Strange to me.
>
> You chatter about new playmates, sing
> Strange songs; you do not know
> *Hey ding-a-ding-a-ding*
> Or where I go
>
> Or when I sang for bedtime, *Fox*
> *Went out on a chilly night,*
> Before I went for walks
> And did not write;
>
> You never mind the squalls and storms
> That are renewed long since;
> Outside, the thick snow swarms
> Into my prints
>
> And swirls out by warehouses, sealed,
> Dark cowbarns, huddled, still,
> Beyond to the blank field,
> The fox's hill
>
> Where he backtracks and sees the paw,
> Gnawed off, he cannot feel;
> Conceded to the jaw
> Of toothed, blue steel.

Not much is said outright. It is winter. A child is now
three. She goes about her business talking, singing. Her

father recalls walks that he has taken, other snows, and songs that she has forgotten or never knew. He also muses on her strangeness and the fact that the snow outside has obliterated his footsteps. Though the metre is primarily iambic, it is also varied; while the lines may run into each other, or run over from stanza to stanza, each stanza moves quietly to its focus on the speaker, the poet. For the child is his daughter. The landscape is that of his separation—cold, dark, closed. The theme is estrangement in this winter of storming parents, though the child seems oblivious to their strife. The tone is wry. Like the fox in the song she has forgotten, he too has gone out on many a chilly night; like the fox he also sees his impression vanish in the storm; and like the fox he has left part of himself—his daughter—to the trap he has evaded. He has also paused to note his loss.

This is one of a cycle of poems that show Snodgrass at his best. The "Heart's Needle" pieces, ten in number, one for each season in a period of two and a half years, begin with the winter of 1952 and end with spring, 1955. All but the ninth were written at Iowa. Looking backward, we may be reminded of such painful Victorian revelations as Meredith's *Modern Love* or Rossetti's *The House of Life;* we certainly are not reminded of the equally Victorian platitudes of Coventry Patmore's *The Angel in the House.* The theme of divorce is, if anything, modern. The pain it creates is ancient: the title is taken from the phrase "an only daughter is the needle of the heart" in an old Irish story. And for the future, the myth of the artist, the great subject of modern literature, is made even more harrowing. The artist is now estranged where once the world had no power. Nor can he further disengage himself. His daughter is partly himself. She is his torment and his solace. Apart from her he is lost, yet she may quicken his art. The honesty, delicacy, and understatement that Snodgrass employs to construct this dilemma are masterful. He could so easily have fallen into the pitfalls of sensationalism or sentimentality. But he does not.

Throughout these poems the now familar images of No Man's land, a city park, the rolling countryside, and a long parade of grotesque animals, dead and alive, help us keep our bearings. The first poem starts much as did the fifth already mentioned. Cynthia, the poet's daughter, born during the Korean War, is also the child of his winter, his own marital cold war. Thus he may see into his child's mind with the eyes of a "chilled tenant-farmer" gazing on his fields covered with un-marked snow:

> . . . Here lies my land
> Unmarked by agony, the lean foot
> Of the weasel tracking, the thick trapper's boot;
> And I have planned
>
> My chances to restrain
> The torments of demented summer or
> Increase the deepening harvest here before
> It snows again.

The second poem moves through spring towards that "demented summer" which the poet had hoped to re-strain after the stealthy winter hostilities. In three sestets we are asked to consider a three-year-old's garden and, indirectly, the girl herself, sprout of another garden bed:

> Someone will have to weed and spread
>   The young sprouts. Sprinkle them in the hour
> When shadow falls across their bed.
> You should try to look at them every day
>   Because when they come to full flower
>   I will be away.

The fatal summer arrives in the third poem. It opens with a child swung between its parents, who are momentarily pulled together and then move apart. The tug of the poem is the pull on the child. Her parents, now separated, are likened to Korean War prisoners returned after a settlement:

> And nobody seems very pleased.
> It's best. Still, what must not be seized
>   Clenches the empty fist.
> I tugged your hand, once, when I hated
> Things less: a mere game dislocated
>   The radius of your wrist.

With fall present, Snodgrass and daughter take a walk in the fourth poem. They snip flowers in a municipal park, blow dandelions, and pocket late buds that they may still bloom despite the recent frost. His hopes remain for his daughter's life in spite of the separation. These hopes also commingle with his fears for the halted scrawl of his own unfinished verses brought home to him by a glimpse of broken morning glories. The last stanza brings the seasonal coda for poet, father, and daughter. Keeping close to a basic syllabic pattern of 6,6,6,8,4 and a rhyme scheme of *ababb*, this stanza, like the rest, allows the last two lines to put enormous pressure on the flattened suggestion of the first three:

> Night comes and the stiff dew.
> I'm told a friend's child cried
>   because a cricket, who
> had minstreled every night outside
>   her window, died.

The remaining five poems are just as wryly involved in grief and the seasons' flow. The last two in particular take us through two of Iowa City's most respected chambers of horrors, also the panorama of Snodgrass' domestic life. In the first, the poet whiles away the time in the third-floor museum of the old library. There, stuffed and resigned, his blessings confront him: two snarling bobcats, a bison confronting its calf, a lioness protecting her cub, two elk locked in mutual hate. Or, respectively, spatting daughter and step-daughter, the poet correcting his child, the envious first wife, she and the poet caught in the old rancor. The final poem, however, discovers father and daughter once again in the park up to their old tricks: roasting hotdogs on old hangers, paying their respects to the animals now beginning their spring rites. Remarried, the poet has survived and suffered, and spring has come again, and so his life must go, the cycle conclude and renew:

> If I loved you, they said, I'd leave
>   and find my own affairs.
> Well, once again this April, we've
>   come around to the bears;
>
> punished and cared for, behind bars,
>   the coons on bread and water
> stretch thin black fingers after ours.
>   And you are still my daughter.

If nothing more, it is the conclusiveness of Snodgrass' last lines that is so arresting. But perhaps this is enough of crude description. The poet's own words may best explain this new excellence. These form the conclusion of his essay towards an explanation of "Heart's Needle, 6" in the *Partisan Review*, spring 1959:

> I am left, then, with a very old-fashioned measure of a poem's worth—the depth of its sincerity. And it

seems to me that the poets of our generation—those of us who have gone so far in criticism and analysis that we cannot ever turn back and be innocent again, who have such extensive resources for disguising ourselves from ourselves—that our only hope as artists is to continually ask ourselves, "Am I writing what I *really* think? Not what is acceptable; not what my favorite intellectual would think in this situation; not what I wish I felt. Only what I cannot help thinking." For I believe that the only reality which a man can ever surely know is that self he cannot help being, though he will only know that self through its interactions with the world around it. If he pretties it up, if he changes its meaning, if he gives it the voice of any borrowed authority, if in short he rejects this reality, his mind will be less than alive. So will his words.

Anything I might add to this would be an anticlimax. So here it is. I am left with the question of who in Iowa will read these poems aside from the teachers and poets? Frankly, I wish many others would, there and elsewhere. Take the typical co-ed from Coon Rapids, who buys her pencils along with her massive social study texts in Gordon's Book Store; who modeled last summer in a Des Moines department store; and who will be off next fall to New York to live with three other co-eds from South Dakota and Illinois, and then maybe wind up married in Scarsdale—she probably ought to read the book. So should some of the bright graduate students in hydraulic engineering from Arabia. The same goes for the boys from those huge uninsistent farms or from those hamlets that tick off the years by decades and have pre-war Rotary magazines in the dentist's office. Then I suppose I also worry about all those people because partly I still miss Iowa City and so often wonder how it's changed. Does the sun still boil the highway, Clabber Girl sign, and dusty green fields into a pollen-thick blue haze? Do the sleety April rains still turn the new housing projects into mud flats stared at by the nervous wife and kids of some new J. C. Penney junior executive just in from Missouri or Nebraska, or by some new university professor, his class pencil still in his hand? Are the parks just as tangled and unkempt, the drinking fountains just as cracked? Do fat ladies still cling two and three together to navigate Christmas ice at the bottom of College Street? Do the poets still read their verses in the hall off the Amvet bar? Are the streets still so empty and solemn after midnight that you can hear a drunk shout from a speeding car at least two blocks away? And how, by the way, is my old record at the Household Finance office? Have the Quonset huts fallen in? Do old men still sit on the hood of the first parked Ford available along Dubuque Street on Saturday mornings? Has the usual spring murder got itself committed yet? I wonder, but I am also somewhat consoled now. For Snodgrass' *Heart's Needle,* apart from its excellence and extraordinary literary promise, has brought all that old foolish life back to me.

NOTES

[1] Quotations from *Heart's Needle* (Copyright 1959 by William DeWitt Snodgrass) are printed with the permission of Mr. Snodgrass and of the publisher, Alfred A. Knopf, Inc.

VII

A PROPHET
ARMED:
AN
INTRODUCTION
TO THE
POETRY
OF
HOWARD
NEMEROV

ROBERT D. HARVEY

HOWARD NEMEROV has referred to himself as a "writer of fictions in verse and in prose," and in evidence for the assertion has published since 1947 three novels, a book of short stories, and five volumes of verse. The last of these, *New and Selected Poems* (1960), offers fifteen new poems (one of which, "Runes," is itself a cycle of fifteen lyrics), together with about forty poems from earlier collections. A few of these are from the early volumes, *The Image and the Law* (1947) and *Guide to the Ruins* (1950), but the bulk of them are divided equally between *The Salt Garden* (1955) and *Mirrors & Windows* (1958). Published as the poet reached the decisive age of forty, *New and Selected Poems* provides a solid retrospective exhibition of Mr. Nemerov's accomplishment in verse.

Nemerov's novels are light, well-plotted comedies, full of pell-mell wit. They are brilliant, epigrammatic satires upon contemporary American life. His fiction shows him as a man of reason who knows very well how to reveal his moral passion beneath a mask of comic satire. His poetry is another matter—but not wholly other. It is easy to sense in the poems the value of his novelists's experience; one recalls Pound's crafty advice that poets try to write verse as good as good prose. The man is far more thoroughly committed in his verse; but indrawing upon the deeper levels of his imagination for his poems, Nemerov does not refuse his wit fair room for play. He composes epigrams and satires as well as serious lyrics, and the instance has arisen when the reviewer has trouble telling one from the other. In his more fully realized work the wit becomes, like miner's dynamite, an energetic and disciplined tool. The verse of the last few years—the verse of *New and Selected Poems*— amply demonstrates his capacity for integrating complex materials by means of a mature and powerful technical equipment of diction, imagery, and rhythm.

Nemerov was born and reared in New York City and graduated from Harvard (1941) just in time for the war. He joined the RCAF, trained in Canada and England, and then in American uniform flew with a RAF squadron over the North Sea in strikes against Nazi shipping. After the spell of violence he returned with an English wife to a quiet life of teaching and writing. He has been a member of the literature faculty at Bennington College since 1948. The three important experiences seem to have been the city childhood, the wartime violence, and the impact after these of nature—the sea and the Vermont hills. Nemerov's imagination has taken city, war, and nature, and shaped from them a complex and compelling world.

The early poem, "Redeployment," [1] which he reprinted in the new volume, is a good introduction to the theme of war:

They say the war is over. But water still
Comes bloody from the taps, and my pet cat
In his disorder vomits worms which crawl

Swiftly away. Maybe they leave the house.
These worms are white, and flecked with the cat's
  blood.

The war may be over. I know a man
Who keeps a pleasant souvenir, he keeps
A soldier's dead blue eyeballs that he found
Somewhere—hard as chalk, and blue as slate.
He clicks them in his pocket while he talks.

And now there are cockroaches in the house,
They get slightly drunk on DDT,
Are hard, fast, shifty—can be drowned but not
Without you hold them under quite some time.
People say the Mexican kind can fly.

The end of the war. I took it quietly
Enough. I tried to wash the dirt out of
My hair and from under my fingernails,
I dressed in clean white clothes and went to bed.
I heard the dust falling between the walls.

The protagonist protests too much: Nemerov's irony depends upon that insistent reiteration. For of course the
point is that the war is *not* over. The hysterical violence
of the imagery imparts a nightmarish quality. We shall
see the poet making more use of this surrealist technique
in later poems. The nightmare is in familiar enough surroundings—cheap metropolitan lodgings are suggested—
there is even an air of domesticity: the faucet, the cat,
the cockroaches, the pervading dirt; we have no trouble
recognizing this "unreal city." The protagonist may have
nowhere to go, but he bathes and dresses to go sleepless
to bed, alone and alert to hear the silence of the dust
falling. He insanely accepts these horrors as a matter of

course: "the water *still* comes bloody"; the cockroaches, yes, are a nuisance, but means are being worked out to deal with them—imperfect means, to be sure; the pet cat "in his disorder" vomits horribly, but the worms "crawl swiftly away," and "maybe they leave the house." The air of the tentative here suggests the similar horror of Kafka, as does also the random incuriosity about that place where the protagonist's friend has found those eyeballs. Throughout, Nemerov manages this juxtaposition of the ordinary and the monstrous or obscene with considerable distinction. He slips perhaps in the brashness of *"pleasant* souvenir." But that "but not without you hold them," is a fine touch of dialect.

"The Soldier Who Lived Through the War" is the title of another early piece. Whether this means simply that the soldier has survived, or that he has really *lived* only in the commitment to violence (both meanings are there), the result is the same: the "war" continues. Life is seen, after the experience of war, as either dangerous and contingent and vital, or a vacant drift to nothingness. Questioning the danger, for a poet, of a career in teaching, Nemerov once remarked, "I have seen dangers in the academic life, but so are there dangers everywhere." This view persists, and in a new poem, "Life Cycle of Common Man," the poet flatly calculates the number of cigarettes and whiskey empties, "bones, broken shoes, frayed collars and worn out or outgrown diapers and dinner-jackets" an ordinary man strews in his wake, then demands that we

Consider the courage in all that, and behold the man
Walking into deep silence, with the ectoplastic
Cartoon's balloon of speech proceeding
Steadily out of the front of his face, the words
Borne along on the breath which is his spirit
Telling the numberless tale of his untold Word

Which makes the world his apple, and forces him to
eat.

The war is not over. The dangers of commitment to the
chaos of "reality" are the same everywhere, but facing
these dangers, accepting the commitment, is what constitutes life; the only ultimate danger is to refuse the
commitment, to stop "walking into the deep silence"; that
refusal, that stoppage, is death.

The thematic differences between the early "Redeployment" and the new "Life Cycle of Common Man" may
be summed up in the difference between hysterical
paralysis and stoical courage. The shabby horror of death
becomes the grotesque and comic absurdity of life; nightmare isolation gives way to man walking and talking—
Joyce's Stephen Dedalus, that narcissistic young madman,
to fortyish, wife-foolish but fatherly-wise Leopold Bloom.

Nemerov himself has remarked that he was a "city
boy who came late to the country; 'nature,' whatever
that is, had a powerful effect for being an effect so long
delayed." I have said that Nemerov composes his imaginative world out of war, city, and nature. In his later verse
he uses the war theme to express the endless struggle
between city and nature, between mind and world. The
title poem of his third volume (1955), "The Salt Garden," presents a concrete image in which the depth of
his city-nature complex can begin to be gauged. A man
having "with an amateur's toil" and "much patience, and
some sweat" made a pleasant greenery

From a difficult, shallow soil
That, now inland, was once the shore
And once, maybe, the ocean floor,

watches his place "bend in the salt wind," and becomes
suddenly aware of the mighty though distant ocean.

Despising for the moment his puny achievement and so
made restless, he rises at dawn and encounters "a great
gull come from the mist." The gull "stared upon my
green concerns" like a "merchant prince come to some
poor province," then "fought his huge freight into air
and vanished seaward with a cry." The poem concludes:

> When he was gone
> I turned back to the house
> And thought of wife, of child,
> And of my garden and my lawn
> Serene in the wet dawn;
> And thought that image of the wild
> Wave where it beats the air
> Had come, brutal, mysterious,
> To teach the tenant gardener,
> Green fellow of this paradise
> Where his salt dreams lie.

There is a suggestion of Yeats' wild swans in this. But
Nemerov's distinct stamp is upon it. What emerges for
the city man's awareness from his encounter with the
great gull is an inexplicable sense of identity with the
bird. Men build cities and so become human. But in
becoming human they enter upon the hazards of the
moral life. In emerging from and building ramparts
against " 'nature,' whatever that is," they lose their innocence—in a word, they "fall." Nemerov draws a good
deal upon the Old Testament, and he is aware that *both*
Jerusalem and Babylon were cities—and so was Sodom.
And so was Nagasaki. In reclaiming a bit of what was
"once the shore and once, maybe, the ocean floor," this
amateur naturalist from the city is bringing his limited
human skill in contact with the great reservoir from
which that very skill—his human consciousness—ap-

pears to separate him. That separation constitutes the fall of man; that contact, his salvation. The feeling of helplessness, of nonentity, while seen to be invalid as a total response to the encounter, is not wholly denied by the poem's resolution. Man's garden is sowed with salt; his only hope, and that a limited one, is in his own effort that makes it anyhow green.

The meanings contained in these symbols cannot be wholly rendered discursively. They are symbols, and out of them the poet is making poems. We can, however, try to indicate how the three basic areas of Nemerov's imagination which I have abstracted from his verse—city, nature, and war—are related, and how in the last few years he has been forcing them to contain at once a broader and deeper range of meanings.

The theme of war develops an ambivalence: its violence kills, maims, destroys; but its violence is also a form of energy, of action, of life. The horror of death—whether physical death or death of the heart or of imagination—is real enough, and it tends to breed more death, to effect a paralysis. To grant that reality, but to face it and endure it, is to find one's identity in terms of the war which produces it. The horror is then strangely transmuted. The war then reveals itself as the inescapable war of the city with nature. It is the action of flinging meaning into the void. It is the experience of committing one's poor human consciousness, one's more or less skilled battalions of intelligence, against the brute forces of nature, whether without or within: for the salt sea flows in our veins. It is the ever-circulating bloodstream whose reverberations we mistake for the sea's surf when we hold the shell to the ear. Only out of the mind's active struggle to order matter can the awareness of a larger reality, containing both mind and matter, emerge. Possessed of such awareness, the poet renders it in poems.

The meanings here suggested may be illustrated quite clearly in a fairly long poem from *Mirrors & Windows*, entitled "The Town Dump." To this poem Nemerov appends an epigraph from *King Lear,* which pungently reflects upon the war of freedom with necessity:

"The art of our necessities is strange,
That can make vile things precious."

A mile out in the marshes, under a sky
Which seems to be always going away
In a hurry, on that Venetian land threaded
With hidden canals, you will find the city
Which seconds ours (so cemeteries, too,
Reflect a town from hillsides out of town),
Where Being most Becomingly ends up
Becoming some more. From cardboard tenements,
Windowed with cellophane, or simply tenting
In paper bags, the angry mackerel eyes
Glare at you out of stove-in, sunken heads
Far from the sea; the lobster, also, lifts
An empty claw in his most minatory
Of gestures; oyster, crab, and mussel shells
Lie here in heaps, savage as money hurled
Away at the gate of hell. If you want results,
These are results.
    Objects of value or virtue,
However, are also to be picked up here,
Though rarely, lying with bones and rotten meat,
Eggshells and mouldy bread, banana peels
No one will skid on, apple cores that caused
Neither the fall of man nor a theory
Of gravitation. People do throw out
The family pearls by accident, sometimes,
Not often; I've known dealers in antiques
To prowl this place by night, with flashlights, on

The off-chance of somebody's having left
Derelict chairs which will turn out to be
By Hepplewhite, a perfect set of six
Going to show, I guess, that in any sty
Someone's heaven may open and shower down
Riches responsive to the right dream; though
It is a small chance, certainly, that sends
The ghostly dealer, heavy with fly-netting
Over his head, across these hills in darkness,
Stumbling in cut-glass goblets, lacquered cups,
And other products of his dreamy midden
Penciled with light and guarded by the flies.

For there are flies, of course. A dynamo
Composed, by thousands, of our ancient black
Retainers, hums here day and night, steady
As someone telling beads, the hum becoming
A high whine at any disturbance; then,
Settled again, they shine under the sun
Like oil-drops, or are invisible as night,
By night.
          All this continually smoulders,
Crackles, and smokes with mostly invisible fires
Which, working deep, rarely flash out and flare,
And never finish. Nothing finishes;
The flies, feeling the heat, keep on the move.

Among the flies, the purifying fires,
The hunters by night, acquainted with the art
Of our necessities, and the new deposits
That each day wastes with treasure, you may say
There should be ratios. You may sum up
The results, if you want results. But I will add
That wild birds, drawn to the carrion and flies,

Assemble in some numbers here, their wings
Shining with light, their flight enviably free,
Their music marvelous, though sad, and strange.

The dump *is* the city, returning to " 'nature,' whatever that
is"—just as the cemetery is a city whose inhabitants are
returning to nature. The dump is not Mr. Eliot's wasteland, from which God has turned away; it is rather itself
God's country, or at least a necessary part of it, and if it
looks like Hell, it is indisputably ours. Like the trail of
debris in "Life Cycle of Common Man" it is our past—it
is history. One recalls the savage pride of Trotsky's triumphant taunt, flung at the departing Mensheviks in the
Petrograd Soviet in 1917, "You are all on the ash-heap of
history." It is a Hell, but Gehenna as a matter of fact was
Jerusalem's town dump. To conclude that what looks like
Hell is Hell only is to conclude too easily and too soon;
"nothing finishes." Any "ratio" will only sum up the results, "if you want results": Nemerov contents himself
with simply adding that the marvel of the birds, too, is
part of the ghastly whole.

In a note to this writer, Mr. Nemerov offered an illu-
minating off-the-cuff statement:

Poetry is a kind of spiritual exercise, a (generally
doomed but stoical) attempt to pray one's humanity
back into the universe; and conversely an attempt to
read, to derive anew, one's humanity from nature, nature considered as a book, dictionary and bible at
once. Poetry is a doctrine of signatures, or presupposes
that the universe is such a doctrine whether well written or ill . . . Poetry is an art of combination, or dis-
covering the secret valencies which the most widely
differing things have for one another. In the darkness
of this search, patience and good humor are useful

qualities. Also: The serious and the funny are one. The purpose of poetry is to persuade, fool, or compel God into speaking.

"Poetry is a doctrine of signatures . . ." In his best work Nemerov presents adumbrations, not a "ratio"; "signatures rather than the Name Itself."

The style of "The Town Dump" is characteristic. In his earlier verse Nemerov was severely criticized for his undisciplined verbal wit. But here the verbal play seems masterfully controlled. "Where Being most Becomingly ends up Becoming some more" is wittily abstract, and the abrupt descent into those raw particulars, rising to "savage as money hurled away at the gate of Hell" expresses a magnificent rage. The flat emptiness of "If you want results, these are results," provides exactly the inane anticlimax he wants. "The serious and funny are one"—a dangerous truth. But the poet seems to me to mix his tonal qualities in this poem in a fully disciplined way. The hysterical soar and swoop of the tonal rhythms correspond exactly to that sustained dynamo hum rising fitfully to a high whine, or that continual smoulder which rarely flashes out and flares.

Nemerov's increasing mastery of his rhythms may be further illustrated by "Trees," also from the 1958 volume. There is a quiet firmness about this fine sentence, which constitutes the entire poem:

> To be a giant and keep quiet about it,
> To stay in one's own place;
> To stand for the constant presence of process
> And always to seem the same;
> To be steady as a rock and always trembling,
> Having the hard appearance of death
> With the soft, fluent nature of growth,

One's Being deceptively armored,
One's Becoming deceptively vulnerable;
To be so tough, and take the light so well,
Freely providing forbidden knowledge
Of so many things about heaven and earth
For which we should otherwise have no word—
Poems or people are rarely so lovely,
And even when they have great qualities
They tend to tell you rather than exemplify
What they believe themselves to be about,
While from the moving silence of trees,
Whether in storm or calm, in leaf and naked,
Night or day, we draw conclusions of our own,
Sustaining and unnoticed as our breath,
And perilous also—though there has never been
A critical tree—about the nature of things.

In this and in a number of other poems from the 1958 volume ("The Map-Maker on His Art," "To Lu Chi," "Writing," "Painting a Mountain Stream," and others), and in
the new poems of the 1960 volume the sonnet-sequence
"Runes," Nemerov develops his concern with the nature
and problems of poetry or of art in general. He never fails
to insist upon the proximate character of art. It is a "generally doomed but stoical attempt," and when it seems to
succeed, miraculous. In "Writing," for instance, he discovers an intelligibility both in Chinese characters and in
the scorings of skaters in ice; both in some way "do world
and spirit wed"; both seem to establish a connection between the mind and external reality—indeed, to leave a
trace of mind out there. But he concludes:

> continental faults are not
> bare convoluted fissures in the brain.
> Not only must the skaters soon go home;

also the hard inscription of their skates
is scored across the open water, which long
remembers nothing, neither wind nor wake.

In "Painting a Mountain Stream" he puts aside the pen-
tameter line, whose resources he has explored most fully
in his later verse, and shifts the thematic emphasis as well.
"Running and standing still at once is the whole truth,"
he begins, and exhorts the painter to "study this rhythm,
not this thing" in his effort to paint the stream:

The brush's tip streams from the wrist
of a living man, a dying man.
The running water is the wrist.

In the confluence of the wrist
things and ideas ripple together . . .

The water that seemed to stand is gone.
The water that seemed to run is here.
Steady the wrist, steady the eye;
paint this rhythm, not this thing.

Here both the mystery of life—of how things can have, or
be, a rhythm, and the mystery of art—of how man can
create things which seem to have, or become, a rhythm,
are presented in curious relationship to each other, for the
painter himself is a rhythm and not a thing, in more ways
than one. In these stanzas Nemerov makes impressive use
of a quiet variation which at once supports and contains
his themes.

Of course the act of the artist is par excellence expressive of the war of city and nature, since it most directly
reveals the difficulty and mystery of mind or spirit penetrating or even perceiving brute matter. In a number of

poems such as "Brainstorm," "Sanctuary," and "Truth,"
the essential irrationality of the attempt to be rational is
presented. To be rational is to attempt to conform the
world to the mind, to reduce William James's "blooming,
buzzing confusion" to a logic. But if the mind itself be
revealed as part of that blooming and buzzing? In "Brainstorm" something like that is revealed step by step as a
man sitting alone in an upstairs room is distracted from
his book first by the rising wind and then by the crows
whose "horny feet so near but out of sight scratched on
the slate" of the roof overhead. He speculates, as the windows rattle and the timbers groan in the wind, that house
and crows are talking to each other:

> The secret might be out:
> Houses are only trees stretched on the rack.
> And once the crows knew, all nature would know.

And this leads him to wonder in turn what's to prevent
nature, not paradoxically endowed with mind, to invade
his artificially ordered world. The poem then gallops to a
nightmarish conclusion:

> He came to feel the crows walk on his head
> As if he were the house, their crooked feet
> Scratched, through the hair, his scalp. He might be
>   dead,
> It seemed, and all the noises underneath
> Be but the cooling of the sinews, veins,
> Juices, and sodden sacks suddenly let go;
> While in his ruins of wiring, his burst mains,
> The rainy wind had been set free to blow
> Until the green uprising and mob rule
> That ran the world had taken over him,

Split him like seed, and set him in the school
Where any crutch can learn to be a limb.

Inside his head he heard the stormy crows.

"The serious and the funny are one": Nemerov has in this purged away the jarring shrillness of his early use of the nightmare. The rhythm's rush is thoroughly under control. He handles that dreamlike imagery with ease under a compression that seems to leave no room at all for maneuver.

A word ought to be said of Nemerov's satirical verse. It depends upon the same use of the world, but with the difference that the poet chooses to indulge his anger rather than attempt to find through it a larger integration. Here is an early example, entitled "On a Text: Jonah IV, xi"— but first let us quote Scripture. God is remonstrating with Jonah, who is angry that sinful Nineveh is being spared: "And should I not spare Nineveh, that great city, wherein are more than sixscore thousand persons that cannot discern between their right hand and their left hand; and *also* much cattle?" Now Nemerov's verse:

The Lord might have spared us the harsh joke;
Many that live in Nineveh these days
Cannot discern their ass from a hot rock.
Perhaps the word "cattle" refers to these?

In one of his new poems, Nemerov comments wryly and at greater length upon a singularly vulnerable remark culled from the Associated Press, datelined Atlantic City, June 23, 1957. The dispatch, headed "SEES BOOM IN RELIGION, TOO," reads, in part: " 'These fruits of material progress,' said the Rev. Edward L. R. Elson of the National Presbyterian Church, Washington, 'have pro-

vided the leisure, the energy, and the means for a level of
human and spiritual values never before reached.' " The
poem, entitled "Boom!" begins this way:

> Here at the Vespasian-Carlton, it's just one
> religious activity after another; the sky
> is constantly being crossed by cruciform
> airplanes, in which nobody disbelieves
> for a second . . .

After a quick look at Job, Damien, St. Francis, and Dante,
the poem returns to the charge:

> But now the gears mesh and the tires burn
> and the ice chatters in the shaker and the priest
> in the pulpit, and Thy name, O Lord,
> is kept before the public, while the fruits
> ripen and religion booms and the level rises
> and every modern convenience runneth over,
> that it may never be with us as it hath been
> with Athens and Karnak and Nagasaki,
> nor Thy sun for one instant refrain from shining
> on the rainbow Buick by the breezeway
> or the Chris Craft with the uplift life raft;
> that we may continue to be the just folks we are,
> plain people with ordinary superliners and
> disposable diaperliners, people of the stop'n'shop
> 'n'pray as you go, of hotel, motel, boatel,
> the humble pilgrims of no deposit no return
> and please adjust thy clothing, who will give to
>   Thee,
> if Thee will keep us going, our annual
> Miss Universe, for Thy Name's Sake, Amen.

The details have their satirical bite, but the heavy rhetorical impact depends on their being piled high and at accelerated speed. We have seen this device at work in "Brainstorm." The fire of Nemerov's indignation is not icy enough to warrant comparison with Swift; it is rather Voltaire's comic grimace with a strong dash of strictly American guffaw.

The element of wit, though hardly in so heavy a dosage as here, is a permanent element in Nemerov's poetry. When it is so wholeheartedly indulged, it has a kind of frenzied purity. This example of *reductio ad absurdum* comes off from sheer (and painstakingly achieved, for all that, one imagines) gusto. Sometimes his verbal wit rattles tinnily in serious lyrics, especially in some of the early work. But in *New and Selected Poems,* consisting mostly of poems written or published within the last five years, he has managed a tighter control, and the results—"if you want results"—are thematically rich and prosodically strong.

Certainly the satirical gusto develops into something rich and strange in "Suburban Prophecy":

On Saturday, the power-mowers' whine
Begins the morning. Over this neighborhood
Rises the keening, petulant voice, begin
Green oily teeth to chatter and munch the cud.

Monsters, crawling the carpets of the world,
Still send from underground against your blades
The roots of things battalions green and curled
And tender, that will match your blades with blades
Till the revolted throats shall strangle on
The tickle of their dead, till straws shall break
Crankshafts like camels, and the sun go down
On dinosaurs in swamps. A night attack

Follows, and by the time the Sabbath dawns
All armored beasts are eaten by their lawns.

War, city, nature—the familiar concerns this time presented as sardonic prophecy. There are so many false-
prophets hawking their stuff in the Great American Wil-
derness these days that the voice of God is hard to distinguish. Nemerov, gifted with patience and good humor
and a mature awareness of his powers, is certainly suc-
ceeding in persuading, fooling, or compelling some genuine voice into speech in his poems. Whether that voice is
in any sense divine may safely be left to his readers to
decide.

NOTES

[1] Poems quoted in this article are copyrighted by Howard Nemerov and are printed here with his permission, and by the cour-
tesy of the University of Chicago Press.

VIII
THE
POETRY
OF
J. V.
CUNNINGHAM

GROSVENOR E. POWELL

WHEN Yvor Winters said in 1947 that J. V. Cunningham "may prove to be the best of his generation," [1] he was speaking of a man who had published one slim volume of verse in 1942, *The Helmsman,* and a second, *The Judge is Fury,* during the year of Winters' pronouncement. Despite the subsequent publication of two more collections, *Doctor Drink* in 1950 and *Trivial, Vulgar, and Exalted* in 1959, Cunningham has continued to exist as a major poet of whom almost no one has heard. During the last year, with the publication of *The Exclusions of a Rhyme,* containing the previously published poetry along with translations from the Latin, the critical silence was broken, most notably by Thom Gunn's excellent consideration of this last volume in *The Yale Review.* According to Gunn, Cunningham "must be one of the most accomplished poets alive, and one of the few of whom it can be said that he will still be worth reading in fifty years' time."

Cunningham is a professional scholar and teacher, the author of a study of Shakespearean tragedy, a former Guggenheim fellow, and at present a professor of English at Brandeis University. Winters says of him that he "seems to show most clearly [of all the young scholars and critics who are also poets] an understanding of the implications of his adherence to the academic profession." It is certainly clear that Cunningham takes scholarly discipline seriously, as we can see from the following lines (from "To a Friend, on Her Examination for the Doctorate in English"):

> When you shall answer name and date
> Where fool and scholar judge your fate
> What have you gained?
>   A learnèd grace
> And lines of knowledge on the face,
> A spirit weary but composed
> By true perceptions well-disposed,
> A soft voice and historic phrase
> Sounding the speech of Tudor days,
> What ignorance cannot assail
> Or daily novelty amaze,
> Knowledge enforced by firm detail.[2]

But, on the other hand, Cunningham can call the scholar a parasite:

> Homer was poor. His scholars live at ease
> Making as many Homers as you please,
> And every Homer furnishes a book.
> Though guests be parasitic on the cook
> The moral is: *It is the guest who dines.*
> I'll write a book to prove I wrote these lines.

It is thus with Cunningham's positions on most matters, and particularly those relating to current literary theory. They cannot be defined simply; they appear at first as contradiction or perversity. Cunningham is not a romantic poet, and yet he would accept the full implications of the following aphorism by that totally committed romantic, Wallace Stevens: "Reality is a cliché from which we escape by metaphor. It is only *au pays de la métaphore qu' on est poète*." [3] In an age in which poetry means romantic poetry—the practice of such a "classicist" as Eliot belies his announced position—Cunningham writes poetry of controlled statement which suggests the Renaissance masters of the short poem. The development is logical rather than associative, and abstract rather than concrete. The introductory poem to *The Helmsman,* in which the reader is told what he must do if he wishes to read poetry, and in which a scholastic vocabulary carries the meaning, illustrates the style:

Poets survive in fame.
But how can substance trade
The body for a name
Wherewith no soul's arrayed?

No form inspires the clay
Now breathless of what was
Save the imputed sway
Of some Pythagoras,

Some man so deftly mad
His metamorphosed shade,
Leaving the flesh it had,
Breathes on the words they made.

When we discover Renaissance influence in a twentieth-century poet, we expect it to be metaphysical, but Cunningham is not affected by the usual influences. Although Cunningham's verse displays a certain home-grown pleasure in metaphysical wit, the most easily traceable influence on his poetry is not that of Donne, but of Donne's contemporary, the plain-spoken Ben Jonson. The laconic precision, the rhythm, and the subject matter are frequently the same. We can compare Jonson's

> Then his chast wife, though Beast now know no
>   more,
> He adulters still: his thoughts lye with a whore.

With Cunningham's

> You ask me how Contempt who claims to sleep
> With every woman that has ever been
> Can still maintain that women are skin deep?
> They never let him any deeper in.

For the casual reader, Cunningham's poetry may provide sufficient pleasure; the verbal wit, the metrical skill, and the precision of statement are apparent in the individual poems considered as impersonal and isolated statements. But Cunningham himself discourages such a reader. In *The Quest of the Opal*, a curious, third person, autobiographical document dealing with the origins of the poems in *The Helmsman*, he speaks of his own attitude toward the reading of poetry and opposes it to the usual view:

> . . . the lyric especially—that is, the short poem—is commonly thought to be of general application. It should be such that the reader can appropriate it as his own, can regard himself as speaking in his own circumstances the words of the poet. He usually intended to disappoint the reader in this expectation also. He wanted him to know that this was his poem.

not yours; these were his circumstances, not yours;
and these were the structures of thought by which he
had penetrated them.

Cunningham suggests clearly that the poems in *The
Helmsman* are intended to form a coherent and unified
body of work. Specifically, they deal with a definition and
resolution of the problem generally thought to be that of
the romantic poet.

The problem, to put it simply, is that which arises
when the traditional categories of thought are recognized
as arbitrary, and when the mind becomes its own place in
a sense more terrifying than that intended by Marlowe's
Mephistopheles. Historically considered, the breakdown
begins with the sharp distinction between mind and reality recognized by Hobbes and Locke. For Hobbes, nothing exists but particulars in motion, and the individual is
himself a particular isolated from all other particulars.
Such a view makes knowledge impossible and establishes
that separation of man from his environment which later
plagued the English empiricists and such poets as Wordsworth and Stevens, who felt profoundly their own isolation within a mechanistic universe.

I hope that this reference to ideas so much lost in the
dark backward and abysm of time will not blind the
reader to their contemporary significance. When the mind
fully recognizes this distinction between itself and the external world, and the arbitrariness of its own organization
of things, it is thrown in upon itself. Without a system of
thought to guide perception, it falls back upon feeling.
The man of sensibility appears, and lives within a solipsis-
tic universe. Cunningham refers to him in his poem,
"The Man of Feeling":

The music of your feeling has its form,
And its symphonic solitude affirms

The resonance of self, remote and warm,
With private acmes at appointed terms.

So yours, so mine. And no one overhears.
O sealed composer of an endless past,
Rejoice that in that harmony of spheres
Pythagoras and Protagoras fuse at last!

Sensibility, as a touchstone for truth, only develops with
the breakdown early in the eighteenth century of the optimism suggested in Pope's couplet on Newton, with its
implication of a shared universe of certain knowledge. In
much of nineteenth-century poetry, sensibility becomes
truth, e.g., Keats's "I am certain of nothing but of the holi-
ness of the Heart's affections and the Truth of Imagination."

The development in Cunningham's first book, The
Helmsman, is toward a discovery of the following historical fact: a period in which knowledge seems possible appeals to that knowledge; a period in which knowledge
seems arbitrary appeals to direct, wordless experience,
which as Cunningham discovers, is the appeal to sensibility. Cunningham finally rejects this appeal, but the interest in his poetry lies in the fact that he does not reject
it at once. His Irish-Catholic background gave him the
habit of solving personal problems through the traditional
categories of Thomistic psychology. Although the habit
never leaves him, he begins in his earliest published poetry to question the traditional absolutes and to consider
the romantic alternatives. That sensibility provides the
principal concern of his first book he tells us himself in
his prose commentary, The Quest of the Opal. Speaking
of an early poem, he says:

The dog-days, then, was the first issue of what he
called privately the quest of the opal: the attempt to
court and possess, and at the same time disinterestedly

to understand, roughly what was then called sensibility: the province of modern art, the deep well of creativity, the secret and sacred recesses of personality, the Gothic chamber of modern psychology, and the fall of light among the teacups. But an opal, particularly the deep fire opal, derives its color and attractions from flaws in the stone. If this were all, the flaws would be virtues. But any accidental sharp knock, as on the side of a basin while one is washing his hands, my cause the stone to crack; and though it remain in its setting for a while, in some unguarded moment the pieces will fall out, and one will have the ring without the jewel, the promise without the fulfilment.

It is necessary, in reading *The Helmsman,* to recognize this abiding preoccupation with sensibility and with lost absolutes. The poems themselves require the context of the sequence in which they appear. Thus, without the context provided by the poems which surround it, the following, "A Moral Poem," might be taken as a dissenting comment on our current habit of solving our problems through psychoanalysis:

Then leave old regret,
Ancestral remorse,
Which, though you forget,
Unseen keep their course;

Shaping what each says,
Weathered in his style,
They in his fond ways
Live on for a while.

But leave them at last
To find their own home.

Inured to the past,
Be what you become:

Nor ungrudgingly
Your young hours dispense,
Nor live curiously,
Cheating providence.

We find support for such a reading of the poem in an epigram published in Cunningham's most recent collection *Trivial, Vulgar, and Exalted:*

The Elders at their services begin
With paper offerings. They release from sin
The catechumens on the couches lying
In visions, testimonies, prophesying:
Not, "Are you saved?" they ask, but in informal
Insistent query, "Brother, are you normal?"

But this epigram appears in a different context, in a sequence dealing with a different subject. Cunningham writes in such a way that he cannot easily be quoted out of context.

The poem preceding "A Moral Poem" in *The Helmsman* has the title, "Hymn in Adversity," and deals with traditional patterns of consolation, concluding with some irony:

Trust in the Lord,
For that is best,
As for the rest,
Though not ignored
  And not forgotten,

The heart not whole
Nor quite at ease,
Here finds some peace,
Some wealth of soul—
    Albeit ill-gotten.

"A Moral Poem" is followed by "Timor Dei," which concludes:

Today, from my own fence
I saw the grass fires rise,
And saw Thine old incense
Borne up with frosty sighs!

Most terrible, most rude!
I will not shed a tear
For lost beatitude,
But I still fear Thy Fear.

Thus, the "old regret," "the Ancestral remorse," the past to which the poet becomes inured in "A Moral Poem" is not anybody's past but his own. It is not "the pack'd/Pollution and Remorse of Time" which an analyst might discover, but the ghosts of the author's own Catholic training. As a comment on experience, it has a certain universality or we could take no interest in it; but, as a statement, it remains the poet's own and has reference to his circumstances.

While reading poetry, of course, we continually find this practice. Every poet alludes, at one time or another, to contexts with which we are unfamiliar—and the practice is particularly strong in the twentieth century, as a reader of Auden's early verse may discover to his discomfort. The point to be made with reference to Cunningham is that he at least provides us with a context. The context is the sequence of poems itself. The careful reader can thus discover all that he need know in order to achieve that most delicate balance between reading particulars and implying universals.

The progress from Catholic unity through romantic multiplicity is traced for us in *The Helmsman* and *The Judge is Fury*. The mapping of that Las Vegas of the soul beyond romanticism we must postpone until we reach Cunningham's most recent work. Cunningham recognizes that, without the traditional absolutes, there is no reason why one experience should be preferred to another, that to create experience through language is arbitrarily to choose the experience to which he will attend. The alternative would appear to be the appeal to sensibility, but this Cunningham rejects as an appeal to nonverbal experience. As he tells us in *The Quest of the Opal*, "the pursuit of sensibility had been the pursuit of an engrossment in immediacy of experience, but immediacy by definition cannot be talked about, cannot yield a line of verse." This problem is the one developed and resolved in *The Helmsman*.

"Choice" is the key term in this development. The first reference to it occurs in "Dream Vision," which concludes with the following lines:

All choice is error, the tragical mistake,
And you are mine because I name you mine.
Kiss, then, in pledge of the imponderables
That tilt the balance of eternity
A leaf's weight up and down. Though we must part
While each dawn darkens on the fortunate wheel,
The moon will not soften our names cut here
Till every sheltering bird has fled the nest.
They know that wind brings rain, and rain and wind
Will smooth the outlines of our lettering
To the simplicity of epitaph.

All choice is error. The idea is one which develops from the scholastic notion, so influential in Elizabethan drama, of evil as privation of being. The contrast in these lines is that between static choice and the fluid and inexorable seasons. Later poems in the sequence are attempts to find solutions to the problem raised by the paradox of choice, its existence as human necessity and necessary privation. The poem entitled "Choice" suggests that the problem can be solved through the regulating effect of human perception, which, by a delicate balance, can mitigate the rigor of an absolute principle:

> Allegiance is assigned
> Forever when the mind
> Chooses and stamps the will.
> Thus, I must love you still
> Through good and ill.
>
> But though we cannot part
> We must retract the heart
> And build such privacies
> As self-regard agrees
> Conduce to ease.
>
> So manners will repair
> The ravage of despair
> Which generous love invites,
> Preferring quiet nights
> To vain delights.

Several poems toward the end of the sequence treat the difficulty in terms of landscape and resolve it only by acknowledging it. Thus, "Unromantic Love" begins with a statement of the distinction between mind and reality:

There is no quiet in this wood.
The quiet of this clearing
Is the denial of my hearing
The sounds I should.

There is no vision in this glade.
The tower of sun revealing
The timbered scaffoldage is stealing
Essence from shade.

The last two stanzas state, nevertheless, the necessity of
choice and the meaninglessness of sensory details taken
alone:

Only my love is love's ideal.
The love I could discover
In these recesses knows no lover,
Is the unreal,

The undefined, unanalyzed,
Unabsolute many;
It is antithesis of any,
In none comprised.

Cunningham's problem, then, is the modern one of seeing through many illusions without being able to name
alternative absolutes. He is reduced to acknowledging
that words are necessary intermediaries between experience and perception, without being able to affirm the
truth of any one choice or statement. His solution is essentially the same as that of a navigator trying to find his
bearings while flying over the North Pole. In these circumstances, the usual absolute becomes meaningless, and
the navigator must find his position with reference to an

arbitrary pole placed at some other point. It is by inferring hypothetical absolutes that Cunningham is able to conduct his moral navigation through the perceptions of his second book, *The Judge is Fury;* as he puts it at the end of *The Quest of the Opal,* "I am the idea that informs my experience."

The Judge is Fury is introduced by the following epigram:

> These the assizes: here the charge, denial,
> Proof and disproof: the poem is the trial.
> Experience is defendant, and the jury
> Peers of tradition, and the judge is fury.

The "fury" is the fury of the obsessive idea, whatever it may happen to be, which Cunningham refers to in one of the last poems of *The Helmsman* ("L'Esprit de Géometrie et l'Esprit de Finesse"):

> Yes, we are all
> By sense or thought
>   Distraught.
> The violence of reason rules
>   The subtle Schools;
> A falling ember has unhinged Pascal.
>
> I know such men
> Of wild perceptions.
>   Conceptions
> Cold as the serpent and as wise
>   Have held my eyes:
> Their fierce impersonal forms have moved my pen.

This, "the idea that informs my experience," is the hypothetical absolute which Cunningham now substitutes for the absolutes of his Catholic training and the non-verbal absolute of sensibility. It provides the substitute North Pole in terms of which moral bearings will be established in that area beyond Catholic dogma and beyond romantic sensibility. It is with such ideas in mind that Cunningham tells us, at the end of *The Quest of the Opal*, that his second book will develop relationships between the terms sympathy and judgment: since judgment will be in terms of hypothetical absolutes, it cannot occur without sympathy.

Reality and the language which describe it are not the same thing, but for human perception the former can exist only through the medium of the latter. It is never possible to maintain this distinction with any ease. If the self is recognized as the only arbiter of experience and of choice, then one choice is as good as another, or, as Cunningham puts it in "The Solipsist": "Your *hence*/Is personal consequence,/Desire is reason." The problem can be solved only by recognizing that, though perception is determined by the scheme of thought in terms of which it is apprehended, the two must somehow be kept distinct. This distinction is the subject of the following poem, "The Metaphysical Amorist":

> You are the problem I propose,
> My dear, the text my musings glose:
> I call you for convenience love.
> By definition you're a cause
> Inferred by necessary laws—
> You are so to the saints above.
> But in this shadowy lower life
> I sleep with a terrestrial wife
> And earthly children I beget.
> Love is a fiction I must use,

A privilege I can abuse,
And sometimes something I forget.

Now in the heavenly other place
Love is in the eternal mind
The luminous form whose shade she is,
A ghost discarnate, thought defined.
She was so to my early bliss,
She is so while I comprehend
The forms my senses apprehend,
And in the end she will be so.
Her whom my hands embrace I kiss,
Her whom my mind infers I know.
The one exists in time and space
And as she was she will not be;
The other is in her own grace
And is *She is* eternally.

Plato! you shall not plague my life.
I married a terrestrial wife.
And Hume! she is not mere sensation
In sequence of observed relation.
She has two forms—ah, thank you, Duns!—,
I know her in both ways at once.
I knew her, yes, before I knew her,
And by both means I must construe her,
And none among you shall undo her.

But there are times when experience becomes intransigent and refuses to accept any clarifying organization imposed upon it. Such irrational experience must be accepted and somehow weathered, as in "Distraction":

I have distracted time.
In a full day your face

Has only its own place.
Tired from irrelevance
I sleep and dream by chance,
Till passion can exact
No faith and fails in act,
Till timelessness recedes
Beneath the apparent needs
Of a distracted time.

Cunningham recognizes that irrational experience, experience which evades verbal definition, must be faced and can only be imperfectly mastered in language. He is different from many American poets in that he does not confuse irrational experience with super-rational or mystical experience, as the doctrine of sensibility would suggest that he do, to say nothing of the practice of a poet such as Hart Crane, who could be said to court irrationality as the proper subject of poetry and as a means to God. Cunningham is not a romantic poet, despite the fact that his subject is the problems raised by romanticism. He does not seek the irrationality of experience, and we can assume that he is not comfortable with it. As he puts it in one of the epigrams toward the end of *The Judge is Fury*:

If wisdom, as it seems it is,
Be the recovery of some bliss
From the conditions of disaster—
Terror the servant, man the master—
It does not follow we should seek
Crises to prove ourselves unweak.
Much of our lives, God knows, is error,
But who would trifle with unrest?
These fools who would solicit terror,
Obsessed with being unobsessed,
Professionals of experience

Who have disasters to withstand them
As if fear never had unmanned them,
Flaunt a presumptuous innocence.

I have preferred indifference.

The style of these poems may trouble the reader brought
up on the view which has gained authority from the critical pronouncements of Pound and Eliot (most impres-
sively stated in Pound's *ABC of Reading*) that only sensory images are capable of producing anything vivid and
real. Cunningham would agree with Wallace Stevens' assertion that "The momentum of the mind is all toward
abstraction." And, in doing so, he would have ample precedent in the best English poetry of the Renaissance. Cunningham writes "literary" poetry in the good sense in
which Stevens did: the language of the poem itself is
solidly within a tradition of good writing, and is itself a
development of that tradition. Poetry of the past is not
present as information or as allusion: Cunningham has
assimilated his reading, his mind has been changed by
what he has read, and the change is apparent in the maturity of the poetry. This poetry has its native roots in the
abstract vocabulary of the greatest poets of the sixteenth
and seventeenth century. Consider Fulke Greville's

The Mind of Man is this worlds true dimension;
And *Knowledge* is the measure of the minde:
And as the minde, in her vaste comprehension,
Containes more worlds than all the world can finde:
So Knowledge doth it selfe farre more extend,
Than all the minds of Men can Comprehend.

This, though not the source, is certainly the vocabulary of
Cunningham's most characteristic work.

The elements apparently foreign to this abstract style, the rhetoric and imagery of some of the early poems, are there either as a parody of romantic attitudes or as a part of Cunningham's own quest of the opal. Thus, in his early poetry, he shares with Wallace Stevens a tendency toward romantic rhetoric which is justified through self-parody. In "Obsequies for a Poetess," a comment on *fin de siècle* self-deception is put in language which is a parody of late romantic rhetoric:

> Pale Aubrey
> Finds there his faint and final rest; there Dowson
> Pillows his fond head on each breast. For them
> And their compeers, our blind and exiled ghosts
> Which nightly gull us with oblivion,
> Weave we this garland of deciduous bloom
> With subtle thorn. Their verse, sepulchral, breathes
> A careless scent of flowers in late July,
> Too brief for pleasure, though its pleasure lie
> In skilled inconscience of its brevity.

The best of Cunningham's poetry, however, uses a style which seems totally mastered from the moment of its first appearance. It is a poetry in which image and statement are so closely joined as to be inseparable from one another. An example is "The Dog-Days," one of the earliest poems in *The Helmsman*:

> The morning changes in the sun
> As though the hush were insecure,
> And love, so perilously begun,
> Could never in the noon endure,
>
> The noon of unachieved intent,
> Grown hazy with unshadowed light,

Where changing is subservient
To hope no longer, nor delight.

Nothing alive will stir for hours,
Dispassion will leave love unsaid,
While through the window masked with flowers
A lone wasp staggers from the dead.

Watch now, bereft of coming days,
The wasp in the darkened chamber fly,
Whirring ever in an airy maze,
Lost in the light he entered by.

The poem moves from morning to evening and from potentiality through act, and suggests the cyclical nature of things. The dog-days coincide with the end of the Athenian year in late summer, the time of the dog-star, Sirius. Thus, the various cycles within the poem arrive at that time at which no further development is possible (though still "of unachieved intent")—noon, late summer, the end of the year. "Love," within the terms of the poem, is the energy of life—directed, unconscious, predestined; and the wasp is a symbol for this life impelled by love and, hence, going "through the window masked with flowers," and "lost in the light he entered by," i.e., lost in its own directed, unconscious impulse. The wasp, as an image, provides an illustration of the general statement made by the poem, and, at the same time, carries that general statement implicit within itself.

A poem almost totally abstract in its vocabulary, and one which illustrates Cunningham's finest qualities is "Agnosco veteris vestigia flammae," which appears toward the end of *The Judge is Fury*:

I have been here. Dispersed in meditation,
I sense the traces of the old surmise—

Passion dense as fatigue, faithful as pain,
As joy foreboding. O my void, my being
In the suspended sources of experience,
Massive in promise, unhistorical
Being of unbeing, of all futures full,
Unrealized in none, how love betrays you,
Turns you to process and a fluid fact
Whose future specifies its past, whose past
Precedes it, and whose history is its being.

Here we find, concentrated into several sentences, themes
introduced in other poems earlier in the volume. The
poem deals with the recurrence of passion, as the title suggests (more or less paraphrased by the second line of the
poem) with its description of Dido's feelings while listening to Aeneas. It deals further with the paradox of choice,
and the fact that life, or potentiality, consumes itself in
the act of realizing itself.

The subject matter of Cunningham's poetry since 1950
seems less abstruse, and is indicated in the first poem of
his latest collection, *Trivial, Vulgar, and Exalted,* in
which he speaks of his own book, concluding:

The trivial, vulgar, and exalted jostle
Each other in a way to make the apostle
Of culture and right feeling shudder faintly.
It is a shudder that affects the saintly.
It is a shudder by which I am faulted.
I like the trivial, vulgar, and exalted.

The style of these recent poems is the terse abstraction of
the Jonsonian epigram, the subject matter that of a man
who finally has "preferred indifference":

All in due time: love will emerge from hate,
And the due deference of truth from lies.

If not quite all things come to those who wait
They will not need them: in due time one dies.

The attitude could be seen as early as *The Helmsman*
("Elegy for a Cricket"), and could be found throughout
The Judge is Fury ("Experience"). But in these latest
poems it provides the consistent subject.

With a final disillusion like Raleigh's, Cunningham
gives the world the lie:

Of marriage,

I married in my youth a wife.
She was my own, my very first.
She gave the best years of her life.
I hope nobody gets the worst.

Of the single life,

Career was feminine, resourceful, clever.
You'd never guess to see her she felt ever
By a male world oppressed. How much they weigh!
Even her hand disturbed her as she lay.

And of early illusions,

Lady, of anonymous flesh and face
In the half-light, in the rising embrace
Of my losses, in the dark dress and booth,
The stripper of the gawking of my youth,
Lady, I see not, care not, what you are.
I sit with beer and bourbon at this bar.

Cunningham has considered and rejected the dominant literary tendencies of our time. He has seen that they lead to that imprecision of statement which grasps at the ineffable. His own achievement has been that of knowing where he is. The value of this poetry lies in its total honesty to the experience it describes. The mind builds within itself heaven and hell: "I am the idea that informs my experience." In arriving at this position, and in exploring beyond it, Cunningham has written some very great poems.

NOTES

[1] *The Anatomy of Nonsense,* by Yvor Winters, New Directions, 1947.

[2] Quotations from J. V. Cunningham's poetry are reprinted from *The Exclusions of a Rhyme: Poems and Epigrams* by J. V. Cunningham, by permission of the publisher, Alan Swallow. Copyright 1942, 1947, 1950, 1957, 1960 by J. V. Cunningham.

[3] Quotations from Wallace Stevens are from *Opus Posthumous,* Alfred A. Knopf. Copyright 1957 by Elsie Stevens and Holly Stevens.

IX
"TO CHANGE, TO CHANGE!": THE POETRY OF RANDALL JARRELL

WALTER B. RIDEOUT

It is a fact of more consequence to me than it could be to Randall Jarrell that once several years ago, in company with some other professors of English, I had lunch with him on the occasion of his coming to Northwestern to give a lecture. Since I recall the event itself but few of the specific details—I haven't the slightest remembrance of what or how the poet ate—it will not be necessary for his future biographers to interview me, but a few things do stick in my mind. Jarrell, a short, slender man, was wearing a trim, handsome, auburn beard, which, in those innocent days before one asserted his rebellion against conformity by growing a beard like every other rebel's, made him look like a man willing to go his own way all the way. As we sat down about him at a circular table in that respectable hotel dining room, I suppose we were all a bit nervous that he would cast a cold eye on us as being simply pictures, mere sketches even, from a nonfictional institution—his satirical novel, *Pictures from an Institution,* had been published some months before—and that he would immediately obliterate us with a bomb-load of devastating quips before we could organize our academic defenses against him. But nothing like this happened at all. Although I don't recall the subjects of conversation, I do remember that Jarrell was a most pleasant table companion, quite as eager to be agreeable to us as we were to be agreeable to him. He was witty, but not at the expense of anyone, not even the absent and deserving; he was intelligent, humane, and interested in the lives of others. He showed, in short, some of the qualities that characterize his poetry and make the best of it so durable.

For what good it may do those biographers I can report the one remark by Jarrell that I do recall. The talk had turned temporarily to, of all things, sports cars; for *Pictures from an Institution* had sold well, and Jarrell admitted to having purchased a Jaguar and found it good, particularly its well-designed dashboard and its low-slung frame. "It's very pleasant," he said, and I report the sense accurately if not the exact words, "to be able to put your arm outside the car and actually touch the road as you swoop around a curve." Just what to say of this casual, unserious remark I'm not quite sure. If I were a different kind of critic, I would here bring in a fancy passage about the poet as a motorized Antaeus needing constant return to his mother the earth, or the macadam, to renew his creative force; but I am not a different kind of critic and shall only say that the remark has stayed in my mind because it seems to me to typify a quality both of Jarrell's mind and his poetry. The intelligence and the humanity are not bland or neutral; they are spotted and streaked with the unexpected, the idiosyncratic, even the quixotic and contradictory. Jarrell, both as man and poet, commits himself willingly to experience as a thing often not to be understood rationally yet always to be curiously examined and tested on one's own terms.

As might be expected, Jarrell's commitment to testing experience on his own terms is least obvious in his first volume of poems, *Blood for a Stranger*, published in 1942.[1] (Two years previously a selection of his work had been included in the first New Directions book of *Five Young American Poets,* but these poems were incorporated into his own 1942 volume.) It has always been hard for young poets to avoid conscious or unconscious imitation of their established predecessors, especially when, as was the case with such figures as Eliot and Auden, these predecessors had actually explored and opened up exciting new poetic lands. One hears the echoes on page after page of Jarrell's first book. Occasionally the note of Eliot sounds, more often that of John Crowe Ransom, under whom Jarrell had taught English for two years at Kenyon, or of Allen Tate, to whom the volume is dedicated. The verse tends to be hard and dry, the images relentlessly metaphysical, the thought deliberately "difficult"; but what had been functional, necessary parts of the technique of Ransom and of Tate too frequently become borrowed decorations in *Blood for a Stranger.* The most constant influence of all seems to be that of Auden. Like him, Jarrell experiments with ballad forms and half-rimes; juxtaposes learned with colloquial language; yokes the big abstract with the small concrete; and links politics, economics, and psychiatry in an analysis of the decadence of the age. Such elements, sometimes skillfully dealt with even if at second hand, make up poems like "On the Railway Platform," "The Lost Love," "Because of Me, Because of You . . . ," and "Love, in Its Separate Being . . . ," the last two Audenesque to their very titles.

But besides the fact that, imitative or not, these are still far better poems than most young English teachers write, one can make several favorable observations on *Blood for a Stranger.* First, the book shows considerable technical virtuosity. For instance, many different stanzaic forms are used, even to variations of the sestina in "A Story" and "The Refugees." Second, in making his choices some dozen years later for his *Selected Poems,* Jarrell proved himself to be one of his own best critics by choosing only ten from this first volume, but these the most successful even before revisions for the 1955 collection. Finally, in the best as well as in some of the second-best poems in the book Jarrell began to establish his own voice and some of his own attitudes.

Despite the wit that occasionally snaps like a whip in *Blood for a Stranger*, the mood of most of the poems is somber and the subject of many of them is literally pain, the pain, not only of death, which Jarrell seems to have sensed as infecting the whole world in the 1930's, but the pain of life as well, its disillusion, emotional loss, physical decay, alienation of the self from others and from itself, all the afflictions that make up for Jarrell the inevitable human lot. So "The Memoirs of Glückel of Hameln" ends:

> Glückel, Glückel, you tell indifferently
> To ears indifferent with Necessity
> The torments and obsessions of our life:
> Your pain seems only the useless echo
> Of all the evil we already know.

Several poems deal with what, in "Children Selecting Books in a Library," Jarrell calls "the child's peculiar gift for pain"; in fact, childhood suffering becomes a synecdoche for all human suffering in a world where people are subject to a Necessity as unpredictable and all-powerful as the authority of the parent over the child. What seems to me the best poem in *Blood for a Stranger*, "90 North," is concerned with this theme, wherein innocence and the imagined fuse with experience and the real. Despite its echoes of Stephen Spender's "Polar Exploration," the poem is so expert in its control of the basic metaphor, its preparation for the "moralized" conclusion, and its use for emphasis in the last stanza of pause, balance, and repetition, that it is worth quoting as a whole:

At home, in my flannel gown, like a bear to its floe,
I clambered to bed; up the globe's impossible sides
I sailed all night—till at last, with my black beard,
My furs and my dogs, I stood at the northern pole.

There in the childish night my companions lay
    frozen,
The stiff furs knocked at my starveling throat,
And I gave my great sigh—the flakes came huddling;
Were they really my end? In the darkness I turned to
    my rest.

Here, the flag snaps in the glare and silence
Of the unbroken ice. And I stand here,
The dogs bark, my beard is black, and I stare
At the North Pole. And now what? Why, go back.

Turn as I please, my step is to the south.
The world—my world spins on this final point
Of cold and wretchedness: all lines, all winds
End in this whirlpool I at last discover.

And it is meaningless. In the child's bed
After the night's voyage, in that warm world
Where people work and suffer till the death
That crowns the pain—in that Cloud-Cuckoo-Land

I reached my North and it had meaning.
Here at the actual pole of my existence,
Where all that I have done is meaningless,
Where I die or live by accident alone—

Where, living or dying, I am still alone;
Here where North, the night, the berg of death

Crowd to me out of the ignorant darkness,
I see at last that all the knowledge

I wrung from the darkness—that the darkness flung
me—
Is worthless as ignorance: nothing comes from nothing,
The darkness from the darkness. Pain comes from the
darkness
And we call it wisdom. It is pain.

Over many of the poems in *Blood for a Stranger* hangs
the sense of a whole world sleep-staggering through the
nightmare of history toward the inevitable catastrophe of
war. The tormented foreigner in "For an Emigrant" leaves
Europe, over which "death/Moves like an impulse," and
reaches America, only to find that "You escaped from
nothing; the westering soul/ Finds Europe waiting for
it over every sea." In "The Winter's Tale," Jarrell scorn-
fully addresses the inhabitants of western civilization as
"We who have possessed the world/ As efficiently as a
new virus," and says that we can think:

> "Tomorrow we may be remembered
> As a technologist's nightmare, the megalomaniacs
> Who presented to posterity as their justification
> The best armies that the world ever saw."

However just or unjust the accusation, the poet's anger
tends to be "too much up in his head." Though he enters
imaginatively the experience of the emigrant faced with
"old and comfortable injustice," he has not yet suffered
such an experience himself. The actual coming of World
War II, during which Jarrell served in the Army Air
Forces, brought him a more immediate involvement and

a consequent deepening of poetic insight and sympathy. These were to show in his next volume, *Little Friend, Little Friend,* published in 1945.

In every way this second volume is an advance over the first. The actual condition of military life in wartime— the necessary submission to a rigidly hierarchical system, a consequent sense of rootlessness and impermanence, long stretches of routinized boredom alternating with periods of intense, dangerous activity—all this is less conducive to the immediate production of good literature than we may like to think. Jarrell's, however, is certainly among the best poetry to come directly out of World War II and is indeed in an absolute sense very impressive, partly because it does face the actual condition honestly. The many war poems in *Little Friend, Little Friend,* varied as they are in particular subject and form, are consistent in tone. Neither "patriotic" nor "unpatriotic," they try deliberately to understand the war in terms of the individual human beings tombed alive in a social system and a routine or tossed like "things"—the word recurs again and again in the poems—into situations of extreme violence. Always Jarrell makes us aware of the fragile human flesh and the delicately complicated human mind encased in the steel and plexiglass of destruction, the minute fragments of human life within the great metallic machine of war.

It has been suggested that readers, particularly those who saw service in World War II, may find these poems "powerful" partly because of "extra-poetical associations." It is a possible argument. Re-reading *Little Friend, Little Friend* in preparation for writing this article, I suddenly found myself reliving a brief moment of my own safe and undramatic war experience. Some time in 1945 I was invited to a "bottle party" in another room of the Navy B.O.Q. where I was quartered, not far from the entrance to Pearl Harbor. (Was this so long ago that I must identify "B.O.Q." as "Bachelor Officers' Quarters"?) As I opened the door on the crowded, noisy party, a young lieutenant, whom I had never seen and never saw again after that afternoon, stepped quickly up to me, cupped his hand around my ear against the racket, and shouted: "Did you know Joe Robbins?" I started to say that I didn't, but the man hadn't stopped talking: "He was a friend of mine. He came in too fast on the flight deck and crashed into the island and we all watched him burn." Whatever conventional thing one says when impaled on such moments I probably said, but he wasn't listening. The door to the room opened, another man entered, and the young lieutenant stepped to his side. I was close enough to hear him shout over the noise: "Did you know Joe Robbins? He was a friend of mine. He came in too fast on the flight deck and crashed into the island and we all watched him burn." Then I moved away, shocked by the kind of knowledge from which Jarrell was to make poetry.

Possibly, I say, the "extra-poetical associations" intensify our response, but I don't think they are essential to it. Except for a very few poems where the emotion becomes sentiment—as in "Mother, Said the Child," for example —the poet controls his own feeling in various ways so that the statement of it remains honest, appropriate, and hence explosively effective. Leaving aside that famous five-line autobiography of modern man, "The Death of the Ball Turret Gunner," which M. L. Rosenthal has admirably analyzed in *The Modern Poets,* consider the poem "A Lullaby":

For wars his life and half a world away
The soldier sells his family and days.
He learns to fight for freedom and the State;
He sleeps with seven men within six feet.

He picks up matches and he cleans out plates;
Is lied to like a child, cursed like a beast.

They crop his head, his dog tags ring like sheep
As his stiff limbs shift wearily to sleep.

Recalled in dreams or letters, else forgot,
His life is smothered like a grave, with dirt;
And his dull torment mottles like a fly's
The lying amber of the histories.

This is indeed a lullaby, as the references to sleep in lines
four and eight and to both death-in-life and actual death
in the last stanza indicate; hence the form is properly that
of the song, and the vocabulary is for the most part simple
and concrete. But the subject, or "object," of this ironic
cradle-song is not some baby bunting but a grown man
who is driven like a beast through a stupefying, humiliat-
ing routine; so it is appropriate that the monotonous meter
should show few variations and that the rimes should
have the semi-discord of half-rimes. Deliberately unsong-
like too are the compressed juxtapositions of ideas. The
soldier must sell not only himself but his family, and,
carefully propagandized, he fights ostensibly for freedom,
actually for the aggrandizement of that which takes away
his freedom. Just as these contradictions prepare us to accept the conclusion of the argument, "The lying amber of
the histories," so the simple-worded complexity of line
four foreshadows the images of stanzas two and three; to
sleep "within six feet" suggests both a beast-like life and a
constant closeness to the grave, to the emptiness of which
the soldier's life is so startlingly compared in line ten.
There is considerably more to this extraordinary "small"
poem, but perhaps enough has been said to indicate the
skill with which in an apparently simple way Jarrell has
suggested not only the soldier's condition in our time, but
his condition in any time.

By concerning himself with the human being's reaction
to war Jarrell was able to bring to focus the preoccupation

with pain and suffering that had marked but had sometimes been blurred in his earlier poems, and in so doing he
was able to consider the question of guilt. To what extent, if any, does one have ethical responsibility even
though he is part of a system and a machine? Is not killing
an enemy or assisting in killing him murder even though
one justifies it, as most of us do, under the excuse of war?
Such considerations complicate the theme of "2nd Air
Force," in which a woman visits her son at an air base in
the United States. As she watches the men "pass like
beasts, unquestioning," she recalls the newspaper account
of a crippled bombing plane being escorted home by a
fighter craft, thus demonstrating the paradox of human
community in the midst of hate and destruction. She
thinks of the men now about her on the ground and of
the crews "in the steady winter of the sky" and feels for
them

The love of life for life. The hopeful cells
Heavy with someone else's death, cold carriers
Of someone else's victory, grope past their lives
Into her own bewilderment: The years meant *this?*
But for them the bombers answer everything.

"2nd Air Force" is an instance of another way in which
Jarrell's poetry in *Little Friend, Little Friend* had developed out of and improved on that of *Blood for a Stranger.*
Even more than in the first volume the poems of the second are likely to be what Jarrell once described as "dramatic speeches or scenes." It is not clear whether he was
influenced directly by the Robert Browning of *Men and
Women* or indirectly by way of Eliot's "Prufrock" and
"Gerontion" or of Frost's dramatic verse, or whether indeed the dramatic came naturally as a response to temper-
amental necessity; but the fact remains that poem after
poem is a dramatic monologue or, more frequently, a so-

liloquy, though the fictional terms "interior monologue" or "subjective point of view" fit more exactly what the poet is doing. Thus in "2nd Air Force" we see the external scene as the woman herself observes it and are then given her feelings and thoughts as prompted by the scene. A few poems are presented as actual subjective narratives, compressed stories in verse. "A Pilot from the Carrier," for example, describes through the pilot's consciousness how, wounded, he struggles from his burning plane, parachutes down toward his carrier, which is under attack, and then faces his death as a "fragile sun-marked plane/ . . . grows to him, rubbed silver tipped with flame." With *Little Friend, Little Friend* the dramatic clearly becomes Jarrell's favorite way of organizing his material.

"Half my poems are about the war, half are not," Jarrell wrote in commenting on the group of his poems included in John Ciardi's anthology, *Mid-Century American Poets* (1950). This accurately enough describes his third volume, *Losses,* published in 1948; though in subsequent collections, except for *Selected Poems,* he was largely to abandon the subject of war. The "losses" in this third book are of various kinds. In "Pilots, Man Your Planes" they are of a direct military, or rather naval, sort; a fighter pilot ditches his plane in combat, sees his carrier explode and sink, and is rescued among the survivors. But the war produces wounded minds as well as wounded bodies. So in "The Dead Wingman," as Jarrell notes, another pilot "keeps searching in his sleep for his shot-down" fellow-flyer. The losses spread out to include the figurative as well as the literal. In "Eighth Air Force" the speaker, presumably the poet, first presents a scene of casual common life in an encampment, where a puppy laps water from a can and a drunken sergeant shaves. Then, quite as casually, the poet sees "The other murderers troop in yawning"; and with the introduction of the word "murderers" the poem expands into a further questioning of human guilt in war, coming to its damning climax when the poet himself joins mankind, as it were, by speaking the words of Pontius Pilate. The greatest loss is indeed the human being's loss, by choice or by coercion, of his humanity. This is the theme of "A Camp in the Prussian Forest," one of the book's finest and most terrible poems, from the necessarily ugly images in the first stanza to the speaker's horrified hysteria in the last. (Though Jarrell's note is not essential for an understanding of the poem, it may help the reader "get into it" more quickly: "An American soldier is speaking after the capture of one of the great German death camps. The Jews, under the Nazis, were made to wear the badge of a yellow star. The white Star of David is set over Jewish graves just as the cross is set over Christian graves"):

> I walk beside the prisoners to the road.
> Load on puffed load,
> Their corpses, stacked like sodden wood,
> Lie barred or galled with blood
>
> By the charred warehouse. No one comes today
> In the old way
> To knock the fillings from their teeth;
> The dark, coned, common wreath
>
> Is plaited for their grave—a kind of grief.
> The living leaf
> Clings to the planted profitable
> Pine if it is able;
>
> The boughs sigh, mile on green, calm, breathing
>   mile,
> From this dead file

The planners ruled for them. . . . One year
They sent a million here:

Here men were drunk like water, burnt like wood.
The fat of good
And evil, the breast's star of hope
Were rendered into soap.

I paint the star I sawed from yellow pine—
And plant the sign
In soil that does not yet refuse
Its usual Jews

Their first asylum. But the white, dwarfed star—
This dead white star—
Hides nothing, pays for nothing; smoke
Fouls it, a yellow joke,

The needles of the wreath are chalked with ash,
A filmy trash
Litters the black woods with the death
Of men; and one last breath

Curls from the monstrous chimney. . . . I laugh
  aloud
Again and again;
The star laughs from its rotting shroud
Of flesh. O star of men!

It is not only the losses of war that Jarrell describes in
this somber book; peace—ordinary life, in other words—
has its losses too. So "Lady Bates," the initial poem in the
book, is an elegy for a little dead Negro girl; "Money"—
in my opinion, the weakest in the volume—is the solilo-
quy of a spiritually dead, spiritually never born, million-
aire; "Loss," a wonderfully put together variation on the

sonnet, deals unsentimentally with the death of a small
bird. Yet despite this preoccupation with suffering and
death, this sad conviction that as "The Place of Death"
concludes, " 'Only man is miserable,' " Jarrell's poems in
Losses and his other mature books are not depressing
when taken as a whole, though the reader of this article
may have so decided. For one thing, though Jarrell is
often ironic, he is much less frequently satiric; irony may
cut painfully to the bone, but at least it does not inflict
the burning smart that satire does. Again, even while re-
proaching us and himself for our inhumanity, Jarrell usually tempers his anger with compassion; like Mark Twain
he feels pity for the "poor damned human race." Furthermore, he is aware of the humanity that may paradoxically
exist in conjunction with or in spite of inhumanity. The
code name of the fighter plane to which the crippled
bomber calls is "Little Friend"; even "A Camp in the
Prussian Forest" ends with the anguished naming of a
yet uneradicated ideal of human community, "O star of
men!"; and if one person, the poet, can sympathize with
the "dull torment" of the soldier, then other persons
among his readers can as well. Finally, Jarrell manages in
some of his poems to convey a kind of irrational sense of
limited hopefulness, a sense that, despite man's external
subjection to the State or to economic forces and his internal subjection to his own nature, life is nevertheless an
open affair rather than a closed one if only because of
man's imaginative powers.

It is in this last context that we can perhaps best understand Jarrell's long preoccupation with fairy tales, a preoccupation evident as early as *Blood for a Stranger*, where
he writes of "Children Selecting Books in a Library":

Their tales are full of sorcerers and ogres
Because their lives are: the capricious infinite
That, like parents, no one has yet escaped
Except by luck or magic; and since strength

And wit are useless, be kind or stupid, wait
Some power's gratitude, the tide of things. . . .

One of the best poems in *Losses* is "The Märchen," in which, recreating the atmosphere of Grimm's fairy tales, he suggests their links with religious motifs and their symbolic representation of constantly repeated human experience. The poem concludes:

> Hänsel, by the eternal sea,
> Said to the flounder for his first wish, *Let me wish*
> *And let my wish be granted;* it was granted.
> Granted, granted. . . . Poor Hänsel, once too power-
> less
> To shelter your own children from the cold
> Or quiet their bellies with the thinnest gruel,
> It was not power that you lacked, but wishes.
> Had you not learned—have we not learned, from tales
> Neither of beasts nor kingdoms nor their Lord,
> But of our own hearts, the realm of death—
> Neither to rule nor die? to change, to change!

Change and transformation, Jarrell argues here and elsewhere, are at the very heart of the fairy tales, and, logical or not, the fairy tale is a metaphor for life. The prince is transformed by magic in the tale, the child's self or way of living is changed by the unintelligible powers of adults, we change by some incomprehensible process of necessity, which grants our wishes provided we know what to wish.

For an author to consider life so metaphorically can be irritating to those who prefer a more rationalistic philosophy, and I must admit myself 'to accepting Jarrell's fairy-tale metaphor primarily as a sort of "as if" assumption that helps him to get some of his poetry written. That such an assumption does help, however, is indicated by his fourth volume, *The Seven-League Crutches* (1951). Despite a tendency to let some of his poems relax into interesting talk—for example, "An English Garden in Austria" with its scraps of German and French and of curious lore—Jarrell in this volume, as the title suggests, is trying to push old preoccupations in new directions. Fairy tale materials form the basis for his dramatic lyric "The Black Swan," but while the haunting quality of these materials is preserved, the poem makes the psychology of a bereaved child both immediate and believable. In the moving conclusion to the long poem "The Night Before the Night Before Christmas," another of Jarrell's subjective narratives, the fairy tale elements fuse with dream sequences; while in "Hohensalzburg: Fantastic Variations on a Theme of Romantic Character," the author combines these elements with folk lore and fantasy.

Varied and even bizarre as these poems may be on their surfaces, underneath they are linked by a common and quite serious purpose. Like the writers of the German Romantic period Jarrell interweaves fairy tale, folk lore, fantasy, and dream in order to explore both inner and outer "reality," to apprehend, if possible, both the human psyche and the external world in which it exists. Significantly the three poems just mentioned are all narratives, of one sort or another, in verse; and we know that the author has commented directly about the function of a narrative in his introduction to *The Anchor Book of Stories:*

A story, then, tells the truth or a lie—is a wish, or a truth, or a wish modified by a truth. Children ask first of all: "Is it a *true* story?" They ask this of the storyteller, but they ask of the story what they ask of a dream: that it satisfy their wishes. The Muses are the daughters of hope and the stepdaughters of memory. The wish is the first truth about us, since it represents not that learned principle of reality which half-governs our workaday hours, but the primary principle of pleasure which governs infancy, sleep, daydreams—and, certainly, many stories. Reading stories, we cannot help remembering Groddeck's "We have to reckon with what exists, and dreams, daydreams too, are also facts; if anyone really wants to investigate realities, he cannot do better than to start with such as these. If he neglects them, he will learn little or nothing of the world of life."

One notes that this passage documents Jarrell's interest in Freudian psychology, for it draws directly on Freud's distinction between the reality principle and the pleasure principle; yet Jarrell, like Groddeck—and Freud, for that matter—is concerned with "the world of life." He is at once psychologist and philosopher.

Several poems in *The Seven-League Crutches* unite psychology and philosophy in other ways than by the use of fairy tale or similar materials. In one of the best of these, "*Seele im Raum*" ("Soul in Space"), the monologue of a wretched, mentally disturbed woman, the speaker tries to describe accurately a vivid delusion and then breaks in on herself to say: "This is senseless?/ Shall I make sense or shall I tell the truth?/ Choose either—I cannot do both." The woman's hallucinated mind is capable of such a sudden, provocative insight because it is working within a private world freed of the conventional rational strictures. The insight itself appears to echo Jarrell's own questioning of experience as well as his still tentative conclusions about the irrational dilemmas it poses. A quite different poem, "The Knight, Death, and the Devil," attempts another questioning and tentative conclusion, this time by the close observation and interpretation of a work of art, a device frequently employed by Rainer Maria Rilke, whose growing influence on Jarrell's sensibility and technique is in several ways apparent in this volume.

"The Knight, Death, and the Devil" reproduces verbally the visual detail, at once fantastic and photographic, of its subject, the Albrecht Dürer engraving by the same name, and suggests the meaning of the whole picture for the poet observer. The poem begins with a strikingly "unpoetic" line, in which assonance and consonance produce a deliberate cacophony:

Cowhorn-crowned, shock-headed, cornshuck-bearded,
Death is a scarecrow. . . .

Death rides beside the Knight, while the Devil insidiously "trots behind" in deformed bestiality:

His eye a ring inside a ring inside a ring
That leers up, joyless, vile, in meek obscenity. . . .

So accompanied rides the Knight, "In fluted mail," his eyes steadily ahead, looking "At—at—/ a man's look completes itself." And Jarrell's poem completes its own meaning by asserting the paradox of fate and free will that man lives without solving:

The death of his own flesh, set up outside him;
The flesh of his own soul, set up outside him—
Death and the devil, what are these to him?
His being accuses him—and yet his face is firm
In resolution, in absolute persistence;
The folds of smiling do for steadiness;
The face is its own fate—*a man does what he must*—
And the body underneath it says: *I am.*

As "Seele im Raum" and "The Knight, Death, and the Devil" suggest, paradox is as recurrent a motif in The Seven-League Crutches as change and transformation. The title of the collection is entirely fitting; for surely it is "true in fact," however "contrary to common sense," that poetry (art in general) supports the human personality, crippled as it is with outer and inner limitations, by transporting it imaginatively outside itself. It is fitting too that just as Jarrell has widened his range of subject matter in this volume—only three poems out of the book's twenty-nine deal with the war—so he widens his range of tone to include the light as well as the dark: the somberness is now more often touched with humor. From the beginning humor had been a minor note in Jarrell's poetry, somewhat unexpectedly so when one thinks of his reputation for committing witty outrage in prose. Wisecracks and wry observations had appeared occasionally in his first three volumes of verse; but in The Seven-League Crutches humor informs a number of the poems from the somewhat self-conscious wit of "A Conversation with the Devil" to the absurd juxtapositions in "Nollekens," which define the eccentric character of that successful eighteenth-century portrait sculptor, a man as odd as his name. More significantly, humor blends with compassion when Jarrell writes of the unhappy woman in "Seele im Raum" or of the sturdy, convention-bound coed of "A Girl in a Library," in whom he nevertheless sees a flash of the archetypal Woman. In The Seven-League Crutches humor has become part of the poet's way of looking at life. It is a means of coping with what the old woman says to her mirror in "The Face," that "Living is more dangerous than anything. . . ." To put it paradoxically, as Jarrell would wish, humor helps one to understand the seriousness and sadness of things.

Since The Seven-League Crutches Jarrell has published disappointingly little poetry, considering that his first four books came out within only ten years. The Se-

lected Poems of 1955 included only two new poems; and a new collection, *The Woman at the Washington Zoo,* did not appear until late in 1960. Furthermore, five of the thirty-one poems in this latest volume had received magazine publication a decade or more earlier. Jarrell was busy enough during the Fifties, of course. He completed a third of the essays and reviews that make up *Poetry and the Age,* taught regularly at the Woman's College of the University of North Carolina and was visiting professor at several other institutions, spent two years as Consultant in Poetry in English at the Library of Congress, lectured widely, and wrote and published *Pictures from an Institution.* The range of his literary activities in fact indicates that he is one of those rare persons of our specialized era, the man of letters; but these activities have limited the time he has been able to give to poetry.

The *Woman at the Washington Zoo* reveals that one of Jarrell's increasing interests has been in the difficult art of translation. Twelve of the poems are translations, most of them not previously published, nine being from Rilke, an English version of whose *"Der Ölbaumgarten"* ("The Olive Garden") had appeared in *The Seven-League Crutches.* I doubt whether translations can be perfect reflections of their originals, but having applied my own uncertain knowledge of German to several of the poems and compared Jarrell's with other English renderings, I find his to be at least as close to Rilke's meaning and spirit as anyone else's.

I feel safer in asserting that in *The Woman at the Washington Zoo* Jarrell's more recent interests are mixed with earlier ones. "Cinderella" manipulates the fairy tale into an illumination of a woman's inward-grown personality; while "The Elementary Scene," which moves from sharply-outlined, concrete sense details to a deliberately vague emotive state, evokes the special pathos of childhood in a Rilkean manner. (One of Jarrell's best translations is of Rilke's *"Das Kind."*) "The Bronze David of

Donatello," like "The Knight, Death, and the Devil," describes a work of art with vivid meticulousness and speculates without sententiousness on its implications. "Deutsch Durch Freud," first published in *Poetry* in 1950, is lightly mocking and self-mocking in its humor, as its punning title, "German Through Freud," suggests; while at the end of "Jamestown" an ironically witty confrontation occurs between past and present. The longest poem in the book, "The End of the Rainbow," successfully unites discordant elements through its suppleness of tone. This portrait of an aging, New England-born lady painter living out her primly bohemian, solitary life in "a turquoise, unfrequented store" on the coast of Southern California, is at once sympathetic and satiric, charming and disturbing, solid with objective detail and, by its mixture of dream and fairy story motifs, revelatory of the shadowy world of conscious and unconscious motivation.

The best poem in this volume, a volume that received the National Book Award in verse for 1960, seems to me the title one, "The Woman at the Washington Zoo":

The saris go by me from the embassies.

Cloth from the moon. Cloth from another planet.
They look back at the leopard like the leopard.

And I. . . .

        this print of mine, that has kept its color
Alive through so many cleanings; this dull null
Navy I wear to work, and wear from work, and so
To my bed, so to my grave, with no
Complaints, no comment: neither from my chief,
The Deputy Chief Assistant, nor his chief—
Only I complain . . . this serviceable

Body that no sunlight dyes, no hand suffuses
But, dome-shadowed, withering among columns,
Wavy beneath fountains—small, far-off, shining
In the eyes of animals, these beings trapped
As I am trapped but not, themselves, the trap,
Aging, but without knowledge of their age,
Kept safe here, knowing not of death, for death—
Oh, bars of my own body, open, open!

The world goes by my cage and never sees me.
And there come not to me, as come to these,
The wild beasts, sparrows pecking the llamas' grain,
Pigeons settling on the bears' bread, buzzards
Tearing the meat the flies have clouded. . . .
                                        Vulture,
When you come for the white rat that the foxes left,
Take off the red helmet of your head, the black
Wings that have shadowed me, and step to me as
   man:
The wild brother at whose feet the white wolves
   fawn,
To whose hand of power the great lioness
Stalks, purring. . . .
                          You know what I was,
You see what I am: change me, change me!

One can admire the poem for many reasons—for its com-
passionate understanding of a woman's life; for the fresh-
ness of its variation on an old theme; for the structural
skill whereby from the beginning the poet uses images of
color, of cages, and of beasts and birds to build toward the
dramatic climax; for the control of alliteration and repeated vowel sounds that make memorable such lines as,
"Oh, bars of my own body, open, open!" Reading so satis-
factory a poem, one may recall that Jarrell has defined po-

etic excellence in a meteorological metaphor: "A good poet is someone who manages, in a life time of standing out in thunderstorms, to be struck by lightning five or six times; a dozen or two dozen times and he is great." I can only hope that, with all his varied activities as man of letters, he himself will continue to stand out in the dirty weather of life and let the poetic lightning strike him again and again and again.

NOTES

[1] Grateful acknowledgment is made for permission to reprint the following poems: "90 North" and the quotations from "Children Selecting Books in a Library," "The Winter's Tale," and "The Memoirs of Glückel of Hameln": from *Blood for A Stranger* by Randall Jarrell, copyright, 1942, by Harcourt, Brace & World, Inc., and reprinted with their permission. "A Camp in the Prussian Forest" and the quotation from "The Märchen": from *Losses* by Randall Jarrell, copyright, 1948, by Harcourt, Brace & World, Inc., and reprinted with their permission. "The Knight, Death, and the Devil" from *Seven League Crutches* by Randall Jarrell, copyright, 1951, Harcourt, Brace & World, Inc., and Faber & Faber, Ltd. "A Lullaby" and the quotation from "2nd Air Force": reprinted from *Little Friend, Little Friend* by permission of Randall Jarrell. "The Woman at the Washington Zoo": from *The Woman at the Washington Zoo: Poems & Translations* by Randall Jarrell, copyright, 1960, by Randall Jarrell and reprinted with permission of the author and of Atheneum Publishers.

X
MYTH
IN
THE
POETRY
OF
W. S.
MERWIN

ALICE N. BENSTON

W. S. MERWIN, born in New York City, educated at
Princeton, has moved rapidly into a world larger and less
provincial than the East and academia. He has already
published four volumes of verse, as well as a translation,
The Poems of the Cid, and has made his home in Boston,
Spain, France, and England. From the publication [1] of
his first volume, which was selected for Yale's series of
younger poets, he has been recognized as a poet of accomplished craftsmanship and of fresh vision. His second volume, *The Dancing Bears,* won him the Kenyon Review
Fellowship for poetry, and *Green with Beasts* was a British Poetry Book Society choice. In 1956 he was awarded
both a Rockefeller playwriting grant and a playwriting
stipend from the Arts Council of Great Britain, and in
1957 he received a $1000 award from the American So-
ciety of Arts and Letters.

I.

In his foreword to Merwin's first book, *A Mask for
Janus,* W. H. Auden remarked on the turn toward mythic

statement in contemporary poetry, and on the auspicious-
ness of this shift for the work of this particular young
poet. Merwin's verse showed the impulse to escape the
miasma of personal statement and to find a sense of personality, a self, in reference to universal experience. Certainly, as Auden observed, neither the mythic nor the personal and occasional poetry was intrinsically better than
the other, and neither was free from aesthetic snares.
According to Auden, the young poet's use of the mythic
allowed him to escape the mistake of devoting himself
to the transitory. Furthermore, it was the kind of verse
which is most appropriate to modern, democratic man.
Auden quoted de Tocqueville's prophecy that poetry
would eventually turn from the individual, since we find
ideals and heroes anathema, and find its most powerful
expression in man's common nature, in his internal (and
eternal) struggles of the spirit.

Now that ten years have passed, and Merwin has
advanced both in diversity of theme and in strength of
style, it is clear that this gifted poet has continued to be
deeply concerned with mythic vision. Indeed, for those
who may now be making a first acquaintance with him,
it seems desirable further to explore his conception of
the poet as myth maker. For this conception is his aesthetic premise for poetry itself. I see him as especially
concerned with myth and language as the media of creation, with myth and sign as devices which structure experience, and with myth as a sign in the problem of
belief.

What is fascinating about Merwin's use of myth is that
he goes well beyond the retelling of old fables (old wine
in new bottles) and, as an artist, seems to take myth as a
creed. Thus the element of romantic self-consciousness is
part of his poetry. For when the subject is the myth itself, we are at the beginning of beginnings, at creation.
And when we are dealing with a creation which is con-
tinuous, that is, when the nature of the act is stressed

rather than the specific accomplishment, we are more concerned with the creator, who must either be God or the artist. Merwin's emphasis on this aspect of modern myth-making is certainly in the tradition established by the Romantics.

It is a fertile tradition. For with the emphasis on creation, the artist and art are given a pivotal position in all experience. This leads inevitably to the self-consciousness of the artist, so apparent in Romanticism, and has become a fundamental condition of contemporary art. But Merwin is "contemporary" rather than "romantic," in so far as this self-consciousness is rarely expressed in terms of the personal plight of the individual artist seen as sufferer and hero. In "Sestina" (*A Mask for Janus*), dedicated to Robert Graves, he voices some of this attitude:

Have I not also willed to be heard in season?
Have I not heard anger raised in song
And watched when many went out to a wild place
And fought with the dark to make themselves a
name?
I have seen of those champions how thin a share
After one night shook off their sleep at morning.

But the poem ends with lines that express a sentiment closer to Merwin's prevailing position on this theme:

A breathed name I was with no resting-place,
A bough of sleep that had no share of morning,
Till I had made body and season from a song.

The struggle, rather than the glories, of this process of "creation" is emphasized, and it is this struggle which gives the major tension to his earlier verse.

"On the Subject of Poetry" (*The Dancing Bears*) expresses an essential humility in Merwin's attitude toward his role as poet. He tells of a man sitting at the end of a garden, listening to a revolving mill wheel which is not there:

I do not think I am fond, father,
Of the way in which always before he listens
He prepares himself by listening. It is
Unequal, father, like the reason
For which the wheel turns, though there is no wheel.

I speak of him, father, because he is
There with his hands in his pockets, in the end
Of the garden listening to the turning
Wheel that is not there, but it is the world,
Father, that I do not understand.

He can speak of the man in the listening attitude, because "he is there," because he is apparent. But explicitly what the poet wants to grasp is the unseen, which he acknowledges remains a mystery, and for which the listening man is only the sign.

Fundamentally, Merwin views reality as an inchoate mass of possibilities, of a chaos fraught with alternatives and populated by shadows that have substance—a reality which is grasped through belief and through the *pronouncement* of that belief. An unstated first line that the reader comes to hear behind the poems is the New Testament's "In the beginning was the word." This emphasis on the word, on the necessity as well as the creative power of language, is constantly stressed in Merwin's first two volumes, *A Mask for Janus,* and *The Dancing Bears,* where metaphors based on language are pervasive. Thus in "Canso," in the latter volume, he says:

> Creation waits upon
> The word; but you in silence are the conception
> And the consent of speech, the metaphor
> In the midst of chaos, whose world is love.

"Canso" is an example of Merwin's handling of traditional myths, for it is a kind of Orpheus poem. But it is
not a mimetic poem in which the poet-hero's story is re-
told. Compromised in time, man's love itself presupposes
death in its inception so that "love/ Became itself a
sense of leave-taking." The poem explores the nature of
the condition in which the death of the beloved would
leave the lover, whose existence is predicated on her love.
It is written in the future tense, for it involves the speaker
in an abstract discussion of his condition and a discovery
of what action would be left to him when, inevitably,
his love has died:

> If you, if you my word and so my life
> And so the mode and vessel of my death,
> Should die before me, I would not go
> —Although turned phantom by your truancy—
> Calling the earth of you . . .

The speaker, whose condition is death, has no sympathy
with doctrines of promised future resurrection or the idea
that a life exists despite the loss of his love. What is
needed is a full understanding, a grappling with this
condition:

> There must be found, then, the imagination
> Before the names of things, the dicta for
> The only poem, and among all dictions
> That ceremony whereby you may be named

Perpetual out of the anonymity
Of death. I will make out of my grief
A river, and my rage shall be the coin
To catch its ferryman; out of my fear
A dog shall spring; I will fling my bitterness
To stop his throats. I will myself become
A Hades into which I can descend.

And so the Orphic myth itself becomes the subject of the poem, the necessity and condition of its formulation. The myth is its source, and its implications are the subject of the speaker's inquiry.

Similarly, in "East of the Sun and West of the Moon" (*The Dancing Bears*), Merwin retells the ancient Psyche myth. The poem tells the story and is less abstract than "Canso"; but even so the story has a preface which relates both this poem and "Canso" to the question of myth itself. In this prefatory stanza the poet asks,

What is a man
That a man may recognize, unless the inhuman
Sun and moon, wearing the masks of a man,
Weave before him such a tale as he
—Finding his own face in the strange story—
Mistakes by metaphor and calls his own,
Smiling, as on a familiar mystery?

In Merwin's story a young girl accompanies her lover, a young man forced by a curse to appear as a bear, to a nether region. The girl's discontent, which leads to the disaster of the burning tallow, stems from her curiosity about the land she's come to, a country of the changeless, only "miming at mutability." This leads to her tragic questioning:

> But a day
> Must dwindle before dawn be real again;
> And what am I if the story be not real?

And so doubt leads to discovery and loss, which sets her on the pilgrimage through a country where,

> in a landscape of exceptions
> Where no evening came but a shadowy
> Skeptical bird who settled in a tree
> And sang, "All magic is but metaphor."

She must wander and complete her ordeal, winning her love finally when time has brought her to the understanding that she must play her part in the story lest she "walk multifarious" among earthly objects, and "fall an utter prey to mirrors." At this point the skeptical bird gets his answer:

> "All metaphor," she said, "is magic." Let
> Me be diverted in a turning lantern,
> Let me in that variety be real.
> But let the story be an improvisation
> Continually, and through all repetition
> Differ a little from itself, as though
> Mistaken . . .

The poem closes as it was opened, with comment on the story:

> Now, even now, over the rock hill
> The tropical, the lucid moon, turning
> Her mortal guises in the eye of a man,
> Creates the image in which the world is.

The poet is concerned here with the necessity of belief and I will return to this theme in a moment. What is of interest to me now is the example these two poems provide of Merwin's insistence on myth-making as a creative process by which existence is reduced from chaos to order through the ordering principle of language itself. Thus his own art is his subject; but because language is a universal medium, not only an artist's material, and because of the mythic scope of his poetry, Merwin gives us an account of the human condition rather than a justification for the poet *per se*. It is somewhat similar to what Pirandello does in his self-consciousness as an artist. In writing about the theatre, Pirandello postulates that all life is involved in role playing.

Not unlike others who are involved in a doctrine of personal creation, Merwin is automatically involved in the problem of solipsism, of being embroiled in a universe self-defined and isolated. Without outside reference, the self becomes undefined, multiple, or utterly lost. But Merwin's poetry gains much of its excitement for us (especially those who feel that the arts have been led in circles on the illusion-reality, search-for-self track) from his awareness of this problem, his terror of it, and his attempt to break out of it. In several poems Merwin has captured the haunted feeling, the abhorrence, of one who struggles to learn the world and finds only himself. In the most powerful of these, "Proteus" (*The Dancing Bears*), the speaker struggles with the sea beast. Having subdued the elusive figure, he says, "The head he turned toward me wore a face of mine." Here the self cannot get away from self. Conversely all change, implied in the Proteus image, is illusion, since it is an aspect of the same self.

But the girl in "East of the Sun and West of the Moon" sees that she must seize the fixed image given her in order to escape the fate of living by multiple images. And so one justification of myth is that it comes from outside the individual, from tradition and the community. Certainly the emphasis on language seems to indicate that this contact with community, in order to be created, must be communicated. "Learning a Dead Language" (*Green with Beasts*) is a lovely statement of the sense of order implicit in language:

There is nothing for you to say. You must
Learn first to listen. Because it is dead
It will not come to you of itself, nor would you
Of yourself master it. You must therefore
Learn to be still when it is imparted,
And, though you may not yet understand, to remember.

What you remember is saved. To understand
The least thing fully you would have to perceive
The whole grammar in all its accidence
And all its system, in the perfect singleness
Of intention it has because it is dead.
You can learn only a part at a time.

What you are given to remember
Has been saved before you from death's dullness by
Remembering. The unique intention
Of a language whose speech has died is order
Incomplete only where someone has forgotten.
You will find that that order helps you to remember.

What you come to remember becomes yourself.
Learning will be to cultivate the awareness
Of that governing order, now pure of the passions
It composed; till, seeking it in itself,
You may find at last the passion that composed it,
Hear it both in its speech and in yourself.

What you remember saves you. To remember
Is not to rehearse, but to hear what never
Has fallen silent. So your learning is,
From the dead, order, and what sense of yourself
Is memorable, what passion may be heard
When there is nothing for you to say.

Since the poet is working towards this order rather than assuming it (and since it cannot be assumed), his poetry is fraught with the combat of the soul and mind with the as yet unshaped, uncontrolled universe. This, understandably, makes much of his poetry constrained, especially in his first volumes. But the intensity and power of the poetry conveys a passion for experiencing the world. And much of the lyricism of Merwin's mature and more relaxed verse comes from his nature imagery, which celebrates, as a sign, the beauty of experience even while it includes the destructive.

II.

With Merwin's attitude toward the mystery of the world, coupled with his belief in language and gesture as a means of creation and understanding, it seems appropriate that he should have tried his hand at a bestiary. In the first part of his third volume, *Green with Beasts,* he gives us five such animal poems. The first of these, "Leviathan," is one of his best poems. I think it illustrates well how the poet manages his own mythic statement as well as the control he has achieved at the same time that he has been able to relax the verse, dispensing with an archness of tone found in his earlier work. The relentless piling of image on image, the effective use of alliteration, as well as the hyphenated compounds of the long, first periodic sentence capture not only the enormity and power of this beast of Merwin's creation but its duplicity. The rhythms of the verse suggest the thrashing of the Leviathan and help Merwin create a startlingly concrete picture of a beast we've never seen:

> This is the black sea-brute bulling through wave-
>   wrack,
> Ancient as ocean's shifting hills, who in sea-toils
> Travelling, who furrowing the salt acres
> Heavily, his wake hoary behind him,
> Shoulders spouting, the fist of his forehead
> Over wastes gray-green crashing, among horses un-
>   broken
> From bellowing fields, past bone-wreck of vessels,
> Tide-ruin, wash of lost bodies bobbing
> No longer sought for, and islands of ice gleaming,
> Who ravening the rank flood, wave-marshalling,
> Overmastering the dark sea-marches, finds home
> And harvest. Frightening to foolhardiest
> Mariners, his size were difficult to describe:
> The hulk of him is like hills heaving,
> Dark, yet as crags of drift-ice, crowns cracking in
>   thunder,
> Like land's self by night black-looming, surf churning
>   and trailing
> Along his shores' rushing, shoal-water boding
> About the dark of his jaws; and who should moor at
>   his edge
> And fare on afoot would find gates of no gardens,
> But the hill of dark underfoot diving,
> Closing overhead, the cold deep, and drowning.
> He is called Leviathan, and named for rolling,
> First created he was of all creatures,
> He has held Jonah three days and nights,
> He is that curling serpent that in ocean is.

Sea-fright he is, and the shadow under the earth.
Days there are, nonetheless, when he lies
Like an angel, although a lost angel
On the waste's unease, no eye of man moving,
Bird hovering, fish flashing, creature whatever
Who after him came to herit earth's emptiness.
Froth at flanks seething soothes to stillness,
Waits; with one eye he watches
Dark of night sinking last, with one eye dayrise
As at first over foaming pastures. He makes no cry
Though that light is a breath. The sea curling,
Star-climbed, wind-combed, cumbered with itself still
As at first it was, is the hand not yet contented
Of the Creator. And he waits for the world to begin.

The first sentence, which combines images of land and sea, farming (or peace) and war (or disaster), immediately indicates the universal scope of pre-creative energy for which this huge shape is the sign. And the brooding shape, both angel and monster, "sea-fright" and "shadow under the earth," created before man, waits as emblem of all the possibilities, the conditions of the world that wait for man.

In each of his animal poems, Merwin establishes a similarly enclosed universe. Thus the animal is caught in a moment of timelessness which implies all time. In "Blue Cockerel," the bird is pictured in brilliant colors that fill the imagination's eye. His shout "frames all the silence." After this picture is drawn of the bright bird framing a rich spring-to-autumn fecundity, Merwin speaks of the bird's call, or prophecy:

A cry must be painted silent: the spread red hand
Of his comb thrown back, beak wide, and the one
   eye

Glaring like the sun's self (for there is no other),
Like the sun seen small, seen rimmed in red secret,
May be the shape of jubilation crowing,
Or the stare and shriek of terror.

So into the pastoral the demonic is introduced:

And whose body
Is this in the foreground lying twisted sideways,
Eyes glazed, whose stiff posture would become
The contorted dead? Though its face gleams white
It might be the self of shadow we have not seen,
Night who was never here, or the hour itself
There to be sung unmoved. Surely it is
The eye's other center, and upon this,
This only, the bird stares, and for this cause
Cries, cries, and his cry crashes
Among the branches, the blades of great leaves
Looming like towers, the fruits and petals, green
Thickets of light deeper than shadows, the moon-
    white
Ears of that body lying, and makes
And lends echo and moment to all that green
Watery silence. But does he scream
In joy unfading that now no dark is,
Or what wakening does he herald with all terror?

I take this to mean that in the most harmonious moment
there is the possible intrusion of terror and death. Just
as the world of spring and morning is green with possibility, so the shadows and night are "green with beasts."
The line that gives the title to this book comes from the
poem on horses, where a pastoral scene of two tethered
horses is interrupted abruptly:

> The haze of summer
> Blows south over the garden terraces,
> Vague through the afternoon, remembering rain;
> But in the night green with beasts as April with grass
> Orion would hunt high from southward, over the
> hill,
> And the blood of beasts herald morning.

Now the horses, descendants of the beasts of the dawn countries, are remembered in their historical role as companions to battle and destruction.

The world, then, constantly holds these polar possibilities, and if the demonic most frequently breaks forth in Merwin's poems, it is, one would think, because evil rather than good is always the aspect of experience that seems to require explanation and ordering. Perhaps evil is the wrong word to use. It is, rather, that the mystery of the truth that each act may engender its destruction and that destruction accompanies creation, which seems to be Merwin's point. The mystery is an essential part of experience. Expression of it is necessary, for even if this does not reduce the mystery, the recognition makes it less terrifying. Certainly the mysterious or unpredictable part of experience is not avoided. Thus in "Fog" (*Green with Beasts*) Merwin seems to be saying that this aspect of experience is to be met, if one wants to live:

> Ships were not shaped for haven but if we were
> There will be time for it yet. Let us turn head,
> Out oars, and pull for the open. Make we
> For mid-sea, where the winds are and stars too.
> There will be wrung weathers, sea-shakings, calms,
> Weariness, the giant water that rolls over our fathers,
> And hungers hard to endure. But whether we float
> long
> Or founder soon, we cannot be saved here.

So in another sea poem, "Cape Dread" (*The Drunk in the Furnace*),

> Three ships we lost
> And many of their men there, and only we
> Because we were driven far to port, almost
> To the drag of the cliff's foot, and made in
> Through the very spray, found the channel.

Through this danger, surviving because accidentally they were so close to it, the mariners find a cove where there is sweet water and fruit.

The sea is a perfect symbol for Merwin. Even the bestiary is heavily dependent on sea imagery, and it is hardly surprising to find that a good number of his poems are sea poems. Traditionally a symbol of creativity and fecundity, and continually beguiling in its restless state of change, the sea serves to describe the double-edged reality Merwin wants to capture. The sea, as a life-providing element, has always bewitched men in its duplicity, for its treachery is as great as its good, and is as unexpected as it is unknowable.

But this primary condition can be found on land as well. Merwin's conception of experience is expressed succinctly in this four-line poem called "In Stony Country" (*The Drunk in the Furnace*):

> Somewhere else than these bare uplands dig wells,
> Expect flowers, listen to sheep bells.
> Wind; no welcome; and nowhere else
> Pillows like these stones for dreaming of angels.

Unfertile territory is the best for contemplation: use in disuse.

Merwin's most forceful statement of the idea of experiencing all aspects of life is a Dionysian poem, "The
Drunk in the Furnace." Here he comments tersely on
those who, shocked at the irrational aspect of life, are
powerless in preventing its appearance or appeal. In this
poem, the dark, eruptive elements are pictured as the
town's derelict, an unwanted, uncouth stranger. Ironically he appears in the midst of the townsmen's own
rubble, out of the odds and ends of their lives which they
had discarded, hoping to forget. Pictures of this rubble
heap and of the alarming appearance of the drunk are
captured with vivid intensity. I quote the whole of the
poem as a fine example of Merwin's ability to empower
colloquial diction with mythic scope:

> For a good decade
> The furnace stood in the naked gully, fireless
> And vacant as any hat. Then when it was
> No more to them than a hulking black fossil
> To erode unnoticed with the rest of the junk-hill
> By the poisonous creek, and rapidly to be added
>   To their ignorance,
>
>   They were afterwards astonished
> To confirm, one morning, a twist of smoke
>   like a pale
> Resurrection, staggering out of its chewed hole,
> And to remark then other tokens that someone,
> Cosily bolted behind the eye-holed iron
> Door of the drafty burner, had there established
>   His bad castle.
>
>   Where he gets his spirits
> It's a mystery. But the stuff keeps him musical:
> Hammer-and-anvilling with poker and bottle

To his jugged bellowings, till the last groaning clang
As he collapses onto the rioting
Springs of a litter of car-seats ranged on the grates,
    To sleep like an iron pig.

    In their tar-paper church
On a text about stoke-holes that are sated never
Their Reverend lingers. They nod and hate
  trespassers.
When the furnace wakes, though, all afternoon
Their witless offspring flock like piped rats
  to its siren
Crescendo, and agape on the crumbling ridge
    Stand in a row and learn.

Elsewhere Merwin comments on the destructive-creative aspects of fire, and here it issues from a wasteland. But with the words "gully," "resurrection," and "mystery," and the pun on "springs," he converts the town dump, a natural wasteland, into a symbolic underworld. First of all, the city dump, because of the fire issuing from it, is analogous to the Hebrew city dump, Gehenna, which came to symbolize a sort of hell. The words "mystery" and "resurrection," along with the fact that this denizen of the city dump is singing, point to the identification of the drunk with Dionysus, the mystery cult god, who is resurrected in the spring during festivals of fertility, wine and song. Inveighed against by the order-bound righteous religionists, this drunk, half Dionysus, half pied-piper, is teacher to the innocent. (It seems to me that the obvious combination of myths here, exemplified in "Canso" and "East of the Sun and West of the Moon" discussed above, shows that Merwin's intention is to explore the common ground of all myths and not to give weight to the particular truth of a single tradition.) The children, warned to stay away from the drunk, find his song irresistible. Not only is it useless to turn one's back on the irrational, but it will mean rejection of the world's creative urge. Although the diction and locale are contemporary, the allusion to Dionysus shows us that the circumstances are as universal as human experience itself.

The universe, then, is to be embraced in all aspects and the only fear is of the negative aspect, the desert of non-experience. The only kind of hell that Merwin envisions seems to be the condition of nothingness. In an animal poem, "Dog" (*Green with Beasts*), Merwin pictures the dog lying idly in a vacant, hot day. He seems as impotent as the dust of the day until,

> But wrong:
> Look again: it is through you
> That he looks, and the danger of his eyes
> Is that in them you are not there.

This Cerberus guards a Hades that is an oblivion and a vacancy.

III.

The counterpart of this impulse to embrace all experience is the realization of the depths of that experience and the necessity to make some sense of it. This, of course, is the necessity of myth-making and the necessity for belief. Here again, Merwin never stresses any particular belief. He does not become the preacher, dogmatically espousing a system. More frequently his subject is the foolishness of disbelief in the realm of experience beyond the empirical ("No One," *Green with Beasts*):

> Who would it surprise
> If (after the flash, hush, rush,

> Thump and crumpling) when the wind of prophecy
> Lifts its pitch, and over the drifting ash
>   At last the trump splits the sky,
>   No One should arise?

The language of the poem stresses the ambiguity of a belief, half believed, since the "No One" is Someone, "before ourselves whom we had considered/And (after ourselves) had loved/Constantly and well." Still, the surprise ambiguously might be ours or His.

In a trenchantly ironic poem, "The Mountain" (*Green with Beasts*), Merwin explores the attitude of the hill creatures who inhabit it:

>   Of course to each of us
> Privately, its chief difference from its peers
> Rests not even in its centrality, but its
> Strangeness composed of our own intimacy
> With a part of it, our necessary
> Ignorance of its limits, and diurnal pretense
> That what we see of it is all.

The tone of the poem is the calm, objective voice of the historian or social scientist, which is ironically undercut with statements about the mystery of the mountain's essential nature:

>   At a relatively slight distance
> Above us, apparently the whole aspect and
>   condition
> Of the mountain changes completely; there is
>   ceaseless wind
> With a noise like thunder and the beating of wings.

The disappearance of those who have sought the higher reaches of the mountain, the loss of our language of those who returned, the myths that have evolved about the mountain are told in the jargon of that scientific observer. Then, in conclusion, the speaker says:

> Shadows
> Are not without substance, remind and predict:
> And we know we live between greater commotions
> Than any we can describe. But, most important:
> Since this, though we know so little of it, is
> All we know, is it not whatever it makes us
> Believe of it—even the old woman
> Who laughs, pointing, and says that the
>   clouds across
> Its face are wings of seraphim? Even the young
> Man who, standing on it, declares it is not
> There at all. He stands with one leg habitually
> Bent, to keep from falling, as though he had grown
> That way, as is said of certain hill creatures.

Merwin doesn't tell us what the mountain is; none of the attitudes expressed in the poem, whether the mythology of mountain kings or scientific observation, is sufficient. What is stressed is the essential mystery and, as these final lines indicate, that any vision one might hold of the mountain has a reality. It is an image cast by the mountain which provides a meaning for the life of the hill people. Even those who disbelieve live as though they believe.

Just as our lives must be lived by the signs of the mystery by which we are surrounded, so, it would seem, there is a possibility that man himself lives in a design, though his life seem without reference to any pattern. In the last poem of his bestiary, "White Goat, White

Ram," Merwin explicitly states his concept of signs. First he describes the goat leading her contented animal existence. "So broadly is she blind/Who has no names to see with: over her shoulder/She sees not summer, not the idea of summer,/But green meanings." But her inability to put names to things does not deny their being. So, too, the ram, separated from the goat by a road, lives his existence by habit in an unquestioning way. And it is because of their condition that we human beings have taken them as signs of innocence:

> They are white, these two
> As we should say those are white who remember nothing,
> And we for our uses call that innocence,
> So that our gracelessness may have the back
> of a goat
> To ride away upon . . .

> There is no need
> Even that they should be gentle, for us to use them
> To signify gentleness, for us to lift them as a sign
> Invoking gentleness, conjuring by their shapes
> The shape of our desire, which without them
> would remain
> Without a form and nameless. . . .

Then the poet likens us all to the goats, acting in a dumbness:

> For our uses
> Also are a dumbness, a mystery,
> Which like a habit stretches ahead of us
> And was here before us; so, again, we use these

> To designate what was before us, since we cannot
> See it in itself, for who can recognize
> And call by true names, familiarly, the place
> Where before this he was, though for nine months
> Or the world's full age he housed there?

Still, we are different from the animals, because the road
to them is less than a road, since they cannot have a concept "road":

>   For a mystery
> Is that for which we have not yet received
> Or made the name, the terms, that may enclose
> And call it.

But this is only a matter of degree; as the road is a
mystery because they cannot name it, so too is the "path"
we walk on a mystery. And it is the use we make of them,
not the animals as animals, which is the sign of our dumbness. The gesture of sacrifice is what we know of innocence. And as we are above the animals, so, above us,

> There are the angels. We are dumb before them,
>   and move
> In a different mystery; but may there be
> Another road we do not see as a road:
>   straight, narrow,
> Or broad or the sector of a circle, or perhaps
> All these, where without knowing it we stand
> On one side or another? I have known such a way
> But at moments only, and when it seemed
>   I was driven
> Along it, and along no other that my preference

Or kind had made. And of these others above us
We know only the whisper of an elusive sense,
Infrequent meanings and shadows, analogies
With light and the beating of wings. Yet now,
  perhaps only
A few feet away in the shaking leaves they wait
Beyond our words, beyond earthquake,
  whirlwind, fire,
And all the uncovenanted terror of becoming,
And beyond the small voice. Oh we cannot know
  and we are not
What we signify, but in what sign
May we be innocent, for out of our dumbness
We would speak for them, give speech
  to the mute tongues
Of angels. Listen: more than the sea's thunder
Foregathers in the grey cliffs; the roots of our hair
Stir like the leaves of the holly bush where now
Not games the wind ponders, but impatient
Glories, fire: and we go stricken suddenly
Humble, and the covering of our feet
Offends, for the ground where we find we stand
  is holy.

This poem is complex, with an extraordinary balance between guilt and determinism. There is guilt towards the
animals used for our purposes as well as the incom-
pleteness of our innocence. We may not be any more innocent than the goat chosen to signify our unclear notion
of innocence. But, by the analogy Merwin draws, we may
be victims of the same kind of capriciousness, chosen as a
sign for something greater than ourselves.

Merwin's concept of signs is important in maintaining
that the *essence* of mystery cannot be reduced, but that
the sign, the gesture, the naming of that mystery is an

essential part of human experience. Despite the Christian symbolism, he preserves a kind of agnosticism concerning the central mystery of our condition. In this way the poet avoids the limitation of personal solution. In our age, especially, where traditional beliefs have long wavered and cross-cultural pictures of the universe are presented as though with equal validity, the problem of belief remains universal, but the statement of any one, doctrinaire faith seems to be personal. Thus, in concentrating on the conditions that necessitate belief, Merwin avoids the personal and maintains his grasp on a universal problem, one which is most pertinent for our contemporary world.

There is a certain comfort, too, that Merwin seems to derive from affirming the mystery of the universe and giving his signs for it, although he realizes they may be partial. Although the ease of his later poetry may be accounted for by the general trend of contemporary verse, or the maturity of the poet, I feel that it is in part due to a reconciliation to partial "dumbness." The spirit that I am trying to describe is exemplified in a poem, "To Dido," in which he dedicates the volume *Green with Beasts*:

With dumb belongings there can be
The gesture that bestows, for its own reasons;
Its mumbled inadequacy reminds us always
In this world how little can be communicated.
And for these, they too are only tokens
Of what there is no word for: their worth
Is a breath or nothing, and the spirit
  who can convey?
I have doubts whether such things can be dedicated.
They themselves determine whose they are,
Announcing unbidden their conception
In a still place of perpetual surprise.
Can one offer things that know their own way

And will not be denied? These were bodied forth.
In the country of your love: what other
Landscapes they may name, from that place
Is their language. In the cadences of that tongue
They learned what they are. How more can I
    make them yours?

Admittedly the circumstances of this poem are unique,
yet I feel it addresses itself to the central question of
creativity, knowledge, and the power of language.

It seems to me also that something of the same spirit
may be observed in Merwin's few poems about individ-
uals. An uncle, a grandfather, a grandmother—all
seem boldly etched in heroic proportions, because they
lived by a single idea, unquestioning, and to the point
where their bodies and gestures incorporate that idea.
Again, they are not heroic because of the intrinsic nature
of the ideas which motivate them. Somehow they are
bizarre and gothic, as though they were second cousins to
Sherwood Anderson's grotesques, or, perhaps more accurately, like the figures in Grant Wood's *American
Gothic*. It is, rather, their intensity which gives them
their stature.

All that I have said here about Merwin's use of myth
would not, in itself, make him the kind of young poet
who captures our attention and praise. Were it not for
his skill in infusing what I have given here in abstraction with fresh, imaginative pictures and an emotional
quality, both gripping and restrained, he would remain
an interesting "thinker," but he would not be a poet.
However, this underlying "system" gives Merwin certain
advantages which add a unique excitement to his poetry.
In dealing with words and what they can and cannot do
for us, he has the immediate advantage of a subject
ideally suited to his medium, like a sculptor working
with marble who wants to portray strength. In reading

Merwin's poetry, we are immediately involved in the *process* of poetry as well as with the finished product. For as he evolves his myths, the reader becomes involved in the myth-making process which is closely related in impulse or motivation to the poetic process itself. Finally, as I have suggested earlier, this traditional alliance between myth and poetry gives Merwin perspective and scope which allows him to write pertinently about the contemporary world without succumbing to the fallacy of assuming that his problems are unique.

NOTES

[1] Merwin's four volumes of verse are: *A Mask for Janus,* Yale University Press (1952), *The Dancing Bears,* Yale University Press (1954), *Green with Beasts,* Alfred A. Knopf, Inc. (1960), and *The Drunk in the Furnace,* The Macmillan Co. (1960). All quotations are from these volumes and are printed with the permission of Mr. Merwin and the publishers respectively.

XI
DENISE
LEVERTOV:
THE
POETRY
OF THE
IMMEDIATE

RALPH J. MILLS, JR.

AMERICAN poetry at the present time sustains two extremes, with a wide range of practice in between in
which the best—as well as the most truly advanced—
writing is usually done. One extreme is represented by
the academic poets. The term does not necessarily apply
to all poets who happen to teach in universities for their
living, but denotes those writers whose materials are
often selected from the history of literature and culture,
and whose methods are dictated by critical theories of
what poetry ought to be. At the opposite extreme, the
Hip writers mistake the exhibition of hysteria and the
release of invective, unhindered by the requirements of
craft, for poetry. Whitman and Rimbaud, the "true gods"
the Hip writers claim for their masters, had both the
genius and the strength to navigate the rapids of emotion
and vision in which these self-styled successors capsize
and drown.

At the same moment—around 1957—that such figures
as Ginsberg and Kerouac began to make news, a number
of other, previously little-known, poets also published
their own books and caused a less sensational but more
worthy stir. Some of them may even have been loosely

associated in the minds of their audience with the Hip writers next to whom they were occasionally printed; but there is little resemblance except in their mutual rejection of the ruling literary and critical modes. And these poets differ greatly among one another as well. All of them, however—and include here poets such as Robert Creeley, Paul Carroll, Frank O'Hara, John Ashbery, Barbara Guest, Gary Snyder, David Ignatow, Brother Antoninus, Galway Kinnell, and John Logan, in addition to Denise Levertov—aim at an expression of the most personal kind of experience, an authentic statement about themselves, what they see and know, suffer and love; their responses to the things, relationships, and heightened instants of their lives. The tendencies of these poets lead them to the repudiation of Eliot's belief in an "objective correlative" that screens the artist from his work and maintains the privacy of his life as an individual. The idea of masks that explains so much modern poetry of the post-Symbolist generation has no value for these younger poets, who really walk naked, as Yeats said poets should.

We have considered in a previous chapter how the poetry of Robert Lowell moves into this same area of the highly personal or confessional, though he comes from a very different corner of the literary map than does Denise Levertov or Robert Creeley or David Ignatow. The latter have steeped themselves for a long time in that tradition of modern writing whose pioneers are William Carlos Williams, Ezra Pound, and H. D.

Among her fellow-poets in this tradition, Denise Levertov stands out as one whose art, fresh and compelling, convinces us of her genuine rapport with the reality she presents as its core. Her poetry is frequently a tour through the familiar and the mundane until their unfamiliarity and otherworldliness suddenly strike us. Her imaginative gaze feasts on the small objects we usually treat as insignificant appendages to our lives, or pauses with affectionate interest on the seemingly trivial activities in which we spend so much of those lives. Thus she engages very naturally in a persistent investigation of the events of her own life—inner and outer—in the language of her own time and place, and completes that investigation in the forms emerging from what she discovers as it is translated into words. Miss Levertov shares the spirit of Martin Buber, for she always says "thou" to the persons, occasions, and objects she encounters; that is her imagination's essential humanizing gesture toward every aspect of existence.

As I have already indicated, Miss Levertov, along with a variety of other poets, departs sharply from the poetic and critical line passing down through Yeats, Eliot, Auden, and the critics who have developed aesthetic views from their initiative. In the introduction to his anthology *Contemporary American Poetry*, Donald Hall offers a good summary description of qualities emphasized by the poets working in the opposing tradition, with its foundation in the example of William Carlos Williams. "This poetry," Hall tells us, "is no mere restriction of one's vocabulary. It wants to use the language with the intimacy acquired in unrehearsed unliterary speech. But it has other characteristics which are not linguistic. It is a poetry of experiences more than of ideas. The experience is presented often without comment, and the words of the description must supply the emotion which the experience generates, without generalization or summary."

In allying herself with this movement, Miss Levertov had to grapple with prevailing literary modes and, finally, to discard them. A struggle of this sort, the purpose of which is to open a way for poetic development, normally makes or breaks a writer—that is, if he or she dares to undertake it, as many do not—and it is a real sign of Miss Levertov's abilities that she has returned victorious. But the effort to win a voice of one's own amounts to nothing or becomes artificial unless it has been prompted by the conditions of human experience itself, by all that is cast into the poet's field of vision in the course of living. Poetry, if it will earn its name, must never begin with experience at second hand, but with a steady eye on what surrounds us everywhere. As the French philosopher Jacques Maritain says in his *Art and Scholasticism*, "Our art does not derive from itself alone what it imparts to things; it spreads over them a secret which it first discovered in them, in their invisible substance or in their endless exchanges and correspondences." Miss Levertov has learned this lesson well, and it is identical to the one her art teaches us. The conclusion of her "Note on the Work of the Imagination" (*New Directions 17*, edited by James Laughlin) adds to the quotation from Maritain a consideration of this spiritual faculty which makes the poetic object possible; she writes, "What joy to be reminded . . . that the Imagination does not arise from the environment but has the power to create it!"

Some poets make their published poems the battleground for style and individuality, and the reader can witness the spectacle, and its success or failure. In Denise Levertov there is an unseen conflict which occurred somewhere in the eleven-year span between her first book, *The Double Image* (1946), published in England before she came to the United States, and her next, *Here and Now* (1957), issued by Lawrence Ferlinghetti's City Lights Bookshop in San Francisco. Kenneth Rexroth, who anthologized her work some years ago in his *New British Poets*, placed her then as one of the most promising neo-romantics of the war period; but his later statements about her writing, collected in *Assays* (1961), indicate that he believes—as I do—Miss Levertov's full powers as a poet began to unleash themselves only after she had been in America awhile and, as Rexroth says, had come "to talk like a mildly internationalized young woman living in New York but alive to all the life of speech in the country."

The poems included in *The Double Image* give evidence of a true poetic gift in their author, though they are not marked with those characteristics of thought and rhythm and speech that would insure them as her handiwork, and hers alone. I don't mean that the poems are imitations; on the other hand, they seem to partake of a general mood in English poetry of the time, owing, no doubt, to the war. Here is world-weariness, disenchantment, a flirtatiousness with death and the twilight regions of the spirit. Somehow a vein of uncertainty runs through these pieces, as if the poet almost suspected herself in what she was doing. I am sure, however, that I could never gain such an impression if Miss Levertov had published only that single volume or if she had continued in her initial style. She served her poetic apprenticeship in works suffused with vague emotion, filled with whispers of mortality and unrest, the damp vegetation of England, and murmurs of perishable love. I will quote just a few lines from one of these early poems, "Five Aspects of Fear," before approaching her more central productions:

In fear of floods, long quenched, waves fallen,
shattered mirrors darken with old cries;
where no shot sounds the frightened birds go flying
over heights of autumn soft as honey:
each country left is full of our own ghosts
in fear of floods quenched, waves fallen.
Rags of childhood flutter in the woods
and each deserted post has sentinels;
bright eyes in wells watch for the sun's assassin:
the regions bereft of our desires are haunted,
rags of childhood flutter in the woods.

Something of the Georgians lingers on in this passage with its rural withdrawal from contemporary affairs, but the strongest and most obvious pull is toward Surrealism, which had crossed the Channel in the 1930's and was still a strong influence during the war. Miss Levertov tries, by means of dreamlike associations and indefiniteness of imagery, to articulate as nearly as possible the purity of her emotions, unsoiled by the concrete or the particular. That vagueness is far removed from what we have come to know as the essential poet in her, the poet whose sleeves are rolled and who wrestles up to her elbows in the dust of a common world. In this poem the effects are atmospheric; the words, I believe, are supposed to bear a cumulative weight of feeling *apart* from any denotation. How different from the present Denise Levertov, who senses her materials as a Giacometti or a David Hare senses the materials of his sculpture. Her "Pleasures," as she calls them in the title of a later poem, are now quite altered:

> I like to find
> what's not found
> at once, but lies
>
> within something of another nature,
> in repose, distinct.
> Gull feathers of glass, hidden
>
> in white pulp: the bones of a squid
> which I pull out and lay
> blade by blade on the draining board—
>
>> tapered as if for swiftness, to pierce
>> the heart, but fragile, substance
>> belying design. Or a fruit, *mamey,*

cased in rough brown peel, the flesh
rose-amber, and the seed:
the seed a stone of wood, carved and

polished, walnut-colored, formed
like a brazilnut, but large,
large enough to fill
the hungry palm of a hand.

The reader will not be wrong, I think, if he sees in this
poem, behind its fascination with the beauty of small
objects and concealed things, an allegorical statement of
the poet's own concern with material reality. In forcing
tangible things to disclose their truths and felicities, she
urges human reality to yield some of its secrets—and its
covert analogies and predilections too.

The change that takes place between her first and
second books—in a decade that saw Miss Levertov leave
England, travel in Europe, meet the American novelist
Mitchell Goodman, marry him, and settle in this country—is remarkable and must have demanded no less than
a complete renovation of her poetic values. But this
revolution of the heart, the head, the senses, how worthwhile it all was! She was compelled to start from scratch,
and that meant for Miss Levertov a confrontation of the
happenings of her life. What she so shrewdly observed
was that the ordinary is extraordinarily unusual:

What a sweet smell rises
when you lay the dust—
bucket after bucket of water thrown
on the yellow grass.
     The water

flashes
each time you
make it leap—

> arching its glittering back.
> The sound of
> more water
> pouring into the pail
> almost quenches my thirst.
> Surely when flowers
> grow here, they'll not
> smell sweeter than this
> wet ground, suddenly black.

Of course, as Kenneth Rexroth further noted, Miss Levertov came under novel influences in America that were quite unlike any English ones. He names as a chief influence the poet we have already mentioned, the writer whose lessons she must have learned well, though without sacrificing her own intentions and capacities. That poet is the late William Carlos Williams. It is likely that she also learned from Rexroth's own poetry and from the Imagists; in her moving tribute to H. D. entitled "Summer 1961," she records some of her debts to Williams, Pound, and H. D.:

> They have told us
> the road leads to the sea,
> and given
>
> the language into our hands.

Perhaps if we look at a brief but fairly representative poem by Williams to remind ourselves of certain qualities in his work we will be able to determine, by comparison with Miss Levertov's "Laying the Dust" above, some of their similarities. Williams' poem is called "Between Walls":

the back wings
of the

hospital where
nothing

will grow lie
cinders

in which shine
the broken

pieces of a green
bottle

Clearly, this poem has little relation to the kind of poetry in the ascendency during the first half of the twentieth century; the poetry of the French Symbolists has had no bearing on what we read in these lines. Again, if we try to apply the sort of exegesis to Williams' poetry—or to Miss Levertov's, for that matter—that is used on Eliot's or Rilke's or Valéry's, we shall miss the point and look foolish. Ingenious explication is beside the point here and will bury the meaning of both poems; we should do better to contemplate them as we would a painting. Williams' attraction to the *disjecta membra* of the physical world, particularly of the modern urban setting, set a firm precedent for Miss Levertov's own poetic venture. We should not forget, either, Williams' insistence that the moral responsibility of the American poet lies in using his native tongue "to represent what his mind perceives directly about him," because this endeavor is, to a degree, Miss Levertov's. Yet there is also a gradual inward turning in her latest poetry and an increasing preoccupation with parable, dream, and interior illumination that are foreign to Williams' imagination.

Williams was for years a champion of younger writers in the United States and, further, was a stalwart foe of the post-Symbolist literature of Yeats and Eliot, as well as an opponent of what he thought was an outworn tradition of English verse forms and meters. It is hardly by accident, then, that young poets, in search of a way past the official poetic idiom, looked to Williams' writings and his viewpoint for guidance. The rejection of conventional for organic form; the repudiation of established metrical patterns in favor of what Williams called "the variable foot"; the return to the spoken language, the *American* spoken language—these are some of the most prominent results of the senior poet's influence. These younger poets likewise avoid in general the habit of making their work a repository of intellectual history, learning, and fragments of the European cultural heritage. I should like to call the poetry of Miss Levertov, and that of a number of her contemporaries, "poetry of the immediate."

My term requires some explanation. I do not mean by "the immediate" an art without craftsmanship, an art that fixes on the disorder of sheer impulse or emotional notation. Miss Levertov has never allowed her poetry to become even slightly vulnerable to that kind of charge—a glance at any one of her poems will prove it. Moreover, we need only cite the comment she supplies for Donald Allen's anthology *The New American Poetry 1945–1960,* where there is no mistaking her distaste for sloppy composition: "I long for poems," she writes, "of an inner harmony in utter contrast to the chaos in which they exist." Poetry must not be a shapeless replica of external things but an organically formed transfiguration of them in which the transfiguration, rather than poetic convention, dictates the form. What I call "the immediate," then, signifies the complex of relationships existing between the poet and the elements that are close at hand in her personal experience. The things, the happenings, the thoughts and dreams that are subjective events in themselves—everything that falls within the circumference of the poet's life as an individual—become the matter of poetry. The author's private circumstance is explored, its potentialities drawn out; but however far her speculations lead her, Miss Levertov never oversteps that circumference. Instead, she creates from within herself an attitude with which to face her environment, as in her poem "Something to Wear":

> To sit and sit like the cat
> and think my thoughts through—
> that might be a deep pleasure:
>
> to learn what news
> persistence might discover,
> and like a woman knitting
>
> make something from the
> skein unwinding, unwinding,
> something I could wear
>
> or something you could wear
> when at length I rose to meet you
> outside the quiet sitting-room
>
> (the room of thinking and knitting
> the room of cats and women)
> among the clamor of
>
> cars and people,
> the stars drumming and poems
> leaping from shattered windows.

This poem grows around the mind's self-reflective activity. While poems about poetry, the act of composition, or the mind contemplating its own powers and processes are common in the literary history of the past 170 years— Mallarmé and Wallace Stevens, for example, expended much of their artistic energy on these themes—Denise Levertov treats such matters in a more personal, autobiographical way than most previous poets have done. Mallarmé, in his famous sonnet "La vierge, le vivace et le bel aujourd'hui," depicts the poet's failure of imagination through the remote but lovely symbolic image of a swan trapped in ice and earthbound:

> Un cygne d'autrefois se souvient que c'est lui
> Magnifique mais qui sans espoir se délivre
> Pour n'avoir pas chanté le région où vivre
> Quand du stérile hiver a resplendi l'ennui.

> (A swan of former times remembers it is he
> Magnificent but who without hope gives himself up
> For not having sung of the region where he should
>   have been
> When the boredom of sterile winter was resplendent.)
> (Translation by Wallace Fowlie, from *Mallarmé*, 1953.)

But however acutely the poet has felt the anguish of impotence in his art, he has removed those feelings from the sphere of his own life and incorporated them into the symbolic universe of his poetry. Stevens is less divided; indeed, his notebooks indicate that he wished to have his theory of the imagination become a cosmic view that could be shared by all men. Nonetheless, Stevens' poetry is generally impersonal and almost totally divorced from the important details of his existence as a man. Miss Levertov does not recognize such separations and refuses to hide her life from her imagination. Yet she may have learned from Stevens—as well as from her own thoughts or from other poets' work—that poetry can be involved in the mind's activity as an individual goes about his daily business of registering and interpreting and responding to surrounding reality. The poem "Something to Wear" describes in part the preparations the mind or self makes to encounter this reality ("the clamor of/cars and people . . .") and to elicit from it the substance of art and beauty ("the stars drumming and poems/leaping from shattered windows"). The contemplating self of the poem's beginning does not keep to solitude but, as in "Matins," vii, goes out to meet the world and come upon the stuff of poetry there:

Marvelous Truth, confront us
at every turn,
in every guise, iron ball,
egg, dark horse, shadow,
cloud
of breath on the air,

dwell
in our crowded hearts
our steaming bathrooms, kitchens full of
things to be done, the
ordinary streets.

Thrust close your smile
that we know you, terrible joy.

Thus for Denise Levertov, as for certain other poets, it is proper, even imperative, for the literary enterprise to concentrate on assigning judgment and value, on finding the marvelous, within the particular range of personal observation and knowledge. If such writing is criticized for a lack of ambitious scope, one might reply that it compensates by a penetrating and scrupulous honesty, by a fundamental human resonance that is anything but restricted, and by a fidelity to the experience of contemporary life. Younger writers today, of almost every allegiance or group, have withdrawn their efforts from the elaboration of symbolic systems and mythologies; the *Cantos, The Waste Land, The Duino Elegies,* although they are still widely admired, apparently are looked upon as distant accomplishments. Now the poet believes he must use his art to define the space he inhabits as a person—if I may be permitted the figure—the space in which he exists, chooses and asserts value, loves and hates and dies. And so for Miss Levertov the poem is an instrument of personal measure, of tests and balances, estimating and preserving the valuable in the teeth of a public actuality that day by day magnifies its impersonality, falsity, and unreality. A poem such as "The Instant" rises out of personal experience and the depth of genuine emotion and significance attached to it by the author. As Miss Levertov's own testament the poem cannot be refuted or denied, for it stands well inside the space her poetic imagination circumscribes about her life as she lives it. Here is the complete poem, taken from her third book *Overland to the Islands* (1958); to cut it would be to destroy the form of an experience as she has realized it:

"We'll go out before breakfast, and get
some mushrooms," says my mother.

Early, early: the sun
risen, but hidden in mist

the square house left behind
sleeping, filled with sleepers;

up the dewy hill, quietly with baskets.
Mushrooms firm, cold;
  tussocks of dark grass, gleam of webs,
turf soft and cropped. Quiet and early. And no valley

no hills: clouds about our knees, tendrils
of cloud in our hair. Wet scrags
of wool caught in barbed wire, gorse
looming, without scent.
                  Then ah! suddenly

the lifting of it, the mist rolls
  quickly away, and far, far—

  "Look!" she grips me, "It is Eryri!
                    It's Snowdon, fifty
miles away!"—the voice
a wave rising to Eryri,
falling.
         Snowdon, home
of eagles, resting-place of
Merlin, core of Wales.

         Light
graces the mountainhead
for a lifetime's look, before the mist
  draws in again.

This poem is both an abbreviated narrative, dramatic in
character (in this it resembles many poems by Robert
Creeley, Paul Carroll, and others), and a spiritual adventure of a nearly ineffable sort. Within the tradition of
post-Symbolist literature such a private illumination as
the poet has here would be objectified into the order of a
larger metaphorical universe—which is not to say that its

value would be sacrificed, but that the value would be transmuted. But in the present poem the experience remains unchanged, is viewed in its own terms. Miss Levertov molds the event into art without abandoning the quality of direct utterance or leaving the domain of her life. The instant to which the poem's title refers is the moment of enlightenment that occurs when mist and clouds part to expose the far-off mountain peak shining in the early light of day and richly endowed with legendary meaning. Still, the poem retains its status as a poem of fact, so to speak, emerging from ordinary circumstances and immediate life, and returning there. We are acquainted with this kind of illumination in Blake or Rilke, though for them it confirms the basis of a whole mythological scheme: the world of things ablaze with the eternal Being they mirror. But to find any metaphysical revelation in Miss Levertov's art we must enter the precincts of the poet's own existence, for she justifies her art through that existence, as well as her existence through her artistic perception.

Miss Levertov's primary intention as a poet has not been the statement of visionary experiences but rather the dogged probing of all the routine business of life in search of what she calls "the authentic" in its rhythms and its details. Her marriage may be a subject for investigation:

> I want to speak to you.
> To whom else should I speak?
> It is you who make
> a world to speak of.
> In your warmth the
> fruits ripen—all the
> apples and pears that grow
> on the south wall of my

head. If you listen
it rains for them, then
they drink. If you
speak in response
the seeds
jump into the ground.
Speak or be silent: your silence
will speak to me.

("The Marriage, II")

or the city's winter streets and the snatches of conversation overheard there:

As the stores close, a winter light
  opens air to iris blue,
    glint of frost through the smoke,
    grains of mica, salt of the sidewalk.

As the buildings closed, released autonomous
  feet pattern the streets
    in hurry and stroll; balloon heads
    drift and dive above them; the bodies
    aren't really there.

As the lights brighten, as the sky darkens,
  a woman with crooked heels says to another woman
    while they step along at a fair pace,

*"You know, I'm telling you, what I love best
is life. I love life! Even if I ever get
to be old and wheezy—or limp! You know?*

Limping along?—I'd still . . ." Out of hearing.

To the multiple disordered tones
    of gears changing, a dance
    to the compass points, out, a four-way river.

Prospect of sky
    wedged into avenues, left at the ends of streets,
    west sky, east sky: more life tonight! A range
    of open time at winter's outskirts.
                                ("February Evening in New York")

This delighted involvement with what most of us continually neglect as trivia or noise, and the ability to carry
out, as Marianne Moore and William Carlos Williams
do, poetic conquests in the categories of the prosaic, are so
natural to Miss Levertov's temperament that she seems
scarcely to think of them. She is totally alive to each
fluctuation, each breath and vibration of the atmosphere
through which she moves with watchful ease. Poetry
speaks to her with the innocent tongues of children:

Martha, 5, scrawling a drawing, murmurs
"These are two angels. These are two bombs. They
are in the sunshine. Magic
is dropping from the angels' wings."

Nik, at 4, called
    over the stubblefield, "Look
the flowers are dancing underneath the
tree, and the tree
    is looking down with all its apple-eyes."

Without hesitation or debate, words
used and at once forgotten.
                                ("The Lesson")

Even though I find it hard to picture Miss Levertov as an aesthetic theorist musing abstractly upon the rightful function of poetry in a hyper-industrialized society, I am sure that in practice poetry is for her an integral part of the acts, thoughts, and gestures of living. In many of her poems we cross into a world very like our own, with the same ornaments and refuse, commonplaces and strokes of grace, but it is also a world made splendid and different by this poet's wise and clear apprehension of it, her abundant imagination. Poems do more than leap from windows; they appear in the humblest, most mundane things, such as this image, seized from a minute's glance out of the poet's kitchen window over the city at sunset:

> On the kitchen wall a flash
> of shadow:
> > swift pilgrimage
> of pigeons, a spiral
> celebration of air, of sky-deserts.
> And on tenement windows
> a blaze
> > of lustered watermelon:
> stain of the sun
> westering somewhere back of Hoboken.
> > > ("The World Outside," I)

The quotidian reality we ignore or try to escape, Denise Levertov revels in, carves and hammers into lyric poems of precise beauty. As celebrations and rituals lifted from the midst of contemporary life in its actual concreteness, her poems are unsurpassed; they open to us aspects of object and situation that but for them we should never have known. And that is no mean achievement for any poet, though it is not the only one Miss Levertov can boast. Another side of her work has slowly asserted itself in two later books, *With Eyes at the Back of Our Heads* (1959) and *The Jacob's Ladder* (1961). I have already alluded to this visionary disposition in discussing "The Instant," but the subsequent pieces rely much more on dream, mystical imagery, and meditation than they do on external conditions that are suddenly transfigured. Some of these poems reflect on the sources of art and imagination and are developments in the line of "Something to Wear," though they find their materials in a deeper layer of consciousness. "The Goddess," "The Well," and "The Illustration," from *The Jacob's Ladder,* are excellent representatives of this category. Other poems press forward on a spiritual journey whose purpose is to uncover the nature of self and its destiny. Miss Levertov's father was a Russian Jew who later became an Anglican clergyman; something of this combination, plus her reading in Biblical, Hasidic, and other mystical writings, undoubtedly has had a decisive influence on these poems.

An example of her meditational poetry is the title poem "With Eyes at the Back of Our Heads"; here Miss Levertov brings to focus two planes of reality that seem to be distant but somehow border one another. The problem is how to get from the first into the second, and the poet addresses herself to it:

> With eyes at the back of our heads
> we see a mountain
> not obstructed with woods but laced
> here and there with feathery groves.
>
> The doors before us in a façade
> that perhaps has no house in back of it
> are too narrow, and one is set too high
> with no doorsill. The architect sees

the imperfect proposition and
turns eagerly to the knitter.
Set it to rights!
The knitter begins to knit.

For we want
to enter the house, if there is a house,
to pass through the doors at least
into whatever lies beyond them,

we want to enter the arms
of the knitted garment. As one
is re-formed, so the other,
in proportion.

When the doors widen
when the sleeves admit us
the way to the mountain will clear,
the mountain we see with
eyes at the back of our heads, mountain

green, mountain
cut of limestone, echoing
with hidden rivers, mountain
of short grass and subtle shadows.

Miss Levertov gives us here a parable of the inner life, a
metaphorical presentation of spiritual pilgrimage in the
individual. The heart of the poem appears paradoxical
because the mountain, which is an image of paradisiacal
proportions, a depiction of the Great Good Place, is seen
only within, by intuition (the "eyes at the back of our
heads"), while the obstacles to be overcome and those to
which we have to accommodate ourselves lie before us.
Yet, as in Heraclitus and Eliot's *Four Quartets*, the way

forward and the way back are one and the same. Thus movement ahead, with the alterations of the self it requires, will be completed in a reconciliation of the inner image of a desired goal with a personal condition of life. Perhaps what we are being told is, "The Kingdom of God is within you." In this, as in her other remarkable poems, Miss Levertov subtly points the way to see with our whole sight.

PERMISSIONS ACKNOWLEDGMENTS:

City Lights Books for "Laying the Dust," "Something to Wear," "The Marriage, II" from Denise Levertov: *Here and Now.* Copyright © 1957 by Denise Levertov.

New Directions, Inc., or "Between Walls" from *Collected Earlier Poems* by William Carlos Williams. For "With Eyes at the Back of Our Heads" and excerpts from *With Eyes at the Back of Our Heads* by Denise Levertov, Copyright 1958, 1959 by Denise Levertov Goodman. For excerpts from *The Jacob's Ladder* by Denise Levertov, Copyright 1958, 1959, 1960, 1961 by Denise Levertov Goodman.

The University of Chicago Press for an excerpt from *Mallarmé* by Wallace Fowlie.

Cresset Press, Ltd. (London) for an excerpt from Denise Levertov [Levertoff]: *The Double Image.*

Denise Levertov for "The Instant" and "The Lesson" from *Overland to the Islands,* Jonathan Williams, 1958.

NOTE

In its earliest form this essay appeared in *Tri-Quarterly;* revised and published as "Denise Levertov" (Chapter Ten) of my book, *Contemporary American Poetry,* New York: Random House, 1965.

XII
THE
POETRY
OF
LOUIS
SIMPSON

YOHMA GRAY

THE paradox inherent in objective criticism of lyric poetry is nowhere more apparent than in an analysis of Louis Simpson's poetry. Lyric poetry seeks to describe intense but transient sensations and emotions which prose cannot, seeks to suspend primary experience for a moment in time so that it may be savored and relished. Many primary experiences are basically incommunicable on *any* level. Consider the difficulty of describing, to someone totally ignorant of the experience, how a cello sounds, or how sandpaper feels, or how a puppy's mouth smells. So-called objective or judicial criticism, therefore, which is mere *explication de texte*, is obviously self-defeating because the subject of a lyric poem is, by definition, beyond the ordinary domain of prose. It does not gain its effect through the information it contains but through the feeling it evokes, and the poem exists because poetry is the only medium through which the experience can be shared.

Louis Simpson published his first book of poems, *The Arrivistes,* in 1949, *Good News of Death* in 1955, and *A Dream of Governors* in 1959. Shortly he will publish a fourth volume of verse, *At the End of the Open Road,* and he plans an edition of *Selected Poems* in 1964. Many of his poems have been published separately in *The New*

Yorker, Hudson Review, American Scholar, Paris Review, Partisan Review and in other journals and anthologies. In addition to his poems he has published one novel, *Riverside Drive*, in 1962, one record in the *Yale Series of Recorded Poets*, one critical study, *James Hogg*, in 1963. He edited *The New Poets of England and America*, together with Donald Hall and Robert Pack, in 1957, and he has published critical articles in leading magazines. He is married, has three children, and is currently an associate professor of English at the University of California at Berkeley.

Although any one of his poems is self-sufficient and self-contained, the relationship between the poems, and between his life and the poems, perhaps deserves some mention. With first-person authority he writes primarily about war, love, urbanism, the American dream, and human mortality. He was born in 1923 in Jamaica, British West Indies, of varied national ancestry. He came to New York to study at Columbia College in 1940 but his studies were interrupted by World War II, during which he served in the 101st Airborne Division of the U.S. Army, through the invasion of Europe from Normandy to Berchtesgaden. He emerged from the war with a bronze star, a purple heart, and United States citizenship, not to mention frozen feet and delayed shock. He returned to Columbia to receive bachelor's, master's, and doctor's degrees. He was an associate editor with the Bobbs-Merrill publishing company until 1955, and since then has been teaching. The obvious use he has made, therefore, of all this experience, invites the so-called intentional fallacy, or the use of biographical material and explicit intention, and the so-called affective fallacy, or the use of emotion and association through "objective correlatives."

Formally his poems fall into three general types: short lyrics; longer poems which depend on topical and historical allusions but which are nevertheless more lyrical than academic in tone; and long dramatic poems. His point of view is more subjective than objective; the reader is aware of the intrusion of the poet's private, inner life in the poems rather than the insertion of an invented character from whom the poet is detached. He does not demonstrate what Keats called "negative capability," or what has been more recently called aesthetic distance. Although he sometimes writes in the third person, the reader senses a subjective "I" in the poem, just as Browning often writes in the first person but conveys the sense of an objective "he." (His dramatic poems are no exception; however, the focus of this essay is on the lyrical poems.) In "The Battle," for example, he delays and thereby intensifies the meaning of the experience to the subjective "I":

Helmet and rifle, pack and overcoat
Marched through a forest. Somewhere up ahead
Guns thudded. Like the circle of a throat
The night on every side was turning red.

They halted and they dug. They sank like moles
Into the clammy earth between the trees.
And soon the sentries, standing in their holes,
Felt the first snow. Their feet began to freeze.

At dawn the first shell landed with a crack.
Then shells and bullets swept the icy woods.
This lasted many days. The snow was black.
The corpses stiffened in their scarlet hoods.

Most clearly of that battle I remember
The tiredness in eyes, how hands looked thin
Around a cigarette, and the bright ember
Would pulse with all the life there was within.

In the midst of all that death, the meaning of life becomes momentarily clear in the ordinary act of smoking a cigarette; and in the midst of all those extraordinarily dramatic images, the mundane image becomes extraordinarily intense.

I am not suggesting that the poems are more concerned with literal than artistic truth or that Louis Simpson is masquerading as all the characters he creates; rather, I mean to call attention to the re-personalization which these poems represent in the direct relationship between reader and writer. They seek to create a rapport which has not been generally characteristic of poetry in the first half of the twentieth century. They appeal not to some past, lost, and eternal truth as a means of salvation, but rather to some present, hidden, and internal relationship which can become an effective conspiracy against the dehumanizing forces in the modern world. His intention becomes explicit in "Room and Board":

> The curtained windows of New York
> Conceal her secrets. Walls of stone
> Muffle the clatter of the fork.
> Tomorrow we shall see the bone.
>
> In silence we construct a sect . . .
> Each of us, comrades, has his own.
> Poems that will not take effect,
> Pictures that never will be known.
>
> The landlord wipes his mouth of pork,
> Pauses to eavesdrop, disconnect
> The water and the telephone;
>
> And Death's unmarried daughter crawls
> Along the thin lath of the walls
> And knocks, because we live alone.

Despite the tone, however, there is never a sense of the narrowly parochial nor the embarrassingly intimate. This is not merely self-introspection nor self-analysis. Theodore Hoffman says of the poetry, ". . . nor is it the victim of either of the affable poetic vices of the day, for it neither attempts to buckle its matter into a self-designed system nor is it engaged in a capricious quest for conceits." That, I think, is one of its major achievements as mid-twentieth century American poetry.

Louis Simpson never departs from traditional form and structure and yet he never departs from contemporary themes and concerns. In "The Lady Sings," for example, he handles a modern psychological situation in the delicate cadence of seventeenth century verse:

The lady sings her child
Will be such a one
As the world has not known:
Jesus without tears.

And as her heart goes wild
Between gates of bone
He comes into his own,
Having his own ideas.

The days her lover smiled
Are as a summer gone.
Over a telephone
We talk across the years.

Now she may be beguiled
By apricocks, and groan
Her secret to the sun.
Shake her and she bears.

The central feeling of the defeat of a possessive mother through the independence of her son begins with a reference to the Virgin, ends with an oblique reference to the *Duchess of Malfi,* and contains diction as diverse as "apricocks" and "telephone," yet synthesizes the elements gracefully.

In the last stanza of "Invitation to a Quiet Life" Simpson demonstrates the precision of his ear as well as of his eye as he imitates a traditional pastoral form:

. . . .

Since, Amaryllis, you and I
Adore an advertising sky
And find happiness to stare
At the enchantments of thin air,
Let us go in, and not regret
The endings that we never met,
But in security applaud
The ecstasies we can't afford.
So shall we manage till the day
Death takes the furniture away.

The pastoral form and the urban theme combine ironically and the irony intensifies and clarifies the metropolitan anxieties which are the subject of the poem. Simpson uses a similar device in "Arm in Arm," a war poem:

. . . .

Beside a Church we dug our holes,
By tombstone and by cross.
They were too shallow for our souls
When the ground began to toss.

Which were the new, which the old dead
It was a sight to ask.
One private found a polished head
And took the skull to task

> For spying on us . . . Till along
> Driving the clouds like sheep,
> Our bombers came in a great throng:
> And so we fell asleep.

The tumultuous chaos of the bombing of a churchyard and the grisly mingling of old corpses and new is the subject of the poem, but the fragmentary senselessness of the experience is enhanced by the deliberately measured and regular meter, and the strife of the battle is heightened by the suggestion of sleep and of the calm of the pastoral scene. There is a kind of literary dialectic in these poems . . . thesis, antithesis, synthesis . . . which forms the dynamic process of an "internal colloquy."

In examining the plight of modern man, Louis Simpson finds all the contemporary tensions between imagination and reality, between fragmentation and continuity, between city and country, between Old World and New World, between military and human values, between the American dream and the American actuality; but he neither moralizes nor wails. To him poetry is not the only suitable subject for poetry, nor expressionism the only suitable mode for it. He does indeed juxtapose images which are abstracted from their normal context, creating an apocalyptic quality, but the final effect is to clarify rather than to cloud. If his poems do not always follow an obviously logical progression, the total insight is rational and conscious and the associative progression makes ultimate sense. Throughout his "Jamaica," for example, he relies on metaphors of the body until the final stanza when he shifts to prestige symbols of modern culture:

. . . .

> Life is a winter liner, here history passes
> Like tourists on top-decks, seeing the shore through sun-
> glasses:

And death, a delightful life-long disease,
Sighs in sideways languor of twisted trees.

The shift from organic to mechanistic images is significant in itself and provides an insight into the values of
modern life. The form and theme are skillfully unified by
the unexpected break at the end of the second line,
where the word "sun" (the natural light which makes all
sight possible) is sharply juxtaposed to the word "glasses"
(artificial devices which alter vision) at the beginning of
the third line, with the hyphen intensifying the cleavage.
Thus the very abruptness of the shift in associations has a
logic of its own to modern man. Simpson is not courting
madness in this "multiverse," nor is he insisting that
modern man is forever "caught between two worlds, the
one dead, the other powerless to be born." In the Romantic tradition he is relying on sensibility as a basis for
orientation and movement in a chaotic world, but his
reliance on human viscera and cerebra is neither frightening nor agonizing to him. He is quite explicit in a stanza
from "Islanders":

. . . .

Enough of these images—they set the teeth on
   edge!
Life, if you like, is a metaphor of death—
The difference is you, a place for the passing of
   breath.
That is what man is. He is the time between,
The palpable glass through which all things are
   seen.
Nothing. Silence. A syllable. A word.
Everything.

. . . .

Sensational perception and individual identity are his
broad concerns. His rhetoric is often ironic; that is, a
subtle reversal takes place between the literally expressed

and the implied values, through naive narration, understatement, and romantic illusion and disintegration. His
presentation of these generalities, however, is always
through the animation of particulars. "He who wishes to
see a Vision, a perfect Whole, must see it in its Minute
Particulars," according to William Blake, and Louis
Simpson adheres to that dictum. He sees reality through
particulars; he is a kind of "responsible vagrant" who
finds meaning in any situation. He has the talent, however, to generalize his experience without diminishing its
concreteness. That is why he can be personal but universal in his tone. "Hot Night on Water Street" is little more
than a series of particulars but it conveys the whole of an
American small town, universally recognizable:

> . . . .
> Three hardware stores, a barbershop, a bar
> A movie playing Westerns—where I went
> To see a dream of horses called *The Star* . . .
> Someday, when this uncertain continent
> Is marble, and men ask what was the good
> We lived by, dust may whisper "Hollywood."
>
> . . . .
> At the newsstand in the lobby, a cigar
> Was talkative: "Since I've been in this town
> I've seen one likely woman, and a car
> As she was crossing Main Street, knocked her down."
> I was a stranger here myself, I said,
> And bought the *New York Times*, and went to bed.

"Music in Venice" demonstrates a similar capacity to
evoke wholeness through particulars:

> . . . .
> It's night in the Piazza. Lighted space
> Burns like your brandy. Violins and brass
> Play waltzes, fox-trots. On a cloud, St. Mark's
>   Winged lion perches;

High palaces go sailing to the moon,
Which, as advertised, is perfectly clear.
The lovers rise, moon-struck, and whisper their
    Arrivedercis.

. . . .

Venice, the city built on speculation,
Still stands on it. Love sails from India
And Sweden—every hanging cloud pours out
    A treasure-chest.
It's love on the Rialto, news of love,
That gives Antonio his golden life,
Even to Envy, sharpening a knife,
    His interest.

In "The Inner Part" [1] a few trivial particulars serve to characterize American mentality before her emergence as a world power into the twentieth century, and American maturity and deep disillusionment after the war to make the "world safe for democracy":

When they had won the war,
And for the first time in history
Americans were the most important people—

When the leading citizens no longer lived
    in their shirt sleeves,
And their wives did not scratch in public;
Just when they'd stopped saying "Gosh!"—

When their daughters seemed as sensitive
As the tip of a fly rod,
And their sons were as smooth as a V-8 engine—

Priests, examining the entrails of birds,
Found the heart misplaced, and seeds
As black as death, emitting a strange odor.

In this poem the shift from the naive buoyancy of pre-World War I America to the sophisticated despair of post-World War I America conveys, as a prose paraphrase cannot, a sense of the exchange of innocence for the knowledge of good and evil. The oblique reference to classical civilization ominously suggests the inevitable consequence of that knowledge, death. Ironically it prophesies World War II.

The value of such a talent is inestimable. Every society has areas of gross insensitivity, some of them positively necessary for carrying on the life processes and some of them merely destructive of the subtle nuances of primary experience which comprise human fulfillment, realization, and delight. There are primitive tribes, for example, which have only three words to denote color: one term for white, one term for black, and one term for all others. Assuming that language and perception are inextricably linked, the level of color awareness in these societies is extremely primitive. Reading the poetry of Louis Simpson makes it obvious that some of our perceptions are equally primitive and undeveloped. We are daily bombarded with sensations from which the conscious mind extracts only a few functional impressions, leaving a vast aggregate of experience to be dismissed or buried in the inner recesses of awareness, below the conscious level. The economy of concentration is often practical but it deprives us of our full power and the responsibilities of that power; it makes us "emotional illiterates," often totally out of touch with our own feelings. Even in the most mundane experience there is a vast area of unperceived reality and it is Louis Simpson's kind of poetry which brings it to our notice. It enables us to see things which are ordinarily all about us but which we do not ordinarily see; it adds a new dimension to our sensational perception, making us hear with our eyes and see with our ears. His poem "Frogs," [2] for example, seems to be a recollection of details of ordinary experience and yet subtly becomes an implied metaphor so that in the resolution, both the particular and the general are sharply impressed on the consciousness:

> The storm broke, and it rained,
> And water rose in the pool,
> And frogs hopped into the gutter,
>
> With their skins of yellow and green,
> And just their eyes shining above the surface
> Of the warm solution of slime.
>
> At night, when fireflies trace
> Light-lines between the trees and flowers
> Exhaling perfume,
>
> The frogs speak to each other
> In rhythm. The sound is monstrous.
> But their voices are filled with satisfaction.
>
> In the city I pine for the country;
> In the country I long for conversation—
> Our happy croaking.

The "shock of recognition" in the final stanza is all the more powerful because of our obtuseness and complacency in the first four stanzas and because the subject of the poem is finally an implied obtuseness and complacency.

"Birch" [3] is another poem which depends ultimately on

a metaphor which is really obvious, but only after the reading of the poem:

> Birch tree, you remind me
> Of a room filled with breathing,
> The sway and whisper of love.
>
> She slips off her shoes;
> Unzips her skirt; arms raised,
> Unclasps an earring, and the other.
>
> Just so the sallow trunk
> Divides, and the branches
> Are straight and smooth.

In "The Boarder," Simpson once again selects the most mundane particulars of a situation to convey the most profound of human feelings:

> The time is after dinner. Cigarettes
>   Glow on the lawn:
> Glasses begin to tinkle; TV sets
>   Have been turned on.
>
> The moon is brimming like a glass of beer
>   Above the town,
> And love keeps her appointments—"Harry's here!"
>   "I'll be right down."
>
> But the pale stranger in the furnished room
>   Lies on his back
> Looking at paper roses, how they bloom,
>   And ceilings crack.

The images of the first two stanzas convey the feeling of conviviality and community, and the images of the last stanza convey the feeling of alienation and separation so powerfully because of the contrast between the dynamic processes implied in the former and the static situation implied in the latter. The contrast depends primarily on the jarring tension between the adjective "paper" and the noun "roses," and the implication of disintegration. Simpson is creating meaning from the raw material of experience and is bringing us to a deeper level of awareness.

In the same manner but on a different level of matter, Simpson vivifies experience which is not a part of everyone's ordinary storehouse but which then becomes as real as frogs or birches or paper roses. In short, some of his subject matter is "raw" and some of it is "cooked"; some depends on common experience and some on special knowledge, but the meaning is always universal. "A Story About Chicken Soup," [4] for example, depends on some general knowledge of World War II and on some general association of chicken soup with Jewish customs:

. . . .

In the ruins of Berchtesgaden
A child with yellow hair
Ran out of a doorway.

A German girl-child—
Cuckoo, all skin and bones—
Not even enough to make chicken soup.
She sat by the stream and smiled.

Then as we splashed in the sun
She laughed at us.
We had killed her mechanical brothers,
So we forgave her.

. . . .

Similarly, familiarity with literary history intensifies

appreciation of Simpson's ability to imitate faultlessly. "Invitation to a Quiet Life" reverberates through three centuries of poetry with its echoes of Marlowe:

Come, Amaryllis, let us go
To see the moving picture show
Where the small people, closely pressed,
Walk all together in their best.

. . . .

"Ballad of the Beery Boys" humorously combines strains of Browning and a familiar popular poem:

Up Flotsam, up Jetsam, up Donner and Blitzen!
I galloped, he galloped through barrels of Pilsen
To Maidenhead, Munich, Sversk and Vienna,
(A landscape of umber, a sky of sienna):

. . . .

"Over at the Baroque Ryehouse" is reminiscent of the style of Emily Dickinson:

. . . .

I've had my cut of sin,
A passing glimpse of heaven,
And hope to meet Christ in
The city after seven.

"Room and Board" is suggestive of Auden's "Musée des Beaux Arts" in the stanza

. . . .

The landlord wipes his mouth of pork,
Pauses to eavesdrop, disconnect
The water and the telephone.

Finally "Song: 'Rough Winds Do Shake the Darling Buds of May'" combines Renaissance conceits and modern form:

Rough winds do shake
>> do shake
>>>> the darling buds of May
The darling buds
>> rose-buds
>>>> the winds do shake
That are her breasts.
Those darling buds, dew-tipped, her sighing moods
do shake.

. . . .

On several levels, then, Simpson's poety has an incisive quality which enables us simultaneously to see and to be suddenly aware that we are seeing, and thus to double the delight. Sometimes he gives the reader the relief of "what oft was thought, but ne'er so well expressed," but more often he intensifies particulars which have never been anything but amorphous, which have never taken on the discipline of form. Who does not remember the delight of seeing, on a cold, wintry day, snowflakes under a magnifying glass for the first time, and who has forgotten the awe at the illumination of the hitherto unsuspected and unperceived mystery, both as an external phenomenon of nature and as an internal phenomenon of perception? Perhaps Robert Louis Stevenson was aware of that kind of delight when he said, "The world is so full of a number of things, I'm sure we should all be as happy as kings." Reality, of course, has a dark as well as a light side, and reality in itself is not always delightful to human perception, is often more somber; perceiving and knowing, however, are always an enhancement of human values, whether their objects be beautiful or ugly. Louis Simpson's poetry imparts new sensibility; the heat of his imagination and the pressure of his experience fuse both the raw materials and organized systems of life into lyrical poems which reflect and refract human emotion with the same beauty and brilliance that diamonds do physical light.

Mid-twentieth century society is generally unsympathetic to knowing for the sake of knowing. (Even in the realm of science, pure research has been defined as the name we give any project when we don't know what we're doing.) Useless, that is, inapplicable knowledge is a term of opprobrium. The truth of the human heart is, however, that some things are worth knowing for the sake of knowing, that somehow awareness and perception are fundamental to the quality of being human. There is a value simply in knowing, and Louis Simpson's poetry reflects and refines that value. Descriptions of so-called objective reality, that is, reality irrelevant to human passion, are very recent developments in human evolution, but very powerful developments for all their newness. Man has always tried to resolve the mystery of his environment and himself, but only recently has he sought to do this by discounting and dismissing his own reaction to the world around him, by the so-called scientific method. In many ways, of course, science and art serve the same general function, the penetration and description of reality, but science elevates the fact and submerges the emotion, and art elevates the emotion and submerges the fact. The world within, however, is still as important as the world without, and the publication in the last decade and a half of lyric poetry of the quality of Simpson's is firm testimony to the fact that it is still a lively art whose concern is human feeling and whose instrument is human imagination.

I do not suggest, however, that his poetry inspires only isolated flashes of dissociated insights. Poetry in general and his poetry in particular can and does produce systematic and coherent organizations of reality which take us deeper into the mystery than we could ever go by ourselves. Simpson is an intellectually mature and responsi-

ble poet who is ultimately committed to making human
sense of what *is*, although he is never unaware of the
eternal paradoxes and possibilities of what *ought to be*.
His war poems, for example, intensify particulars but
ominously suggest also in a systematic way that war is a
singularly ineffective behavior pattern if the human animal really wants to improve his condition. "I Dreamed
that in a City Dark as Paris" links both world wars to
suggest the futility:

> I dreamed that in a city dark as Paris
> I stood alone in a deserted square.
> The night was trembling with a violet
> Expectancy. At the far edge it moved
> And rumbled; on that flickering horizon
> The guns were pumping color in the sky.
>
>   . . . .
>
> These wars have been so great, they are forgotten
> Like Egyptian dynasts. My confrere
> In whose thick boots I stood, were you amazed
> To wander through my brain four decades later
> As I have wandered in a dream through yours?
>
> The violence of waking life disrupts
> The order of our death. Strange dreams occur,
> For dreams are licensed as they never were.

Simpson also consistently suggests the futility of heroism
through war, as in "The Heroes":

> I dreamed of war-heroes, of wounded war-heroes
> With just enough of their charms shot away
> To make them more handsome. The women moved
>   nearer

To touch their brave wounds and their hair
    streaked with gray.

. . . .

A fine dust has settled on all that scrap metal.
The heroes were packaged and sent home in parts
To pluck at a poppy and sew on a petal
And count the long night by the stroke of their
    hearts.

In the same manner, Simpson vitalizes the particular
images of love but generalizes about its timeless quality in
"The Green Shepherd":

Here sit a shepherd and a shepherdess,
He playing on his melancholy flute;
The sea wind ruffles up her simple dress
And shows the delicacy of her foot.

And there you see Constantinople's wall
With arrows and Greek fire, molten lead;
Down from a turret seven virgins fall,
Hands folded, each one praying on her head.

. . . .

But the green shepherd travels in her eye
And whispers nothings in his lady's ear,
And sings a little song, that roses die,
Carpe diem, which she seems pleased to hear.

. . . .

The groaning pole had gone more than a mile;
These shepherds did not feel it where they loved,
For time was sympathetic all the while
And on the magic mountain nothing moved.

"The Silent Lover" [5] is more fragmentary in its progression, but it equates love to concrete images which are in

turn associated with eternity, and thus accomplishes the same end:

> She sighs. What shall I say?
> For beauty seems to grow
> In silence, when the heart is faint and slow.
>
> Sing, sing . . . How shall I sing?
> In silent eyes, where clouds and islands gaze,
> The waves bring Eros in.
>
> I think the rustling of her clothes
> Is like the sea, and she
> A wild white bird,
>
> And love is like the sighing of the sand.

Similarly, his poems on an urban theme illuminate the strange, historic dilemma of alienation from and integration with the great masses of people and materials that we call cities; thus in the poem "In California" [6] Simpson combines his urban concern with his feeling of the failure of the American dream as it was articulated by Walt Whitman:

> Here I am, troubling the dream coast
> With my New York face,
> Bearing among the realtors
> And tennis-players my dark preoccupation.
>
> There once was an epical clatter—
> Voices and banjos, Tennessee, Ohio,
> Rising like incense in the sight of heaven.
> Today, there is an angel in the gate.

Lie back, Walt Whitman,
There, on the fabulous raft with the King and the
  Duke!
For the white row of the Marina
Faces the Rock. Turn round the wagons here.

Lie back! We cannot bear
The stars any more, those infinite spaces.
Let the realtors divide the mountain,
For they already subdivided the valley.

Rectangular city block astonished
Herodotus in Babylon,
Cortes in Tenochtitlan,
And here's the same old city-planner, death.

We cannot turn or stay.
For though we sleep, and let the reins fall slack,
The great cloud-wagons move
Outward still, dreaming of a Pacific.

Finally, while Simpson passionately and graphically describes the ugliness of death in particulars, he generalizes
in a more restrained manner about the fact of human
mortality in "Early in the Morning":

Early in the morning
The dark Queen said,
"The trumpets are warning
There's trouble ahead."
Spent with carousing
With wine-soaked wits,
Antony drowsing
Whispered, "It's

Too cold a morning
To get out of bed."

The army's retreating,
The fleet has fled,
Caesar is beating
His drums through the dead.
"Antony, horses!
We'll get away
Gather our forces
For another day . . ."
"It's a cold morning,"
Antony said.

Caesar Augustus
Cleared his phlegm.
"Corpses disgust us.
Cover them."
Caesar Augustus
In his time lay
Dying, and just as
Cold as they,
On the cold morning
Of a cold day.

His tragic sense serves to intensify the quality of life just
as his imagination intensifies the quality of reality.

Simpson's art imposes order from within on chaos
without, gives meaning to the apparently meaningless,
suggests fresh vantage points from which to probe experience. In "Lines Written Near San Francisco"[7] he sum-
marizes the current American condition with oblique
references to our military and material madness, and he
proffers a possible solution which suggests the process

toward individual human realization and maturity as the defeat of death:

. . . .

Every night, at the end of America
We taste our wine, looking at the Pacific.
How sad it is, the end of America!

While we were waiting for the land,
They'd finished it—with gas drums
On the hilltops, cheap housing in the valleys

Where lives are mean and wretched.
But the banks thrive and the realtors
Rejoice—they have their America.

Still, there is something unsettled in the air.
Out there on the Pacific
There's no America but the Marines.

Whitman was wrong about the People,
But right about himself. The land is within.
At the end of the open road we come to ourselves.

Though mad Columbus follows the sun
Into the sea, we cannot follow.
We must remain, to serve the returning sun,

And to set tables for death.
For we are the colonists of Death—
Not, as some think, of the English.

And we are preparing thrones for him to sit,
Poems to read, and beds
In which it may please him to rest.

This is the Land
The pioneers looked for, shading their eyes
Against the sun—the world of flowers and dreams.

Poetry rarely commands the intensity of religious belief, but it seeks the same end, that of using the materials of human life . . . senses, emotions, intelligence . . . to formulate a coherent and significant meaning for life. The poetry of Louis Simpson offers us that meaning.

NOTES

"Arm in Arm," "Ballad of the Beery Boys," "Invitation to a Quiet Life," "Jamaica," "The Lady Sings," "Over at the Baroque Ryehouse," "Room and Board," (© 1949 Louis Simpson), are reprinted with permission of Fine Editions Press from *The Arrivistes* (1949) by Louis Simpson. "The Battle," "Early in the Morning," "The Heroes," "Islanders," (© 1955 Louis Simpson), are reprinted with permission of Charles Scribner's Sons from *Good News of Death and Other Poems* (1955) by Louis Simpson (POETS OF TODAY II). "The Boarder," "The Green Shepherd," "Hot Night on Water Street," "I Dreamed that in a City Dark as Paris," "Music in Venice," "Song: 'Rough Winds Do Shake,'" (© 1949, 1956, 1957, 1958, 1959, 1963 Louis Simpson), are reprinted with permission of Wesleyan University Press from *A Dream of Governors* (1959) and *At the End of the Open Road* (in press) by Louis Simpson. All poems, in whole or in part, are reprinted with permission of Louis Simpson. Five are reprinted with permission of magazines credited in the text.

[1] © 1963 *The Sixties* Magazine.
[2] © 1963 *Prism* Magazine.
[3] © 1963 *Generation* Magazine.
[4] © 1963 Louis Simpson.
[5] © 1962 *The New Yorker* Magazine.
[6] © 1963 Louis Simpson.
[7] © 1963 *Paris Review* Magazine.

XIII
THE
POETRY
OF
ANNE
SEXTON

BEVERLY FIELDS

ANNE SEXTON was born November 9, 1928, in Newton, Massachusetts, and grew up in Wellesley, where she attended local schools. She has been married for fifteen years and has two daughters—Linda, nine, and Joyce, seven. She began writing five years ago. Her poetry has appeared in numerous periodicals and anthologies. Houghton Mifflin Company has published two volumes of her work—*To Bedlam and Part Way Back* and *All My Pretty Ones*. In 1958–59 she won the *Audience* poetry prize and in 1959 she held the Robert Frost Fellowship at Breadloaf, Vermont. She was awarded a grant as assistant scholar to the Radcliffe Institute for Independent Study during 1961–62, and she won the *Poetry* prize in 1962. This year she was awarded the first traveling literary fellowship of the American Academy of Arts and Letters for a year's residence at the American Academy in Rome. When *Poetry* sent her a biographical form to fill out, she wrote under the heading of education "none" and under the heading of occupation she wrote "homebody."

The poetry of Anne Sexton expresses a number of symbolic themes which have been read as literal autobiography. Because her work is difficult, the biographical approach to the poems has been a temptation; but while there are elements of autobiography in it, the poetry cannot always be interpreted in this way. It seems more profitable to credit her with a degree of esthetic distance and to consider some of the recurrent themes that create relationships among the individual poems. What follows is intended to direct readers to the poems as poems rather than as memoirs.

There are no new seasons in hell, but the old ones from time to time toughen up new visitors who are able to describe in verse the climate of descent. Anne Sexton's hell is more like Dante's than like Milton's; her images clarify rather than veil the ineffable. "The Moss of His Skin," for example, is ostensibly a dramatic monologue, its voice started by a quotation from an article in a psychoanalytic journal. The quotation appears as epigraph to the poem:

> Young girls in old Arabia were often buried
> alive next to their dead fathers, apparently
> as sacrifice to the goddesses of the tribes.

But the form of the poem—the dramatic monologue—is a metaphor that reveals naked a personal fantasy:

> It was only important
> to smile and hold still,
> to lie down beside him
> and to rest awhile,
> to be folded up together
> as if we were silk,
> to sink from the eyes of mother
> and not to talk.
> The black room took us
> like a cave or a mouth

or an indoor belly.
I held my breath
and daddy was there,
his thumbs, his fat skull,
his teeth, his hair growing
like a field or a shawl.
I lay by the moss
of his skin until
it grew strange. My sisters
will never know that I fall
out of myself and pretend
that Allah will not see
how I hold my daddy
like an old stone tree.*

The *liebestod* experience here is given more straightfor-
wardly than even Antigone's; none of its elements is in
doubt—the sense of sin, or tabu, that requires the grave
as the most secret bed and also as punishment is directly
produced in the four grave figures that establish sin
(black), privacy (cave), annihilation (mouth), and the
complex female need not only to share the father with
the mother but also to share the mother with the father
(an indoor belly).

Like all her poems, this one doubles its strength and
clarity through sound. There is almost no rhyme except
at the end, where *see* and *tree* reach a climax intensified
by the intervening *daddy*, with its extra syllable that
contributes to the syncopation of the last two lines. The
poem proceeds to this final syncopation from its beginning jump-rope rhythms, expressive of childhood, and
through a meter that is struck almost exclusively with
two beats to a line, expressive of this secret and disastrous
coupling. Where three beats occur in a line the mother is

to be found, an extra yet necessary presence: "to sink from the eyes of mother"; her presence is implied strongly also in the trimeter lines that recognize the need to hide from the sisters and from Allah, since all these censors refer psychologically to the mother, against whom the sin is after all committed:

> . . . My sisters
> will never know that I fall
> out of myself and pretend
> that Allah will not see . . .

It may be no more than coincidence that "The Moss of His Skin" occurs almost at dead center of Anne Sexton's first published volume, *To Bedlam and Part Way Back;* but it is possible to look before and after it to radiant elements in the large discourse of this book. The metaphorical use of the dramatic monologue makes four more poems, of which one, "Where I Live in This Honorable House of the Laurel Tree," speaks in a *double-entendre* of lament both for the cold pastoral, the death-in-life of poetry, and for the erotic paralysis that results from refusing courtship that is divine or otherwise tabu:

> . . . The air
> rings for you, for that astonishing rite
> of my breathing tent undone within your light.
> I only know how this untimely lust has tossed
> flesh at the wind forever and moved my fears
> toward the intimate Rome of the myth we crossed.
>
> . . . .
>
> You gave me honor too soon, Apollo.
> There is no one left who understands
> how I wait

here in my wooden legs and O
my green green hands.

The tree of the father literally imprisons her here, in an
ancient and durable symbol; and in another sense she is
imprisoned in poetry, the shibboleth that promises to
open the gates of the dead.

But a dead voice chants in another monologue, "Portrait of an Old Woman on the College Tavern Wall,"
with the narcotic repetitiveness of a ballad, its refrain the
voices of the living, about poets and about the locks on
the gates of the dead that prevent the poets from really
reaching the deep truth:

> I only said
> how I want to be there and I
> would sing my songs with the liars
> and my lies with all the singers.
> And I would, and I would but
> it's my hair in the hair wreath,
> my cup pinned to the tavern wall,
> my dusty face they sing beneath.
> Poets are sitting in my kitchen.

As in Donne, the dead voice asks a question whose
answer is made impossible by another question:

> Why do these poets lie?
> Why do children get children and
> *Did you hear what it said?*
>
> I only said
> how I want to be there,
> Oh, down at the tavern

where the prophets are singing
around their round table
until they are still.

Poetry is a lying art undertaken perhaps in a witch's
"kitchen," not only because of the nature of the poet,
who is always aware of the lie behind the truth, but also
because the city of the dead, the buried life, is closed, and
because even the dead would lie if they could.

To lie or not, to publish or withhold, is the concern of
the fourth dramatic monologue in this volume. The "Unknown Girl in the Maternity Ward" speaks to her illegitimate infant, six days old. From the dramatic surface of
the poem, however, a lyrical note thrusts up as the girl
tells the infant that

. . . Your lips are animals; you are fed
with love. At first hunger is not wrong.

This is surely out of character; it knows too much; and it
is a direction toward the undramatic pulse that beats *sotto
voce* beneath the monologue where it is not difficult to
detect the poet pinned sprawling to the wall:

The doctors are enamel. They want to know
the facts. They guess about the man who left me,
some pendulum soul, going the way men go
and leave you full of child. But our case history
stays blank. All I did was let you grow.
Now we are here for all the ward to see.
. . . .
. . . I am a shelter of lies.
Should I learn to speak again, or hopeless in
such sanity will I touch some face I recognize?

The decision is made at last, as involuntary and natural
an act as when

. . . I burst empty
of you, letting you learn how the air is so.
. . . .
. . . the doctors return to scold
me. I speak. It is you my silence harms.
I should have known; I should have told
them something to write down. My voice alarms
my throat. "Name of father—none." I hold
you and name you bastard in my arms.

And now that's that. There is nothing more
that I can say or lose.
Others have traded life before
and could not speak. I tighten to refuse
your owling eyes, my fragile visitor.
I touch your cheeks, like flowers. You bruise
against me. We unlearn. I am a shore
rocking you off. You break from me. I choose
your only way, my small inheritor
and hand you off, trembling the selves we lose.
Go child, who is my sin and nothing more.

This is the poem that has led some to speculate whether
or not Anne Sexton has had an illegitimate child—an
interpretation that amuses her. Such error is not merely
simple-minded, however; it is a response to the poet's
trick of investing the experience of *the other* with her
own emotional realities. What is primary in the poem is
of course the experience of childbirth with its essential
pain of separation; but here again, as in many of her
poems, there is a *double-entendre*. The undramatic *sotto
voce* appears to refer associatively to the long poem, "The

Double Image," and to "For John, Who Begs Me Not to
Enquire Further"; and its expresses precisely the problem
that is called attention to in the epigraph to *To Bedlam
and Part Way Back.* The epigraph is a quotation from a
letter of Schopenhauer to Goethe:

> It is the courage to make a clean breast of it
> in face of every question that makes the philos-
> opher. He must be like Sophocles's Oedipus,
> who, seeking enlightenment concerning his terrible
> fate, pursues his indefatigable enquiry, even when
> he divines that appalling horror awaits him in the
> answer. But most of us carry in our heart the
> Jocasta who begs Oedipus for God's sake not to
> inquire further.

This is an afterthought, of course, in the context of the
volume; but it puts neatly the tension that motivates all
the poems. A small composition history may be illuminat-
ing. After Anne Sexton had written the long poem "The
Double Image" she showed it to her teacher John
Holmes, who was angry and dismayed to find her revealing so much of herself in her verse and attempted to
prevent her publishing it. Her answer to him was "For
John, Who Begs Me Not to Enquire Further"; but even
here, in her rebuttal, his censorship appears to be the
voice of her own inner Jocasta. The poem begins in
explanation, justification; and the attempted liberation of
her Oedipus from her Jocasta is reinforced by means of
free verse:

> Not that it was beautiful,
> but that, in the end, there was
> a certain sense of order there;

something worth learning
in the narrow diary of my mind,
in the commonplaces of the asylum
where the cracked mirror
of my own selfish death
outstared me.
And if I tried
to give you something else,
something outside of myself,
you would not know
that the worst of anyone
can be, finally,
an accident of hope.

The movement away from solipsism, the only possibility for a poet who works from the specific to the general, who does not stop at the moment of lyrical narcissism, begins the middle of the poem:

I tapped my own head;
it was glass, an inverted bowl.
It is a small thing
to rage in your own bowl.
At first it was private.
Then it was more than myself;
it was you, or your house
or your kitchen.

The witch's kitchen again. But the poem ends with a return to the lyrical moment, enlarged, however, by the experience of reaching out, so that the final declarative sentence is twice qualified:

There ought to be something special
for someone

in this kind of hope.
This is something I would never find
in a lovelier place, my dear,
although your fear is anyone's fear,
like an invisible veil between us all . . .
and sometimes in private,
my kitchen, your kitchen,
my face, your face.

"My face, your face," Jocasta's face; it is the awareness of "my own selfish death" that sees more than one face in "the cracked mirror"—cracked to reflect both sides of the overwhelming question whether or not to inquire, whether or not to express the results of inquiry.

Like the "Unknown Girl in the Maternity Ward," Anne Sexton makes her decision, but it is a difficult one. The *double-entendre* in "Unknown Girl," made in alternate rhyme to express its internal debate, and in "Where I Live in This Honorable House of the Laurel Tree," is her manner of clarifying the difficulty by means of the metaphors of childbirth and mythology. Equivalence between childbirth and poem-making is by no means new, and neither is the fear of annihilation in poetry that is expressed in the metaphor of the tree. Keats and Tennyson both felt such fear, and so did Frost and Eliot; Plato was impelled to exclude poets from his ideal republic, himself a poet; and it was Vergil, after all, who invented the metaphor of the golden bough.

Just how personally Anne Sexton pursues her fearful inquiry, however, is a matter of more conjecture than most of her readers are likely to understand. Where the lyric leaves off and the dramatic monologue takes up is frequently not clear. "For Johnny Pole on the Forgotten Beach," for example, looks like a lyric: its refrain, "Johnny, your dream moves summers/inside my mind," separates two sections of the poem that are concerned respectively with Johnny on the beach of a resort summer and with Johnny on a "beach of assault" in war, and the voice says that "He was my brother, my small Johnny brother, almost ten." But whose voice tells the truth? The poem's? Or Anne Sexton's, telling an interviewer "something to write down"—that she did not have a brother who was killed during the war?

The answer is irrelevant. The infernal journey requires what can probably be called vision, a state of heightened or intensified perception that can apprehend the nature of both the self and the other, separately as well as together, the kind of ego mobility that can slide freely between inner and outer reality.

One major literary device for attaining and expressing vision, in this sense, is synesthesia, as old as Saint John of Asia and as new as Rimbaud or as Anne Sexton. Her synesthetic figures radiate most frequently from the sense of hearing. In "Music Swims Back to Me," where the synesthesia is at its simplest, she presents the Proustian notion that "the song . . . remembers more than I." The sense of vertigo and of loss is heavy:

Wait Mister. Which way is home?
They turned the light out
and the dark is moving in the corner.
There are no sign posts in this room,
four ladies, over eighty,
in diapers every one of them.
La la la, Oh music swims back to me
and I can feel the tune they played
the night they left me
in this private institution on a hill.

It is loss of the self that you feel here; and in an attempt to find it, the persona is impelled toward pathetic fallacy:

Imagine it. A radio playing
and everyone here was crazy.
I liked it and danced in a circle.
Music pours over the sense
and in a funny way
music sees more than I.
I mean it remembers better;

remembers the first night here.
It was the strangled cold of November;
even the stars were strapped in the sky.

"Stars . . . strapped in the sky" conveys of course the
sense of restraint—literal, physical restraint—"in this private institution"; vision here operates to merge the self
consolingly with elements of the external world. The
result, however, is not consoling, but suggests that the
persona and the stars are fellow inmates in a prison-house,
so that the poem moves, by implication, from the immediate, lyrical moment toward a larger statement about the
nature of the universe.

Like the stars, the persona is strapped in, but paradoxically, since she remarks the lack of sign posts as if she
were able to move like "the dark" itself:

They lock me in this chair at eight a.m.
and there are no signs to tell the way,
just the radio beating to itself
and the song that remembers
more than I. Oh la la la,
this music swims back to me.
The night I came I danced in a circle
and was not afraid.
Mister?

Paradise is lost here too, even though there is irony in the lost circle of dancing confidence where she may have felt preserved like the Old Testament prophets in a circle of flames or like anyone in any magic circle anywhere.

Another ironic paradise lost is evoked in "The Bells," where again sound stirs the memory and where the circle in "Music Swims Back to Me" becomes "three rings of danger":

> Today the circus poster
> is scabbing off the concrete wall
> and the children have forgotten
> if they knew at all.
> Father, do you remember?
> Only the sound remains,
> the distant thump of the good elephants,
> the voice of the ancient lions
> and how the bells
> trembled for the flying man.
> I, laughing,
> lifted to your high shoulder
> or small at the rough legs of strangers,
> was not afraid.
> You held my hand
> and were instant to explain
> the three rings of danger.

There is no narcissism here, only the knowledge of the serpent in paradise, whose wounding nature is made evident by means of the circus poster that is "scabbing off"—still scabbing off the hurt place which is referred to ironically as a "concrete wall." Here, as in "Music Swims Back to Me," the persona "was not afraid"—a phrase that is terrifying in context, since it is perfectly clear that there is in both situations a great deal to fear: in "Music Swims" the fear is of vertigo, restraint, and loss of self; in "The Bells" the fear is of the father's courtship, which is tabu, and which also produces restraint, as the metaphorical paralysis of "Where I Live in This Honorable House of the Laurel Tree" makes plain.

The courtship, and the response to it, is one of the most vivid infernal events in the volume:

> Oh see the naughty clown
> and the wild parade
> while love love
> love grew rings around me.
> This was the sound where it began;
> our breath pounding up to see
> the flying man breast out
> across the boarded sky
> and climb the air.
> I remember the color of music
> and how forever
> all the trembling bells of you
> were mine.

The word choice is designed to understate the elements of the *liebestod* experience that were seen so plain in "The Moss of His Skin," which, by the way, has a kind of tactile association with "the rough legs of strangers"; the reason behind the understatement is the awareness that for children experience has to be toned down in order to be acceptable to the adult world. Thus sin becomes only "naughty" in this poem, and is furthermore projected onto the other, the clown; and the "three rings of danger" which clearly refer to "love love/ love" which "grew rings around me" can be simply the literal circus rings. The divine lover, identified in "Where I Live" as Apollo, is here reduced to the childlike "flying man"—another instance of substituting one image for another: here it is a matter of displacing the divine, or tabu, attribute of the father onto the trapeze artist—and even the need for the mother is timidly expressed in a verb as the flying man is seen to "breast out across the boarded sky" so that the undifferentiated, or hermaphroditic, love object, left over from childhood, is only vaguely indicated, as it is in dreams.

The excitement and suspense (and fear) shared with the father take on an erotic color at the point where the two have only one breath: "our breath pounding up to see"; and it is preparatory to this moment of climax that the perception becomes synesthetic, as music becomes a place—"This was the sound where it began"—and then afterward becomes visual—"I remember the color of music." The equation of the flying man, or divine lover, with the father is firmly established at the conclusion, which reverts to the image of "the bells" that "trembled for the flying man" and which makes the bells the father in liquid consonants and murmuring alliteration that evoke the sense of touch: "all the trembling bells of you/ were mine."

The bells recur in "Said the Poet to the Analyst":

My business is words. Words are like labels,
or coins, or better, like swarming bees.
I confess I am only broken by the sources of things;
as if words were counted like dead bees in the attic,
unbuckled from their yellow eyes and their dry
  wings.
I must always forget how one word is able to pick
out another, to manner another, until I have got
something I might have said . . .
but did not.

Your business is watching my words. But I
admit nothing. I work with my best, for instance,
when I can write my praise for a nickel machine,
that one night in Nevada: telling how the magic
 jackpot
came clacking three bells out, over the lucky
 screen.
But if you should say this is something it is not,
then I grow weak, remembering how my hands
 felt funny
and ridiculous and crowded with all
the believing money.

Two major preoccupations—truth and the father—come together here when the persona, after saying flatly that "I/ admit nothing," does make an admission in her memory of "how my hands felt funny/ and ridiculous and crowded with all/ the believing money." The admission appears to be that the money is the father's love, since it is the result of hitting the jackpot with "three bells." The technique of substitution is at work again here, in the displacement of the attitude of "believing," in the sense of "credulous," from the persona to the money itself, a displacement that operates to strengthen the association of the money with the father's love by suggesting that this literal paternal love believed itself innocent. The displacement also permits the persona to draw back from her own credulousness, to disavow it, as if to say that she had known all along what the analyst had said about her narrative, "that this is something it is not."

The first stanza of the poem prepares the way for the second, in the admission that "Words are like labels,/ or coins," and in the afterthought that a better simile is "bees" which have been "unbuckled" from everything that gave them life in general and from their seeing eyes in particular. There is life behind words too, or separate from them, which the words cannot always see; and in the second stanza there is the knowledge that there is life behind or separate from things and events, life that words, things, events, can only "pick out" or "manner." The limitations of poetry here are almost as strong as they are in "Portrait of an Old Woman on the College Tavern Wall."

The image of the bees recalls the first poem in this volume, "You, Doctor Martin," where a mental hospital is referred to as a "summer hotel":

> You, Doctor Martin, walk
> from breakfast to madness. Late August,
> I speed through the antiseptic tunnel
> where the moving dead still talk
> of pushing their bones against the thrust
> of cure. And I am queen of this summer hotel
> or the laughing bee on a stalk
>
> of death. We stand in broken
> lines and wait while they unlock
> the door and count us at the frozen gates
> of dinner. The shibboleth is spoken
> and we move to gravy in our smock
> of smiles. We chew in rows, our plates
> scratch and whine like chalk
>
> in school. There are no knives
> for cutting your throat . . .

Again the bee is an alternate image, a second thought, chosen perhaps because it can sting like words or like a fatal woman; and it leads to the first of a series of chilling anticlimaxes in the poem. Following the Dantean image of the dead who do not know they are in hell, an image expressed in sexual terms, the "laughing bee on a stalk" suggests pollination, but this expectation is sharply defeated in the next stanza by the qualifying words, "of death," until you recognize that what is given here is another form of the *liebestod*. If there is any doubt that this "summer hotel" is really hell itself, it is dispelled "while they unlock/ the door and count us at the frozen gates"; but again an anticlimax is presented, this time to insist on the ordinariness of hell: the "frozen gates" open only to "dinner." Juxtaposed with the childhood reference to "school," the statement that "There are no knives" is not surprising until you get to the coda: "for cutting your throat."

Various images from childhood pattern through this poem: besides "chalk" and "school" there is "our smock," and in a subsequent stanza the persona remarks, "What large children we are/ here," in the same way that she later observes in "Music Swims Back to Me" that there are in the room with her "four ladies, over eighty,/ in diapers every one of them." The mood of infantile regression among the patients is conveyed not only through such explicit images, however; the rhyme scheme is designed to resemble the repetition of the abc's

To Bedlam and Part Way Back is not wholly separated from Anne Sexton's second volume, *All My Pretty Ones*. For one thing, both the title and the epigraph to the second volume celebrate mourning; and part two of *To Bedlam and Part Way Back,* consisting of "For John, Who Begs Me Not to Enquire Further," "The Double Image," and "The Division of Parts," is a kind of bridge, between the controlling theme of the first volume as expressed in its epigraph and in "For John," and the controlling theme of the second volume, as set out in its epigraph, a quotation from a letter of Franz Kafka to Oskar Pollak:

> . . . the books we need are the kind that act upon us
> like a misfortune, that make us suffer like the death
> of someone we love more than ourselves, that make
> us feel as though we were on the verge of suicide, or
> lost in a forest remote from all human habitation—
> a book should serve as the ax for the frozen sea within
> us.

In the first volume, immediately following the *apologia* of
"For John, Who Begs Me Not to Enquire Further,"
mourning begins freely with "The Double Image," a long
poem in five sections which attempts to get behind words
to the life they represent. Addressed to her second daughter, Joyce, who is now seven, these stanzas set out the
essential counters for the grave game of being a woman.
The fearful inquiry that has been conducted in the volume up to this point now picks up the vague suggestions
of the mother that have appeared thus far and turns the
whole flood of its light upon her. The poem reads like a
personal history; its title, "The Double Image," is ostensibly concerned with a pair of portraits hanging in the
family home—one of the persona, the other of her
mother:

> In north light, my smile is held in place,
> the shadow marks my bone.
> What could I have been dreaming as I sat there,
> all of me waiting in the eyes, the zone
> of the smile, the young face,
> the foxes' snare.

> In south light, her smile is held in place,
> her cheeks wilting like a dry

orchid; my mocking mirror, my overthrown
love, my first image . . .
   . . . .
The artist caught us at the turning;
we smiled in our canvas home
before we chose our foreknown separate ways.

It is the mother who is being mourned here; the poem is written after her death:

You call me *mother* and I remember my mother again,
somewhere in greater Boston, dying.

But the object of mourning is not so simple as that; the mother is after all "my mocking mirror," and in *All My Pretty Ones* there is a poem called "The Housewife" which ends with the statement that

A woman *is* her mother.
That's the main thing.

The mourning then is not only for the mother, but for the self as well, that self "who chose two times/ to kill myself." John Holmes's angry criticism of this poem before publication may have been in response to the narcissism which does break through, not only in the mirror imagery but also in the form of this strange mourning for the self. In advance of her own death she foresees it in the mother's "cheeks wilting like a dry/ orchid; my mocking mirror." It is as if she were psychically dead and believed like Guido da Montefeltro that no one could return from hell to judge her. In a sense she is right, of course, since no one who makes the descent with this poem can say that he has seen someone else's damnation and not his own.

"The Double Image" refers not only to the two portraits, to

> . . . the cave of the mirror,
> that double woman who stares
> at herself,

but also to the double woman whose other part is her daughter. The mother's portrait is

> A cave of a mirror
> placed on the south wall;
> matching smile, matching contour.
> And you resembled me; unacquainted
> with my face, you wore it.

The double image is really a triple image, made up of the persona, the mother, and the daughter; the triptych becomes visible at the end of the poem:

> . . . I didn't want a boy,
> only a girl, a small milky mouse
> of a girl, already loved, already loud in the house
> of herself. We named you Joy.
> I, who was never quite sure
> about being a girl, needed another
> life, another image to remind me.
> And this was my worst guilt; you could not cure
> nor soothe it. I made you to find me.

The ending, unlike the endings of the other poems, seems to be its weakest part, perhaps because it is a

"believing" confession that intends to disarm the charge
of narcissism while it tells only half the truth. Much
more immediately valid is the account of the circumstances that led to the first suicide attempt:

> I . . .
> . . . had said your nickname
> the mewling months when you first came;
> until a fever rattled
> in your throat and I moved like a pantomime
> above your head. Ugly angels spoke to me. The
> blame,
> I heard them say, was mine. They tattled
> like green witches in my head, letting doom
> leak like a broken faucet;
> as if doom had flooded my belly and filled your
> bassinet,
> an old debt I must assume.

This sounds like the truth the Greeks knew; it rattles the
chain that binds the feelings for the mother to the feelings for the infant daughter, for one thing. And for
another, it brings up, in the penultimate line, the possibility that a woman, like Leda, whose belly is flooded by
a divine lover, may be responsible for unanticipated disasters.

The same kind of truth, historical or not, creates two
statements about the mother:

> On the first of September she looked at me
> and said I gave her cancer.
> They carved her sweet hills out
> and still I couldn't answer.

On the other peak of the *liebestod* triangle is the mother, the "overthrown/ love" of an earlier stanza in two senses: the ambiguity brings together the mother as "first image" or first love, "overthrown" by subsequent love for the father, and also the mother as discard, as also-ran, usurped, "overthrown" by the persona in rivalry for the father. The sense of victory over the mother is expressed also in another poem, still uncollected, called "Consorting With Angels":

> There were still men who sat at my table,
> circled around the bowl I offered up.
> The bowl was filled with purple grapes
> and the flies hovered in for the scent
> and even my father came with his white bone.

It is this kind of knowledge that makes her say "I couldn't answer." Given the remark that "a woman *is* her mother" and the admission to Joyce that "I made you to find me," it is fairly clear that "The Double Image" repeats the tension in "For John," but in a new way. Now there are again two faces, and the "mocking mirror" of "The Double Image" is like the "cracked mirror" of "For John"; it reflects two aspects of the persona, but this time they are the persona as mother and as daughter. Seen in the light of this poem, the tension between the inner Oedipus and the inner Jocasta in "For John" looks like an elaboration of what appear to be the essentially undramatic conflicts that underlie "The Double Image."

This poem clarifies the volume's controlling theme, which is the hesitation between the truth and the lie; it is always the mother who is the censor, wherever she may appear, whether in "The Double Image," in "For John," in "The Moss of His Skin," or in the reference to Jocasta in the epigraph.

But the poem also looks forward, in its mourning, to the theme of the second volume; and the anticipation reaches a crescendo in the last poem in *To Bedlam and Part Way Back.* Called "The Division of Parts," this poem continues to mourn, but from beneath a surface of feeling failure that recalls the erotic paralysis of "Where I Live in This Honorable House of the Laurel Tree." Unlike Hamlet, who probably protested too much as he leaped into Ophelia's grave, the persona here acknowledges her material inheritance with discomfort and proclaims that

> . . . Time, that rearranger
> of estates, equips
> me with your garments, but not with grief.

And yet the title of the second volume is *All My Pretty Ones,* the quotation from *Macbeth* amplified on the title page into the fuller speech of Macduff:

> All my pretty ones?
> Did you say all? O hell-kite! All?
> What! all my pretty chickens and their dam
> At one fell swoop? . . .
> I cannot but remember such things were,
> That were most precious to me.

What is not reproduced on the title page is Macduff's conclusion that

> . . . Sinful Macduff,
> They were all struck for thee. Naught that I am,
> Not for their own demerits, but for mine,
> Fell slaughter on their souls,

a conclusion that very likely impels the defensive protes-
tations of lack of sentiment in "The Division of Parts"
where, in a context of Easter imagery, the persona announces that

> . . . I have cast my lot
> and am one third thief
> of you,

as she acknowledges herself to be

> . . . one third
> of your daughters counting my bounty
> or I am a queen alone
> in the parlor still,
> eating the bread and honey.

Here again is the bee, although it is submerged in the
choice of the word "honey"; and again it is an alternate
choice, a second thought, as it was in "You, Doctor
Martin," in "Music Swims Back to Me," and in "Said the
Poet to the Analyst," so that it seems to be the result of
further attempts to get behind words to life. What feelings the persona has that "Not for their own demerits,
but for mine" her dead lie dead, appear to refer to an
awareness of this role of "queen alone," like "a laughing
bee upon a stalk/ of death." The bread and honey are
poisonous because whoever kills a rival must die.

All My Pretty Ones begins with the first knowledge
brought back from the descent into hell, in a poem called
"The Truth the Dead Know," which recalls "Dover
Beach." It is headed by a dedication:

> For my mother, born March 1902, died March 1959
> and my father, born February 1900, died June 1959.

Like the concluding poem of *To Bedlam and Part Way Back*, it is ostensibly a refusal to mourn; what it seizes instead of grief is the day of physical love:

> Gone, I say and walk from church,
> refusing the stiff procession to the grave,
> letting the dead ride alone in the hearse.
> It is June. I am tired of being brave.
>
> We drive to the Cape. I cultivate
> myself where the sun gutters from the sky,
> where the sea swings in like an iron gate
> and we touch. In another country people die.
>
> My darling, the wind falls in like stones
> from the whitehearted water and when we touch
> we enter touch entirely. No one's alone.
> Men kill for this, or for as much.
>
> And what of the dead? They lie without shoes
> in their stone boats. They are more like stone
> than the sea would be if it stopped. They refuse
> to be blessed, throat, eye and knucklebone.

But here again responsibility for death, although it is explicitly denied, is implicit in the line "In another country people die"; the overtones that Browning, Eliot, and Hemingway have given to the fairly neutral Marlowe original of this notion ring loud in the poem, especially as the line follows immediately another literary allusion— the simile of the "iron gate," which refers directly to Marvell's "iron gates of life" in "To His Coy Mistress," another poem about the value of love in the face of death. As in Marvell, however, the overriding emphasis is on the confrontation of death, which alone gives love whatever value it has. The elements of the *liebestod* experience are shifted about here; death is now not effect but cause.

"The Truth the Dead Know" is nothingness, annihilation, refusal "to be blessed"; and it is repeated in several poems in *All My Pretty Ones*. The short poem "Young" ends

> as the crickets ticked together
> and I, in my brand new body,
> which was not a woman's yet,
> told the stars my questions
> and thought God could really see
> the heat and the painted light,
> elbows, knees, dreams, good night.

And "The Fortress," a long poem addressed to the poet's elder daughter, Linda, observes that

> We laugh and we touch.
> I promise you love. Time will not take away that,

echoing "The Double Image," addressed to Joyce, which also fastens onto the day, in lieu of anything further:

> . . . I say today believed
> in itself, or else it fell.

> Today, my small child, Joyce,
> love your self's self where it lives.
> There is no special God to refer to.

"From the Garden" expresses the same theme, simply, like Wordsworth's "The Tables Turned":

> Come, my beloved,
> consider the lilies.
> We are of little faith.
> We talk too much.
> Put your mouthful of words away
> and come with me to watch
> the lilies open in such a field,
> growing there like yachts,
> slowly steering their petals
> without nurses or clocks.
> Let us consider the view:
> a house where white clouds
> decorate the muddy halls.
> Oh, put away your good words
> and your bad words. Spit out
> your words like stones!
> Come here! Come here!
> Come eat my pleasant fruits.

There are several attempts in *All My Pretty Ones* to get beyond the day to a robust religious experience, but they all end either by emphasizing, as a Rouault painting does, the terrible ordinariness of Christ's suffering on the cross, or by invoking a daydream miracle so fanciful as to deny entirely the possibility of mystery. Part two of this volume has its own epigraph:

> I want no pallid humanitarianism—If Christ
> be not God, I want none of him; I will hack
> my way through existence alone . . .
>
> Guardini.

Two crucifixions appear in this section. The first, "For God While Sleeping," is a lament in which the first stanza expresses nostalgia for the absolute at the same time that it denies its possibility:

> Sleeping in fever, I am unfit
> to know just who you are:
> hung up like a pig on exhibit,
> the delicate wrists,
> the beard drooling with vinegar;
> hooked to your own weight,
> jolting toward death under your nameplate.

The second crucifixion, "In the Deep Museum," is a dramatic monologue, beginning with the first awareness of imminent resurrection, in which again the commonplace nature of extreme suffering is emphasized:

> My God, my God, what queer corner am I in?
> Didn't I die, blood running down the post,
> lungs gagging for air, die there for the sin
> of anyone, my sour mouth giving up the ghost?
> Surely my body is done? Surely I died?
> And yet, I know I'm here. What place is this?
> Cold and queer, I sting with life. I lied.
> Yes I lied. Or else in some damned cowardice
> my body would not give me up. I touch
> fine cloths with my hands and my cheeks are cold.
> If this is hell, then hell could not be much,
> neither as special nor as ugly as I was told.

Put beside "You, Doctor Martin," this poem illustrates brilliantly the poetic possibility that the metaphors of the

madhouse and the crucifixion are interchangeable repre-
sentations of hell; and put beside "The Double Image," it
demonstrates also that abortive suicide and resurrection
are imaginative experiences that spring from the same
emotional root.

In part five of *All My Pretty Ones*, in "Letter Written
on a Ferry While Crossing Long Island Sound,"

> The sea is the face of Mary,
> without miracles or rage
> or unusual hope,
> grown rough and wrinkled
> with incurable age.

Longing for miracle, the persona observes four nuns and
asks,

> Oh God,
> although I am very sad,
> could you please
> let these four nuns
> loosen from their leather boots
> and their wooden chairs
> to rise out
> over this greasy deck,
> out over this iron rail,
> nodding their pink heads to one side,
> flying four abreast
> in the old-fashioned side stroke;
> each mouth open and round,
> breathing together
> as fish do,
> singing without sound.

And improbably, the nuns sail forth as in a two-dimensional pre-Renaissance Italian painting and

> They call back to us
> from the gauzy edge of paradise,
> *good news, good news.*

The only real miracle in the poetry, however, is the Christ-like immortality of parents, their reincarnation in the spirit and flesh of their offspring. In a poem that gives its title to the volume, "All My Pretty Ones," and is addressed to the dead father, the persona observes:

> I hold a five-year diary that my mother kept
> for three years, telling all she does not say
> of your alcoholic tendency. You overslept,
> she writes. My God, father, each Christmas day
> with your blood, will I drink down your glass
> of wine?

Mother, father, and aborted child pay supernatural visits in a short poem called "Ghosts"; and in "Old Dwarf Heart" the mother and father appear again. The epigraph to this poem is a tribute to Saul Bellow, a quotation from *Henderson the Rain King*:

> True. All too true. I have never been at home in
> life. All my decay has taken place upon a child.

Recalling the erotic paralysis of "Where I Live in This Honorable House of the Laurel Tree," the first stanza picks up the same theme and begins amplification:

When I lie down to love,
old dwarf heart shakes her head.
Like an imbecile she was born old.
Her eyes wobble as thirty-one thick folds
of skin open to glare at me on my flickering bed.
She knows the decay we're made of.

"Old Dwarf Heart" is the buried self, the recalcitrant child upon whom decay has taken place; "thirty-one thick folds" refer not only to the obvious erotic image but also to the age of this persistent child who,

. . . At her best
. . . is all red muscle, humming in and out, cajoled
by time. Where I go, she goes.

Reincarnation is explicitly given at the end of the poem:

. . . Old ornament, old naked fist,
even if I put on seventy coats I could not cover
you . . .
mother, father, I'm made of.

The last poem in *All My Pretty Ones* is written in the form of a journal addressed to "Dearest"; it begins with a reference to the dead:

It is snowing, grotesquely snowing,
upon the small faces of the dead.
Those dear loudmouths, gone for over a year,
buried side by side
like little wrens.

Appropriately, this final poem picks up the major themes of the volume: mourning, the attempt to reach consolation through religion and through love, and the mystery of family relationships that are as durable as a life after death, their consequences in the individual felt as the effect of doom or of contagion. The first volume is echoed here too, as it has been in many other places; the "stone tree" of "The Moss of His Skin" appears here compared to a crucifix:

> Only the tree has quietness in it;
> quiet as the crucifix,
> pounded out years ago
> like a handmade shoe.

Predestined pain is in that simile; the inferno of these poems is an ancient place, older and truer than any "gauzy edge of paradise." And the possibility of paradise is made to appear weak indeed, in a stanza where it is referred to in an anticlimax that is heavily outweighed by what goes before it:

> Just yesterday,
> twenty-eight men aboard a damaged radar tower
> foundered down seventy miles off the coast.
> Immediately their hearts slammed shut.
> The storm would not cough them up.
> Today they are whispering over Sonar.
> Small voice,
> what do you say?
> Aside from going down, the awful wrench,
> the pulleys and hooks and the black tongue . . .
> What are your headquarters?
> Are they kind?

The tree, however, is not only doom as represented by the ancestor; it is also poetry, as it was in "Where I Live in This Honorable House of the Laurel Tree," "quiet as the crucifix"—we return here to the cold pastoral, the death-in-life of poetry— "pounded out years ago/ like a hand-made shoe." The reference to craft and the reference to antiquity both suggest poetry as a kind of Yeatsean continuum, a witch's kitchen like the kitchens in "Portrait of an Old Woman on the College Tavern Wall" and in "For John, Who Begs Me Not to Enquire Further."

The poem ends, as the volume does, with another *double-entendre* that expresses, as it does in "In the Deep Museum," both nostalgia for and denial of absolute love:

> Dearest,
> where are your letters?
> The mailman is an impostor.
> He is actually my grandfather.
> He floats far off in the storm
> with his nicotine mustache and a bagful of nickels.
> His legs stumble through
> baskets of eyelashes.
> Like all the dead
> he picks up his disguise,
> shakes it off and slowly pulls down the shade,
> fading out like an old movie.
> Now he is gone
> as you are gone.
> But he belongs to me like lost baggage.

So much for hope; but fear remains. Older than the mother and the father, the ancestor here is "actually my grandfather"; and if he has carried off with him the promise of "a bagful of nickels" (to feed the slot machine with the hope of ringing up three bells?), he has not been able to break the chain of contagion that binds the generations. The luggage may be lost, but the persona still holds the check; and hanging around her neck are all the keys.

NOTE

* All quotations from the poetry of Anne Sexton, with the exception of "Consorting With Angels," which appeared in the *Carleton Miscellany*, © Spring, 1963, are taken as indicated in the text from *To Bedlam and Part Way Back* © Houghton Mifflin 1960) and *All My Pretty Ones* (© Houghton Mifflin 1962), with the permission of the poet and of Houghton Mifflin Company.

NOTES
ON THE
CONTRIBUTORS

ALICE N. BENSTON

was born in New York City and attended Queens College. She was married in 1951, while still an undergraduate, and later, because of her husband's service in the Navy, moved to Atlanta, Georgia, where she began her graduate studies at Emory University. She completed her doctorate there in 1962. Mrs. Benston has taught at Northwestern and the University of Chicago and is presently Assistant Professor in the Humanities at the University of Rochester, where her husband also is teaching. She has published on topics having to do with naturalism in the drama.

FREDERIC E. FAVERTY

was Chairman of the Department of English from 1945–58 and is presently the Morrison Professor of English Literature at Northwestern. Born in Chester, Illinois, he studied at Washington University, Western Reserve, and received his graduate degrees at Harvard. He has published critical and scholarly articles and has performed a diversity of services, editorial and bibliographical, for the learned journals and societies in his field of Victorian literature. His *Matthew Arnold the Ethnologist* was published in 1951. In 1958 his *Our Literary Heritage* reprinted his appraisals—some seventy in number—of the most famous men of letters from Homer to our time. These essays had appeared from week to week in the Chicago *Tribune's* "Magazine of Books."

BEVERLY FIELDS

is an Assistant Professor of English at the University of Illinois at Chicago Circle. A native Chicagoan, she has her M.A. and Ph.D. from Northwestern and Lake Forest College. Her book on Coleridge will be published this summer by Kent State University Press. Mrs. Fields was married in 1940, and she and her husband make their home in Evanston. They have two daughters.

YOHMA GRAY

was born in Jamestown, New York, went to school there, and grew up in the beautiful lake country near the old village of Chautauqua. She attended Syracuse University, and has taken both her advanced degrees at Yale (M.A., 1959, Ph.D., 1967), writing on the novels of Richard Wright. She first taught at Northwestern in 1960 and is presently Associate Professor of English at Mundelein College.

JEAN H. HAGSTRUM

Professor of English at Northwestern, was born in St. Paul, Minnesota, and attended the University of Minnesota. His graduate work was at Yale, where he received his Ph.D. degree in 1941 after he had already taught at Northwestern for a year. He served with the civilian Office of Censorship from 1942–44, and as an Army infantry rifleman in Italy from 1944–46. He was again in Italy, 1953–54, as a Fulbright research fellow. His *Samuel Johnson's Literary Criticism* was published in 1952, *The Sister Arts*, a study of the relation of poetry and the visual arts, in 1958, and his *William Blake, Poet and Painter*, in 1964. The latter received the Melville Cane Award of the Poetry Society of America for 1965.

Mr. Hagstrum served as Chairman of the Department of English at Northwestern from 1958 to 1964, and spent the following year in France as President's Fellow from the University.

ROBERT D. HARVEY

was born in Evanston, Illinois, and, after two years' service during World War II in the United States Army Signal Corps, was graduated from Northwestern in 1948. He received both his M.A. and Ph.D. degrees from the University of Chicago, and is presently Professor of English at the University of Nevada. Apprentice teaching was at Valparaiso University, and the University College of the University of Chicago; returning as an instructor to Northwestern, he later taught at the University of California. He has published on Lincoln Steffens, and wrote his dissertation on the "muckraking" journalists.

RALPH J. MILLS, JR.

a native Chicagoan, graduated from Lake Forest College in 1954, received his M.A. from Northwestern in 1956, studied at Oxford on an English Speaking Union fellowship, then returned to teach at Northwestern. He completed his Ph.D. degree there in 1963, taught at the University of Chicago as a member of the Committee on Social Thought, and is presently an Associate Professor at the Chicago Circle of the University of Illinois. The University of Minnesota Press published his *Theodore Roethke* in 1963 and his *Richard Eberhart* in 1966. Other books are *Contemporary American Poetry*, Random House, 1965, and an edition of the selected prose of Roethke, *On the Poet and His Craft*, Random House, 1965. He is at work on an edition of Roethke's letters.

GROSVENOR POWELL

was born in Corregidor in the Philippines, the son of an Army officer stationed there. His schooling, as a result of frequent Army transfers, was scattered through Texas, Massachusetts, California, and Maryland. He received his undergraduate degree at the University of Maryland in 1954, and his M.A. and Ph.D. at Stanford University, the latter in 1965. He wrote his doctoral dissertation on "Romantic Mysticism and the Poetry of Wallace Stevens." He is Assistant Professor at the University of British Columbia, presently on leave as American *lektor* at the University of Stockholm. He has worked with the Swedish International Development Authority training volunteers who were sent to Ethiopia and Zambia.

WALTER B. RIDEOUT
is Professor of English and Chairman of the Department of English at the University of Wisconsin. For thirteen years, 1949–1962, he taught at Northwestern. He was born at Lee, Maine, educated at Colby College (A.B., 1939, Ph.D., 1950). Among his published works are *Letters of Sherwood Anderson,* 1953, in which he was associate editor with Howard Mumford Jones; *The Radical Novel in the United States, 1900–1954,* 1956; *A College Book of Verse,* 1958, with James K. Robinson; *A College Book of Modern Fiction,* 1961, also with Robinson; and, with Robinson and Gay Wilson Allen, *American Poetry,* 1965. He is at work upon a life of Sherwood Anderson.

HUGH B. STAPLES
was born and raised near Boston, educated at Andover and Harvard, and served as an Army Intelligence officer in World War II. He received his Ph.D. from the University of California (Berkeley) in 1954, and has taught at Northwestern and the University of California (Davis). In 1966 he became Director of Graduate Studies in English at the University of Cincinnati. He is the author of *Robert Lowell: The First Twenty Years,* and has written on Roethke, Sillitoe, and Joyce. His critical edition of

Personal Sketches of His Own Times by Sir Jonah Barrington is to be published by the University of Washington Press.

PETER L. THORSLEV, JR.

was born in Iowa, received his early education in Canada, and was graduated from Dana College, Nebraska, in 1950. After three years of Army service in this country and overseas he took his graduate degrees (M.A., 1957, Ph.D., 1959) at the University of Minnesota, where he was Shevlin Fellow in Arts (1956–57) and taught as an instructor for two years. He taught at Northwestern 1959–1960 and is now Associate Professor of English at the University of California at Los Angeles. His *The Byronic Hero* was published by the University of Minnesota Press in 1962, he has contributed to various journals on subjects connected with Romanticism, and is now, through a grant from the Guggenheim Foundation, writing a book on freedom and destiny in Romanticism.

DONALD T. TORCHIANA

was born in Philadelphia, left college at the age of nineteen to serve in the U.S. Army Air Force. Stationed in England from 1944 to the end of World War II, he flew missions over Germany as B-17 pilot with the 8th Air Force. He was graduated from De Pauw University in 1947, and received his advanced degrees (M.A., 1949, Ph.D., 1953) at the State University of Iowa. He came to Northwestern in 1953, and is presently an Associate Professor. For two years, 1960–62, he was on leave from the University to teach at University College, Galway, Ireland. His *W. B. Yeats and Georgian Ireland* appeared in 1966, and he is now at work on a book dealing with the intellectual background of Yeats.

BIBLIOGRAPHY

This selected list contains the titles of volumes of verse by the poets. A few other relevant titles are named, but poems by them printed in periodicals are not included, nor are the names of their novels, short stories, or other prose works, critical or scholarly.

(In the present reprint, bibliographies have not been extended beyond the titles available at the time the Prefaces were completed.)

CUNNINGHAM, JAMES VINCENT

The Helmsman. San Francisco: The Colt Press, 1942. (For Cunningham's commentary on *The Helmsman* See his *The Quest of the Opal,* Denver: Alan Swallow, 1950.)

The Judge is Fury. New York: The Swallow Press and William Morrow and Company, 1947.

Doctor Drink. Cummington, Massachusetts: The Cummington Press, 1950.

The Exclusions of a Rhyme; Poems and Epigrams. Denver: Alan Swallow, 1960.

(Trivial, Vulgar, and Exalted was not separately published, but first appeared in *The Exclusions of a Rhyme.)*

EBERHART, RICHARD

A Bravery of Earth. London: Jonathan Cape, Ltd., 1930; New York: Jonathan Cape and H. Smith, 1930.

Reading the Spirit. London: Chatto and Windus, Ltd., 1936; New York: Oxford University Press, 1937.

Song and Idea. London: Chatto and Windus, Ltd., 1940; New York, Oxford University Press, 1942.

Poems, New and Selected. Norfolk, Connecticut: New Directions, 1944.

Burr Oaks. London: Chatto and Windus, Ltd., 1947; New York: Oxford University Press, 1947.

Brotherhood of Man. Pawlet, Vermont: Banyan Press, 1949.

An Herb Basket. Cummington, Massachusetts: The Cummington Press, 1950.

Selected Poems. London: Chatto and Windus, Ltd., 1951; New York: Oxford University Press, 1951.

Undercliff: Poems, 1946–1953. London: Chatto and Windus, Ltd., 1953; New York: Oxford University Press, 1953, 1954.

"The Visionary Farms" (verse drama), in *New World Writing,* III. New York: New American Library, 1953.

Great Praises. London: Chatto and Windus, Ltd., 1957; New York: Oxford University Press, 1957.

Collected Poems, 1930–1960. London: Chatto and Windus, Ltd., 1960; New York, Oxford University Press, 1960.

JARRELL, RANDALL

Blood for a Stranger. New York: Harcourt, Brace, and Company, 1942.

Little Friend, Little Friend. New York: Dial Press, Inc., 1945.

Losses. New York: Harcourt, Brace and Company, 1948.

The Seven-League Crutches. New York: Harcourt, Brace and Company, 1951.

Selected Poems. New York: Alfred A. Knopf, Inc., 1955; London: Faber and Faber, 1956.

The Woman at the Washington Zoo: Poems and Translations. New York: Atheneum Publishers, 1960.

(Jarrell's *Poetry and the Age,* New York, Alfred A. Knopf, 1953, is a volume of essays of interest to readers of Jarrell's own poetry. A useful bibliography of Jarrell is Charles Marshall Adams' *Randall Jarrell, a Bibliography,* Chapel Hill, University of North Carolina Press, 1958.)

KUNITZ, STANLEY J.

Intellectual Things. Garden City, New York: Doubleday, Doran and Company, 1930.

Passport to the War. New York: Henry Holt and Company, Inc., 1944.

Selected Poems, 1928–1958. An Atlantic Monthly Press
Book. Boston and Toronto: Little, Brown and Company, 1958.

LEVERTOV, DENISE

The Double Image. London: Cresset Press, 1946.

Here and Now. San Francisco: City Lights Books, 1957.

Overland to the Islands. Highlands, North Carolina:
Jonathan Williams, 1958.

With Eyes at the Back of Our Heads. New York: New
Directions, 1959.

The Jacob's Ladder. New York: New Directions, 1961.

O Taste and See. New York: New Directions, 1964.

LOWELL, ROBERT

Land of Unlikeness. Introduction by Allen Tate. Cummington, Massachusetts: The Cummington Press,
1944.

Lord Weary's Castle. New York: Harcourt, Brace and
World, Inc., 1944, 1946.

Poems: 1938–1949. London: Faber and Faber, Ltd.,
1950.

The Mills of the Kavanaughs. New York: Harcourt,
Brace and Company, 1951.

Life Studies. London: Faber and Faber, Ltd., 1959; New
York: Farrar, Straus and Cudahy, Inc., 1959.

Phaedra and Figaro. (A verse translation of Racine's
Phèdre by Robert Lowell, and Beaumarchais's *Le
Mariage de Figaro* translated by Jacques Barzun.)
New York: Farrar, Straus and Cudahy, Inc., 1961.

Imitations. (Free adaptations of various European poets.)
New York: Farrar, Straus and Cudahy, Inc., 1961.

("91 Revere Street," *Partisan Review*, XXIII, Fall 1956, 445–477, is an important autobiographical prose essay by Lowell. It is reprinted, with a few revisions, in the American edition of *Life Studies*. "Robert Lowell," an interview with Frederick Seidel, *Paris Review*, XXV, Winter-Spring 1961, 57–95, is a valuable biographical article. Hugh Staples's "Robert Lowell: Bibliography 1939–1959, with an Illustrative Critique," *Harvard Library Bulletin*, XIII, Spring 1959, 292–318, will be reprinted in a revised and expanded form in his *Robert Lowell: The First Twenty Years*, to be published early in 1962 by Faber and Faber and by Farrar, Straus and Cudahy.)

MERWIN, WILLIAM STANLEY

A Mask for Janus, with a foreword by W. H. Auden. Yale Series of Younger Poets. New Haven: Yale University Press, 1952; and London: Oxford University Press, 1952.

The Dancing Bears. New Haven: Yale University Press, 1954; Toronto: Burns and MacEachern, 1954.

Green with Beasts. New York: Alfred A. Knopf, Inc., 1956; London: Rupert Hart-Davis, Ltd., 1956.

Poem of the Cid (El Poema de Mio Cid); a verse translation. Toronto: J. M. Dent and Sons, Ltd., 1959.

The Drunk in the Furnace. New York: The Macmillan Company, 1960; London: Rupert Hart-Davis, Ltd., 1960.

NEMEROV, HOWARD

The Image and the Law. New York: Henry Holt and Company, Inc., 1947.

Guide to the Ruins. New York: Random House, Inc., 1950.

The Salt Garden. Boston: Little, Brown and Company, 1955.

Mirrors & Windows. Chicago: University of Chicago Press, 1958.

New and Selected Poems. Chicago: University of Chicago Press, 1960.

ROETHKE, THEODORE
Open House. New York: Alfred A. Knopf, Inc., 1941.
The Lost Son, and Other Poems. Garden City, New York: Doubleday and Company, 1948.
Praise to the End! Garden City, New York: Doubleday and Company, 1951.
The Waking; Poems, 1933–1953. Garden City, New York: Doubleday and Company, 1953.
Words for the Wind. London: Secker and Warburg, 1957; Garden City, New York: Doubleday and Company, 1958; Bloomington, Indiana: Indiana University Press, 1961 (a paperback edition).
I Am! Says the Lamb. Garden City, New York: Doubleday and Company, 1961.

(*Twentieth Century Authors*, First Supplement, edited by Stanley Kunitz, 1955, contains an autobiographical letter by Roethke; and a statement by the poet about his own work is included with a selection of Roethke's poetry in John Ciardi's *Mid-Century American Poets*, 1950. Roethke's "Some Remarks on Rhythm" appeared in *Poetry Magazine*, 97, I, October 1960, pp. 35–46.)

SEXTON, ANNE
To Bedlam and Part Way Back. Boston: Houghton Mifflin Company, 1960.
All My Pretty Ones. Boston: Houghton Mifflin Company, 1962.

SIMPSON, LOUIS
The Arrivistes. New York: Fine Editions Press, 1949.
Good News of Death and Other Poems. New York: Charles Scribner's Son, 1955.
A Dream of Governors. Middletown, Connecticut: Wesleyan University Press, 1959.
At the End of the Open Road. Middletown, Connecticut: Wesleyan University Press. 1963.

SNODGRASS, WILLIAM DE WITT
Heart's Needle. New York: Alfred A. Knopf, Inc., 1959.

WILBUR, RICHARD

The Beautiful Changes, and Other Poems. New York: Reynal and Hitchcock, 1947; Harcourt, Brace and Company, 1954.

Ceremony and Other Poems. New York: Harcourt, Brace and Company, 1950.

A Bestiary. Illustrated by Alexander Calder. New York: Printed at the Spiral Press for Pantheon Books, 1955.

Molière's The Misanthrope, a translation in verse. New York: Harcourt, Brace and Company, 1955.

Things of This World. New York: Harcourt, Brace and Company, 1956.

Poems, 1943–1956. London: Faber and Faber, Ltd., 1957.

(Wilbur's lyrics for *Candide* are in *Candide: A Comic Opera* based on Voltaire's Satire. Book by Lillian Hellman. Lyrics by Richard Wilbur [and others]. New York: Random House, 1957.

NOTE ON MANUFACTURE

The text of this book was set on the
Linotype in Fairfield, and the chapter
titles in Cheltenham. The composition,
printing, and binding were done by
Kingsport Press, Inc., and the paper
manufactured by the *S. D. Warren Company.*
Designed by *Stuart Ross.*